The Countertrade Handbook

THE COUNTERTRADE HANDBOOK

DICK FRANCIS

Quorum Books
New York · Westport, Connecticut

Published in the United States and Canada by
Quorum Books, Westport, Connecticut

English language edition, except the United States and Canada,
published by Woodhead-Faulkner (Publishers) Ltd.

First published 1987

Library of Congress Cataloging in Publication Data
Francis, Dick.
The countertrade handbook.

Bibliography: p.
1. Countertrade. I. Title.
HF1414.3.F72 1987 382 87–11867
ISBN 0-89930-320-X (alk. paper)

Library of Congress Catalog Card Number:
ISBN: 0-89930-320-X
Printed in Great Britain

Contents

Preface

A great deal has been written about countertrade over the last few years, covering both the macro-economic effects and the techniques involved. There has been speculation on the volume of trade affected by countertrade and reports of deals have abounded. What characterised much of what was written was the lack of accuracy – ranging from the badly informed to the deliberately misleading.

Against this background, I was particularly pleased to be asked by Woodhead-Faulkner to write a book, concentrating on *practical* aspects of countertrade. My close involvement with a large number of real-life cases had given me a good insight into countertrade and, having spoken to exporters (and importers) in many countries, I felt that I had a good idea of what they hoped to achieve through the use of countertrade.

I hope the book will be useful to people actively involved in international trade, or the financing thereof. In seeking to explain what countertrade really is, as opposed to what some people claim it to be, I have written at length, and in a fair amount of detail. Oscar Wilde said that 'The truth is rarely pure and never simple' so I have not sacrificed veracity for brevity.

My thanks are due to the following people who have provided material for this book, and publications which have allowed me to use their material: American International Underwriters Limited; Dr Michael Beltramo; Michael Boxall; Oswald Burstin; *Countertrade and Barter Quarterly: East-West* magazine; Bert Edwards; *Euromoney Trade Finance Report*; Japan Foreign Trade Council Inc.; Siobhan Menary; Rod Rees; Robert Scallon. Special mention must be made of Sheila Hogg, Lorraine Smillie and Maureen Johnson who typed the manuscript and whose skills were matched only by their great patience.

I have written this book in my private capacity but I should like to acknowledge the very great assistance provided by my employer, Barclays Bank Plc.

Dick Francis
February 1987

Introduction

In his contribution to the Group of 30's report 'Countertrade in the World Economy' David Swanson said 'If Countertrade is the secret to International Trade in the 1980s then it must be done secretly.'

Certainly, the air of secrecy surrounding countertrade makes it difficult for anyone to sort fact from fiction. Companies which have successfully transacted deals are reluctant to talk – partly because they fear other potential buyers will insist on countertrade, and partly because they do not want their competitors to find out how the deal was done.

For those seeking to find out more about countertrade the search is not made any easier by the fact that it is not a science. There is no agreement on terminology nor are there any set procedures or documentation. Each transaction tends to be unique in its construction.

This book will concentrate on practical aspects of countertrade. It does not examine the macro-economic arguments for and against the use of countertrade, because whatever the reason for its use, it is becoming more common in international trade.

Important points to remember from the beginning are as follows:

1. It is not a panacea to all trade ills.
2. It is not a magic wand to wave over impossible trading situations.
3. It is costly and risky.
4. It is time-consuming and cumbersome.
5. Often, it cannot be avoided.

It might be useful to set the scene by saying a little about the current international trading environment.

Since 1985 nearly 30 countries have had to reschedule their debts. Thus many countries are no longer creditworthy, certainly for goods requiring medium- or long-term credit. In the developed countries there is over-capacity in steel, automotive products, agricultural machinery and power generation equipment, etc. Competition, therefore, continues to be fierce for whatever business there is, particularly in the still creditworthy markets of the developing world. A halving in the price of oil during 1985/6 added a new twist to this problem. Some markets already in trouble were pushed into even worse difficulties, e.g. Mexico, Nigeria and Venezuela. Others so far regarded as creditworthy began to feel the pressure, such as Indonesia.

This is the background to developments in export finance in the mid 1980s. The countries needing capital goods and, indeed, imports over a wide range cannot afford them. Sellers with over-capacity cannot find financiers willing to take the risks involved in meeting these needs. Against this background, more countries are moving towards new ways of financing trade and exporting goods. Exporters must come to grips with ideas and techniques which may be inherently distasteful, but which represent what *has* to be done to continue export sales.

Countertrade should not be taken lightly. Patience could be the principal virtue of a good countertrader. A sense of humour would certainly be another. Consider this description of a countertrader from Rod Rees (Countertrade Manager, Smith Kline and French Laboratories Ltd):

> 'Countertrade is to professional management what Dr Jekyll's secret potion was to the medical profession. The mere mention of countertrade is often enough to transform a normally sound and steady executive into a giddy entrepreneur who gaily throws caution (along with profit) to the wind. Countertrade smacks of excitement, of cutting convoluted and complex deals in far-away countries, of rubbing shoulders with such exotic people as commodity brokers, oil traders and the like, and of being able to demonstrate talents and abilities hitherto totally ignored by peers and superiors. To a manager whose life to date has been encompassed by budget performance reports, sales forecasts and cash flow statements, it is a chance to break free and to show that there is a real red-blooded entrepreneur lurking under that drab, unexciting exterior.'

This book should provide a guide to understanding some of the complexities of countertrade.

Part I

CHAPTER 1

Setting the scene

History of barter and countertrade

Money as a unit of measurement overcame many of the problems associated with barter, the oldest form of trade. But barter did not totally disappear. Apart from its continued use within undeveloped societies, it was found to be an appropriate trading device in specific transactions between developed and undeveloped countries. In his essay entitled 'Countertrade in the World Economy' (Report on Countertrade in the World Economy by the Group of 30), Robert V. Roosa traces the origin of many modern countertrade terms back to the inter-war years, and in particular to Hjalmar Schacht. Schacht was President of the Reichsbank under Hitler. He set up clearing systems between Germany and her trading partners, which enabled the countries to settle their net position once a year in hard currency or gold. The world 'compensation' is derived from the German word, *kompensations-geschaeft*, the term used to describe the clearing systems of the 1930s. There was a very positive resurgence in the use of barter after the Second World War. The countries in what we now call collectively Eastern Europe were anxious to rebuild and re-equip industries which were devastated by the hostilities, or which were geared to the manufacture of war material. Post-war attitudes were not conducive to the granting of credit to these countries. Foreign exchange resources were, in any event, very seriously depleted in all countries. Enterprising businessmen in the West saw opportunities to supply the much-needed equipment against payment in kind – raw materials and minerals, for example. It is no coincidence that some of the most active Western countertraders today trace their origins back to Hungary, Czechoslovakia, Romania, etc.

Countertrade is now an integral part of the planning process in Eastern Europe and the balancing of trade between countries is considered to be highly desirable in Socialist thinking.

The second surge in countertrade activity occurred in the early

1980s, when the Debt Crisis in the Third World followed the almost total depletion of foreign exchange reserves and the world was in its worst economic recession since the 1930s (Table 1.1 illustrates this point). At the same time, foreign commercial banks declined to advance new credit, and national export credit agencies like the Export Credits Guarantee Department (ECGD) either withdrew their insurance cover or increased premia for many markets. Countertrade was seen by countries faced with these problems as a way of procuring much-needed imports.

Table 1.1 Outstanding debt of 15 borrowers

	Total debt ($ billion in 1984)	Bank debt
Argentina	47.8	32.0
Bolivia	4.2	1.1
Brazil	102.0	73.7
Chile	20.4	15.6
Colombia	12.6	7.5
Ecuador	7.6	4.7
Ivory Coast	6.2	2.6
Mexico	95.5	77.1
Morocco	13.2	3.4
Nigeria	19.2	5.7
Peru	13.4	4.7
Philippines	26.2	13.4
Uruguay	4.7	2.5
Venezuela	34.9	27.6
Yugoslavia	18.5	7.9
Total	426.5	279.6

What is not widely recognised is that the reduction in the number of creditworthy markets left the stronger countries in an even stronger bargaining position. They were able to exploit their creditworthiness. We will examine this aspect in the next section.

The figures: How much? How big? How many?

The growth in interest in countertrade over the last few years has been fuelled by various 'statistics' on the actual volume of countertrade world-wide. Claims as to the extent of countertrade vary from 3 per cent to 30 per cent of all world trade, although the figure of 30 per cent is probably an exaggeration. Table 1.2 shows Organization for Economic Co-operation and Development (OECD) estimates of the extent of countertrade world-wide. In its study *Countertrade: Developing*

Table 1.2 OECD estimates of countertrade volumes

	$ billion	% of trade involved
Industrial countries with:		
East Europe	15.6	15
Oil exporters	4.3	2
Other lesser developed countries	16.6	5
Among each other	15.7	2
Developing countries with:		
East Europe	14.2	30
Among each other	12.5	10
Total	78.9 (4.8%)*	

*Percentage of overall world trade.

Country Practices (OECD, Paris, 1985) the OECD gave an estimate of countertrade transacted. It was felt that 4.8 per cent was the maximum, or approximately $80 billion.

Trade statistics are gathered principally from customs documents, using trade classification numbers for products. These source documents will not carry any indication that the goods covered are part of a countertrade transaction. As will be illustrated later, countertrade represents two (or more) commercial transactions linked together in some way.

These claims therefore should be treated with caution. Having spoken to many hundreds of major exporters, in many countries, it is hard to find any company where countertrade comprises anything but a relatively insignificant part of its export trade. This is not necessarily true of selected industrial categories such as the defence industry. In the chapter on off-set we will examine this area in greater depth but it is sufficient here to say that in a survey (published in October 1985) by the International Trade Commission (USA), 500 corporations reported that $7.16 billion or 5.6 per cent of their exports involved countertrade. Of those exports 80 per cent were of military equipment.

What is significant, however, is that countertrade is growing. More companies are using countertrade proactively. More countries are using countertrade, and average transaction sizes are getting bigger. For these reasons, a sound knowledge of countertrade is essential so that an exporter will know how to react when faced with countertrade demands, or how to *use* countertrade to gain a competitive edge.

A question that is frequently asked is 'What is the minimum size for a countertrade contract?' – and there are two answers. Countertrade demands are often expressed as a percentage of the export contract. Thus a 5 per cent countertrade demand on a contract valued at

£500,000 represents a relatively small amount. The contract is, of course, still worth pursuing because the profit on the export contract should more than cover the additional costs involved in countertrade.

A 100 per cent countertrade demand on an export contract of £25,000 is another matter. The profit earned on the export may be insufficient to cover the extra costs involved in the countertrade leg of the transaction.

In the next chapter, we will look at which groups of countries use countertrade, and why. But how *many* countries use countertrade? The countries listed in Appendix 1 represent those where countertrade has been used in the recent past. Over 80 countries are believed to have had some countertrade experience and, as already mentioned, the number is growing.

CHAPTER 2

Countertrade: Why and where

An important element in learning how to cope with countertrade is understanding *why* it is used. Once an exporter is aware of what motivates a country to employ countertrade, he will be better placed to respond to countertrade demands if they are made. The more skill an exporter has in these matters, the greater are the chances of success.

The reasons for a country using countertrade reflect in the way deals are put together. We will look at typical transaction structures in Chapter 3, but first of all we should examine the most common countertrade rationales.

Countertrade will be used for one or more of the following reasons:

1. *Where little or no foreign exchange is available*

This is the most obvious reason. The Debt Crisis of the 1970s and 1980s saw many developing countries with depleted reserves. What exacerbated the problem even further was the rapid withdrawal of credit facilities by nervous commercial banks. These banks had become cautious about the extent of their sovereign and foreign commercial lendings, and feared the 'domino' effect should one debtor in a region fail to meet a loan repayment. National export credit agencies like ECGD, Eximbank (Export Import Bank of United States), COFACE (Compagnie Française d'Assurance pour le Commerce Exterieur (France)) and SACE (Sezione Speciale per L'assicurazione del Credito All'esportazione), faced with mounting claims from insured exporters, increased premia and withheld cover for certain markets. This had the effect of reducing the number of exporters willing to export to those markets. Table 2.1 outlines ECGD's claims experience over the past few years, and Fig. 2.1 shows the trend.

What is ironic is that the Debt Crisis was brought about, in part, by loans incurred to establish new projects and new industries. The developed nations had provided the means of production, but had

Table 2.1 ECGD claims experience over the period 1976–85

£ million	Claims paid	Recoveries	Consolidated fund balance
1976/7	63.1	27.1	358.2
1977/8	94.2	26.7	420.4
1978/9	133.6	43.7	470.1
1979/80	263.8	98.6	485.1
1980/1	290.5	80.6	463.4
1981/2	303.5	79.7	481.3
1982/3	584.1	103.6	280.7
1983/4	674.3	132.7	− 42.3
1984/5 (provisional)	834.9	348.6	−392.5

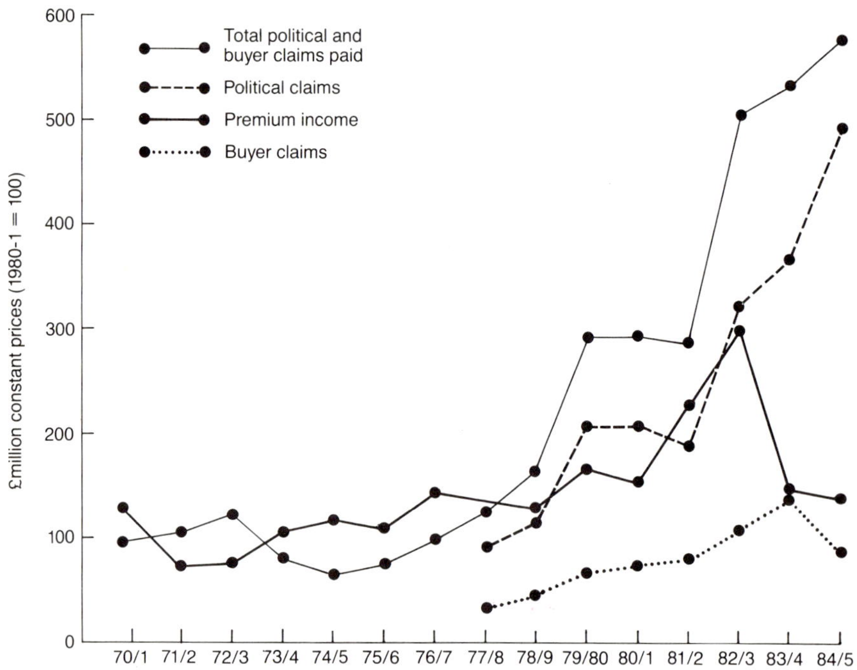

Fig. 2.1 ECGD claims payments and premium income 1970–85

withdrawn the support needed to acquire basic inputs, spares, etc. Many of these new projects and industries were set up to reduce dependence on imports, and have become important employers of local labour. The subsequent run-down and often total closure of these industries threw people out of work. Social unrest followed in some areas.

Governments are under pressure to keep open the factories of their new industrial base, and have turned to countertrade as a means of procuring the inputs they need. In a similar vein, other countries have recognised the need to *conserve* foreign exchange, and may insist on an element of countertrade for their imports.

From the foregoing, it will be apparent that countries using countertrade in this category are largely from the 'developing world', and countertrade is used as a *trade finance* technique.

2. *Where there is a need to create new export products or new export markets*

Those countries able to pay for their imports are in the enviable position of being buyers in a buyer's market for many types of goods. They are able to impose conditions on their suppliers which would, in less competitive times, be unacceptable. Extended credit terms may be demanded, large discounts negotiated and so on. A growing trend is for suppliers to be asked to buy, or to arrange the purchase of goods from their clients directly, or from their client's country generally. But why should this be so?

Many developing or 'newly industrialising' nations have been building up their industrial base for some years. The motivations to invest in industries were, for example, to create employment, to utilise local natural resources and to reduce imports. Initially, many of the goods produced were for domestic consumption. In time it was found that either production exceeded domestic demand or goods were switched to the export market to generate much-needed foreign exchange. This caused problems for a variety of reasons. We will examine what these problems are when we look at the subject of countertrade goods.

Countertrade can be employed for the reasons stated, by any country trying to develop new exports or even protect existing exports. Experience has shown us that newly industrialising countries are most likely to pursue countertrade for this reason, together with some of the Socialist countries of Eastern Europe. Countertrade is, in this context, a *trading* technique.

3. *To balance trade for economic or political reasons*

(a) *Eastern Europe*

The growth in countertrade after the Second World War has already been mentioned. Since that time, the concept of procuring goods by way of countertrade has become rather more entrenched in the planning process of the East European countries. Imports into East European countries are often prioritised. Those of high priority are paid for in cash, with no or very small counterpurchase demands. Goods classed as non-essentials or luxuries may be subject to compensation or at best large counterpurchase demands. The idea of balancing trade is very much a Socialist one. Bilateral trade agreements are a feature of the way business is conducted between Socialist countries. In their trading relations with other countries, they will attempt to balance trade, and countertrade is one way of achieving this.

We look at bilateral clearing accounts, bilateral trading agreements and Eastern Europe in later chapters.

(b) *Other countries*

In the Group of 30's report on countertrade, Professor David Yoffie describes the lack of confidence in international trade. He discusses two most important trends in the employment of restrictions in world trade.

Although the types of restriction vary, there has been a significant increase in the incidence of non-tariff barriers, such as voluntary export restraints, domestic subsidies, anti-dumping actions and countervailing duties. The second trend identified is the growing demand for reciprocity in trade; Professor Yoffie says '. . . and since Countertrade links imports to the export of goods and services, it is one of the strictest forms of reciprocity'.

It is not within the scope of this book to discuss the macroeconomic aspects of bilateralism for the sake of it. Suffice it to say here that countertrade is used as one of a series of techniques designed to manage foreign exchange.

4. To acquire new technology, to create/protect employment, or to reduce reliance on other countries for strategic reasons

Countries importing high-technology, high-value or strategic goods (e.g. for defence) are often able to take advantage of the competitive international environment for the supply of such goods.

It has been a feature of the defence and aviation industries for many years that in supplying goods of this nature, suppliers will be asked by their customers – most often governments or state enterprises – to reinvest part of the sales value in the buyer's country. We will examine in Chapter 4 how 'off-set', as it is called, actually works, but it is interesting to look at the reasons for its use.

The goods acquired are usually of an extremely high value, either individually as with aircraft, or in total when part of a package, such as a complete air defence system. To alleviate the heavy foreign exchange expenditure involved in purchases of this nature, the buying country may insist that a portion of the sales price be comprised of local procurements for the item being acquired. In addition, or alternatively, there could be a requirement that non-related goods be bought to replace the foreign exchange spent on the imported item.

Particularly in the area of defence, many governments are concerned that they are dependent on the supplying country for servicing, technical support and replacement of vital strategic equipment. In the event of war, such dependence could lead to difficulty if supplies are interrupted. Partial local manufacture, assembly, etc., could help to reduce this dependence.

To take advantage of the buyer's market which exists in the defence and aerospace industries, buyers can often insist on acquiring technology or at the very least insist on co-production of part of the item purchased.

Off-set policies exist in many developed countries – partly because they are major buyers of high technology goods and partly because such countries are able to take advantage of the technology transferred, in their industries. The earlier comment on the strength of the negotiating position of creditworthy countries is also relevant.

There is a growing trend for off-set demands to be applied to procurements of lower-level technologies. Australia has applied its policy to imports of buses and power-station equipment. New Zealand imported coal-mining machinery and called for off-set proposals, whilst Denmark did the same when buying railway engines. (Chapter 4 examines off-set in greater detail.)

CHAPTER 3

The terminology and methodology

Terminology

One of the reasons why countertrade is, at first sight, rather difficult to understand is the lack of agreement on a common terminology. Some of the words used mean different things to different people. Some of the words mean the same thing.

The following list gives just a selection of the terms used:

Barter	Buy-back
Counterpurchase	Triangular deals
Compensation	Parallel deals
Off-set	Switch
Linked deals	Reciprocal deals
Co-operation	Bilateral deals

It is absolutely vital that the exporter looks beyond the terminology to assess exactly what the proposer means by the word used. Countertrade is not a science; there are no internationally accepted words for the various techniques. There is, however, a case for adopting a terminology for use within one's own company, not least to assist communication. This chapter covers compensation, counterpurchase and switch. Off-set and buy-back will be discussed in Chapter 4, while the types of transaction variously described as 'reciprocal' and 'bilateral' are covered in Chapter 15.

In applying the terms shown in the following transaction structures, not everyone will agree, but they represent what is believed to be the most widely accepted usage.

Methodology

We will now look at basic transaction structures. They are simplistic in their presentation so that we can see what each involves as far as flows of goods or cash are concerned. We will elaborate on how these are built on in real-life situations, when we examine the roles of other parties.

Compensation

This is a barter-like arrangement whereby the goods exported are 'paid for' by a countersupply of goods. Figure 3.1 shows how this looks in diagrammatic form. One might ask why it is not called barter since it seems to be a direct exchange of goods. There are differences, albeit fine ones. Barter represents an exchange of goods, possibly of unequal value. There may be no underlying valuation of the goods and no alternative means of payment in cash. Barter often takes place between governments, rarely between commercial entities. Money plays no part

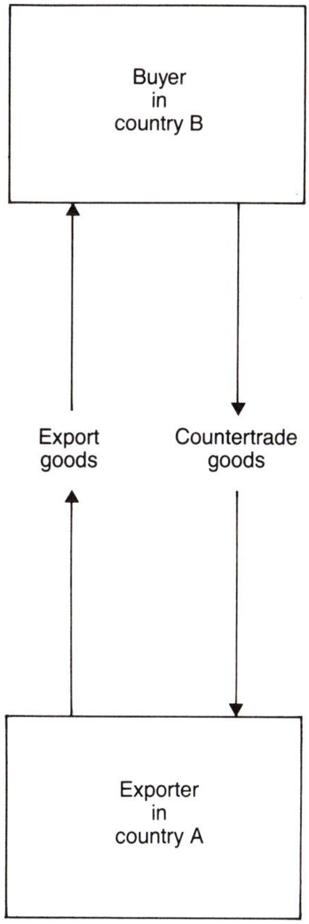

Fig. 3.1 Compensation in simple form

and there are usually only two countries involved. For these reasons we will not examine how barter deals are put together.

Compensation has certain features which distinguish it from other varieties of countertrade, particularly counterpurchase. The following notes describe these features:

1. *Values*

   As the sale of the countertrade goods provides the hard currency to pay for the export, the value of the countertrade goods should at least equal that of the export. This may be a statement of the obvious, but it is important to recognise this when comparing compensation with counterpurchase (see page 42).

2. *Timing*

   As the sale of the countertrade goods is needed to provide the hard currency for the export, the shipment dates should be closely linked. The exporter would not want to be at risk by despatching his goods to the buyer, against a mere promise by the buyer to provide countertrade goods at some time in the future. So many factors could affect the supply of the countertrade goods, and only a few of the risks can be covered by insurance.

   In addition there is the fundamental problem of financing the gap between the date of supply by the exporter, and the subsequent arrival of the sales proceeds for the countertrade goods.

3. *Insurance*

   National export credit agencies such as ECGD, COFACE and SACE will not insure contracts for exports where payment is to be made in kind rather than cash. It may be possible to insure such contracts against certain of the risks on the Private Political Risks Market. The subject of private market insurance is an interesting one, and will be looked at in Chapter 9.

4. *Contract structure*

   Almost invariably compensation transactions are framed in one single contract. This can cause problems when the countertrade side of the transaction is to be discharged by a third party. Not only will there be the problem of preserving the confidentiality of the principal export deal but it will prove difficult to arrange for a third party to be a principal to only one part of the contract.

selected goods are available for export from Hungary to Brazil and which can be financed through the clearing system. The next step, therefore, is that suitable goods will be identified in Hungary, and the switch dealer lines up a buyer in a third country.

This buyer will give the switch dealer a letter of credit, expressed in hard currency. The transaction is finalised by the Hungarian supplier shipping goods ostensibly to Brazil, via a freight forwarder in, say, Rotterdam. Here the goods are diverted to the ultimate buyer, and the switch dealer is able to draw on the letter of credit in hard currency.

In Hungary, the supplier of the goods receives a payment from the Hungarian Bank for Foreign Trade (managers of the clearing arrangement with Brazil), from the bilateral payments account. In Brazil, the importer pays local currency to the Central Bank where it is credited to the bilateral payments account. These two payments will correspond, and the effect will be that the clearing imbalance – the swing – will be reduced. Although this is a complex matter, the exporter will not be involved in the arrangements to any great extent. The important points to note are that the right switch dealer must be identified and recruited, and that the exporter must allow sufficient in his price to cover the switch dealer's fee.

There are several variations on this basic idea. Chapter 15 examines the various types of bilateral agreement.

CHAPTER 4

Off-set and buy-back

One of the most disturbing, and yet understandable, trends in countertrade over recent years has been the growth in the use of off-set. It is important to remember that countertrade represents a necessity to engage in *reciprocal activity*, and off-set is just that.

Put simply, in making a sale of a medium- to high-technology capital item, the seller has to undertake some sort of activity in addition to the supply of the item in question. Much of what has been written on the subject in the press has concentrated on the macro-economic effects of off-set. Examples of the off-set transactions are quoted, without explaining the rationale, the technique or the cost.

As in the rest of this book, no effort will be made here to *justify* off-set, or to comment on its impact on industrial economics.

Off-set activity can fall into two areas: indirect and direct.

Indirect off-set

This represents activity involving products and technology *unrelated* to the product being sold.

Direct off-set

This is the opposite of indirect off-set, where the activity undertaken *is* related to the product being sold.

The rationale for off-set policies

Before elaborating on the ways in which off-set is carried out, a few words on the reasons for its use. Countries are able to impose such demands because of the over-capacity which exists in many industries. Although originally found in contracts for the supply of high technology goods – usually defence and aerospace – it can now be found in contracts for the supply of lower levels of technology. Countries buying high-value capital goods are able to demand the very latest technologies, concessionary prices, long credit periods at fine interest rates and *also* off-set arrangements.

The Greek and Korean off-set policies described in Appendix 1 illustrate the way in which off-set will be used to gain concessions from suppliers. These concessions are designed to:

(a) limit foreign exchange expenditure on high-value imports;
(b) replace foreign exchange;
(c) protect/increase local employment;
(d) improve local industrial technological capabilities;
(e) reduce technological dependency for strategic reasons;
(f) increase export markets for domestic goods;
(g) increase levels of local investment by foreign companies.

In seeking to gain such benefits, therefore, countries will establish off-set policies which will impose on suppliers a range of obligations. Whilst each of the activities listed below can apply to direct *and* indirect off-set, there may be a system of weightings used in the evaluation process which will favour direct off-set activity. Such weightings vary from country to country, but the Korean and Greek policies referred to above are good examples of how weightings are applied.

The terminology used in describing various types of off-set will vary, but the following represent the common terms in use.

Licensed production

This is the authorisation of local industry to manufacture equipment, such authority being granted by industries or the government in the selling country. There may be parallel agreements in place whereby production from the licensed entity will be

(a) incorporated in the item being sold;
(b) bought by the licensee;
(c) sold to third parties.

The relationship between licensor and licensee could take many forms and could entail the transfer of technology, on a temporary or permanent basis.

Co-production

This involves the establishment of a relationship between the exporter (or a third party) and a company in the buyer's country. Once again, the type of relationship will vary from case to case but could range from a simple agreement to a full joint venture. Output from the venture may be used in the same way as listed under 'Licensed production' above.

Subcontractor production

This is the placing of contracts for the manufacture or assembly of goods, with companies in the buyer's country. Output could be used in the same way as mentioned above.

Local infrastructure

The exporter may be required to set up local establishments, such as training schools, regional sales offices, research establishments and so on.

Counterpurchase

A final concession which may be demanded from the exporter is a requirement to purchase goods from the buyer, or from other companies in the buyer's country.

Figure 4.1 shows off-set in diagrammatic form. There are several important points to note:

1. The off-set activity could involve the exporter (including subsidiaries and associates), its subcontractors *or* unrelated industries/companies.
2. The receiver of the off-set benefit could be the buyer (including subsidiaries and associates), its subcontractors *or* unrelated industries/companies.
3. The off-set package will often be a mixture of the various types.
4. Production of components for the goods being sold could be on a long-term basis which will involve the purchase of the additional production by the 'giver' of the off-set benefit.

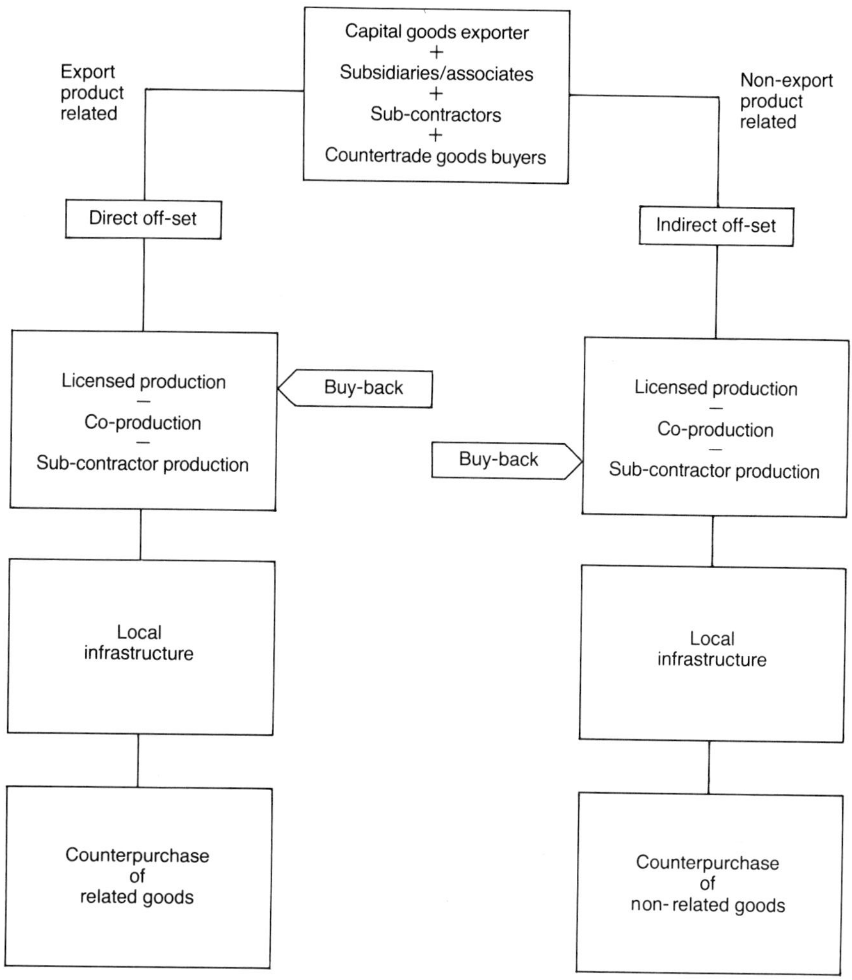

Fig. 4.1 Off-set

Constructing an off-set offer

There are as many different ways to put an off-set programme together as there are contracts involving off-set. The extent to which a company is able to transfer technology, employ local contractors or invest money will be determined by a number of factors, most of which can only be decided on the facts of each case:

1. Corporate policy on off-set.

2. Corporate understanding of the off-set demands.
3. The uniqueness of the company's technology.
4. Limitation on the ability to transfer technology on the grounds of national security, or patent restrictions.
5. The ability to persuade subcontractors to join in the off-set programme as a condition of working with them.
6. The ability to persuade third parties to join in the off-set programme if they are not involved in the export sale.
7. The practicalities of re-sourcing (e.g. tooling, training, unique subcontractor capability).
8. The cost of re-sourcing, transferring technology, etc. and the ability to absorb/pass on the extra cost to the buyer.
9. The company attitude to overseas investment.
10. The safety of and potential return from the overseas investment.
11. Consideration must be given to the selection of a partner in the buyer's country – including an evaluation of the buyer's capabilities.
12. Recipient of off-set benefit should have the required technical capabilities, together with the necessary capital (plus capital equipment) and manpower.

Once again, the team approach is the right one. Dr Michael Beltramo – a leading US expert on off-set – suggests that personnel with the following responsibilities should be chosen:

1. Marketing.
2. Purchasing.
3. Engineering.
4. Production.
5. Contracts.
6. Countertrade.
7. Cost analysis.

Figure 4.2 is a decision tree, showing the steps leading up to the initial presentation. Within this exercise, reference must constantly be made to the needs of the buyer, the effect of the programme on the price, and on the product, and the activities of the competition. Figure 4.3 shows a matrix devised by Dr Beltramo, which illustrates the process of evaluating the various criteria.

This section of the chapter will not, however, provide the answer to all of the problems likely to face an exporter in constructing an off-set programme. The purchase of goods from the buyer/buyer's country

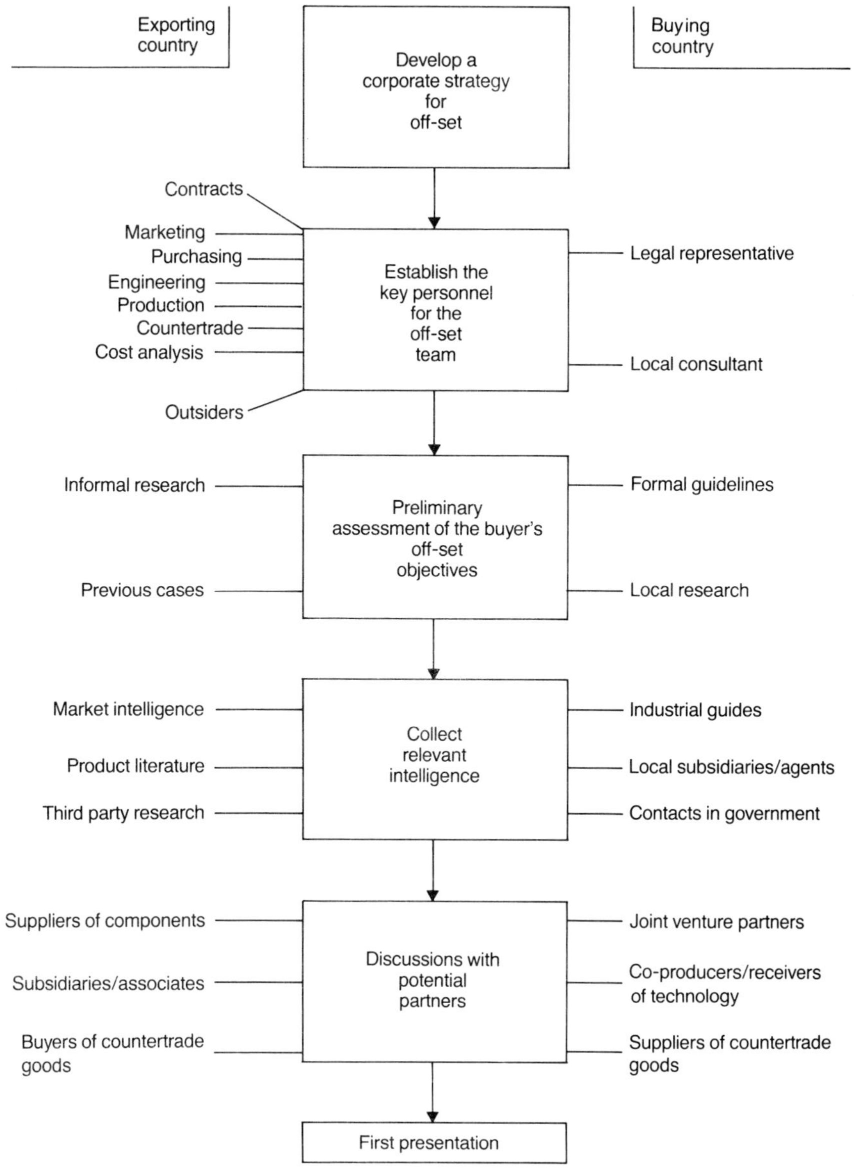

Fig. 4.2 Off-set – decision tree

Issues \ Participants	Customer	Competitor(s)	You
Product			
Price			
Off-sets			

Fig. 4.3 Off-set – evaluation matrix

could be handled in the same way as counterpurchase. The other aspects of off-set will require individual treatment. Reference to the policies of Greece and Korea will illustrate the complexities of off-set (see Appendix 1).

Buy-back

Of growing interest to countries seeking new inward investment is the concept of 'buy-back'. In simple terms, companies establishing manufacturing concerns in foreign countries are asked to accept resultant production as a way of:

(a) generating foreign exchange for the concern through export sales;
(b) receiving profits from the investment;
(c) receiving loan or capital repayments.

An increasing number of East European countries including the USSR have entered into such arrangements, but China represents the country most active in seeking investments based on buy-back agreements. The nature of the initial investment could be through a joint venture, with capital provided in the form of cash and/or capital plant, technology transfer (in a type of licensing operation) or capital investment in an existing enterprise.

Like contracts involving off-set, there are as many different approaches to buy-back as there are contracts. A few points of a general nature may serve to underline the complexities of such arrangements.

1. The supplier of the capital plant may be the manufacturer thereof, and *not* a producer of the end product. It will not have the necessary marketing skills or infrastructure. The question which must be considered is how the supplier's existing clients will react if it starts competing with them for the sale of the end-product.
2. The time lag between the investment and commencement of production may be considerable, e.g. mining ventures. This raises questions regarding finance.
3. The end-product to be used to 'pay' the investor may only be available *after* domestic demand has been satisfied.
4. There are the obvious questions on such things as quality control, availability of raw materials, sustainability of markets, updating technology (e.g. investment in research and development), and other production/marketing related problems.
5. Finally, there is the question of security. It may be possible to take out investment insurance to cover against such risks as sequestration, blocking of dividends, cancellation of export licençes, impounding of plant and so on.

The subject is far too wide to be discussed here in the detail it deserves and in any event, each case will be constructed in a unique way.

CHAPTER 5

Putting a deal together: 1

In this chapter an attempt is made to set out how a typical countertrade deal could be structured. Guidance is given on the approach most likely to lead to success.

A few words of warning are necessary first:

1. No two transactions are the same.
2. Each will have unique features.
3. It is difficult to share the experiences gained by other companies.
4. Some basic techniques are transferable.
5. Knowledge gained in one country may not be valid in another.

For the sake of clarity, some of the aspects mentioned in this chapter are elaborated on in later chapters, e.g. sources of help, trading houses, insurance, costs, risks, etc. These notes are also arranged in the approximate order in which the action should be undertaken.

Getting advice

The number of countries where countertrade is likely to occur is growing. There are a few surprises too. It is no longer safe to assume that because the buying country is classed as 'developed', countertrade will not be an issue. Seeking advice at the outset will save time and money later and could improve the chances of success.

Typical early questions might include the following:

1. Is countertrade likely to occur?
2. Is it government policy or a commercial necessity?
3. What is the administration/approval process?

Sources of such information are diverse, but will include the following:

1. Countertrade consultants.
2. Banks.
3. Trading houses.

4. Insurance brokers.
5. Government/national organisations.
6. The media.
7. Local agents.
8. In-house knowledge.

In Chapter 12, further information is given on the services provided by most of the 'external' sources of help, and Chapter 16 looks at managing countertrade in-house.

Whoever is to undertake negotiations with the foreign buyer should be aware of the current countertrade situation, and be ready to respond accordingly. Except in those isolated cases where countertrade is offered to 'sweeten' a tender, the first golden rule is:

Resist countertrade – cash is best.

Prior knowledge of the countertrade situation is important in some countries – particularly in Eastern Europe – as the subject may not be raised at the outset of negotiations. If, therefore, a cash price is quoted, there will be no scope for recovering the extra costs of countertrade through inflating the sales price when countertrade is demanded later.

The second golden rule is:

Do not quote prices until the countertrade situation is clear.

Is countertrade obligatory? (1)*

In some countries, governments have a formal countertrade policy or law (2). This may or may not be translated into a full procedural process. If it is, copies of the appropriate documentation should be obtained, translated where necessary and studied. Care should be taken to ensure that the documents are current. Changes in procedure or law are not always widely publicised.

It is likely that the documents will include the title and office of the administrative body involved. Through local agents, or from general enquiry, the names of the key figures should be ascertained.

Discussions with countertrade advisers could reveal whether the policy is strictly adhered to, optional or avoidable. Where other firms are known to have undertaken transactions, discreet enquiries may yield valuable information.

If draft countertrade contracts form part of the procedural guide, copies should be given to the company's legal advisers for comment.

* The numbers in parenthesis refer to the stages shown in Fig. 5.1.

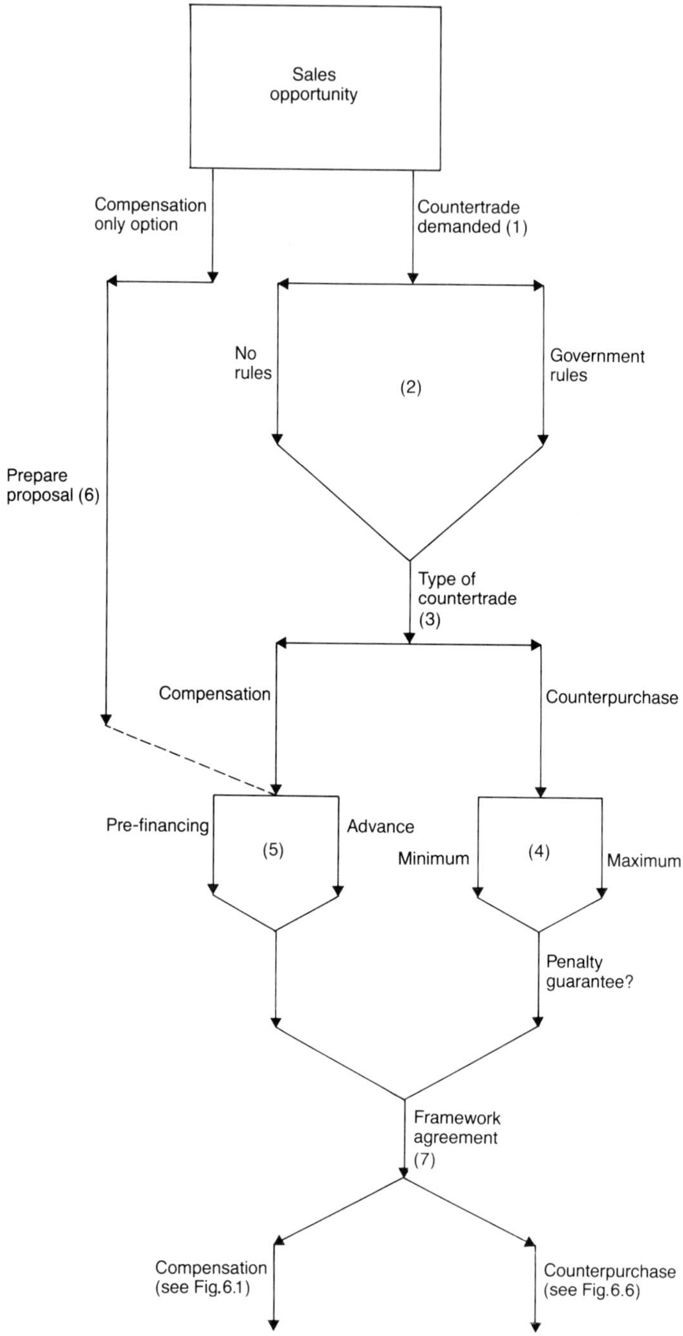
Sales
opportunity
Compensation
only option
Countertrade
demanded (1)
No
rules
(2)
Government
rules
Prepare
proposal (6)
Type of
countertrade
(3)
Compensation
Counterpurchase
Pre-financing
(5)
Advance
Minimum
(4)
Maximum
Penalty
guarantee?
Framework
agreement
(7)
Compensation
(see Fig.6.1)
Counterpurchase
(see Fig.6.6)

Summary of process for negotiating a countertrade deal

A sales opportunity for an exporter in country A arises in country B.

(1) Countertrade is *demanded* by the buyer acting on his own initiative or on the direction of his government.
(2) The exporter ascertains whether there is an established procedure in country B, or whether countertrade is an *ad hoc* arrangement.
(3) The type of countertrade must be established: Is it to be compensation (receiving goods in 'payment') or counterpurchase (a parallel obligation)?
(4) If it is counterpurchase, the exporter must determine the level of purchases to be undertaken.
(5) If it is compensation, the exporter must decide who ships first. If he does, then there will be a need to finance the export pending receipt of the countertrade goods.
(6) If no countertrade rules exist, or there is no other way to finance the export, the exporter will need to prepare a countertrade proposal, as a way of financing the export sale. This will include consideration of the same point as in (5).
(7) The exporter should try to sign a framework agreement setting out the way in which the business will be transacted.

Thereafter, matters will proceed on the basis of compensation or counterpurchase transactions.

Fig. 5.1 Negotiating a countertrade deal

Occasionally, a list of possible countertrade goods is also provided. Unfortunately such lists are often unrepresentative of what is actually available, and will almost always include a depressing array of low-quality, overpriced, unsaleable goods. As an initial guide, however, the list should be given to the company's countertrade advisers, trading house, etc., for scrutiny and comment. An indication of preferred goods could be suggested.

Not all countries have a formal policy, and will limit their 'demand' to a fairly simple statement that countertrade offers must be made. Without the benefit of a procedural guide, it is all the more important for advice to be sought early on. The comments made above on finding names of countertrade administrators and examining previous cases obviously apply here too. The lack of formal rules can, in some cases, be turned to the exporter's advantage.

Where there are no formal rules, there is a tendency for companies to build in contingencies for the unknown, thus adding to their price and reducing competitiveness. A well-researched and well-prepared proposal can avoid this problem. Prior to despatching the sales personnel abroad, the company must decide on its strategy if it transpires that countertrade is indeed an issue.

What sort of countertrade is being demanded? (3)

Off-set is a more specialised area, and has already been discussed in Chapter 4. Chapter 3 set out the differences between counterpurchase and compensation. It is vital to find out at the earliest possible time which is to apply – is countertrade a parallel issue, or a means of finance? The implications, risks and costs associated with each are different.

If the government policy is directed towards *counterpurchase*, the company's main aim must be to pitch its counterpurchase offer at a level (4) which:

(a) satisfies the government's requirements
(b) is equal to, or better than, that of any competitor;
(c) generates the lowest additional cost; and
(d) is achievable.

The company's attitude will be influenced by its assessment of where it stands with regard to its competitors, if any. If it is known to be leading the bidding on price and/or technology, and these are perceived to be the key issues, then a bare minimum level of counterpurchase could be offered. If the company is obviously *not* the preferred tenderer, bidder or supplier, a larger-than-expected offer could be submitted, perhaps involving 'distressed' goods (see Chapter 10).

Counterpurchase is often stipulated as a percentage of the sales contract. Care must be exercised in determining the base figure on which the percentage is calculated. (This point is considered in Chapter 7, on documentation.)

Having established the general level of counterpurchase to be offered, the question of penalty guarantees must be considered. A penalty guarantee is merely a performance bond. It is requested by countertrading countries as a way of ensuring that the counterpurchase obligation is actually fulfilled. (See Chapter 7.)

Once the basic points have been considered, the exporter would move towards a framework agreement (or memorandum of understanding, protocol, etc.).

Compensation is the use of countertrade as a trade finance technique. In simple terms, the sale of the countertrade goods will provide the hard currency to pay for the goods exported. Note the difference between counterpurchase and compensation. In the former, the export will be paid for in the normal way with countertrade a parallel issue.

The latter is very different, with a much closer relationship between the export and the countertrade leg.

If it is determined that compensation is the system directed by government regulations, the company would need to examine various matters which do not necessarily apply in counterpurchase deals:

1. Availability of saleable countertrade goods.
2. Timing of deliveries (i.e. who ships first).
3. Funds flow management procedure.
4. Recourse in the event of non-fulfilment.
5. Financial standing of potential third-party partners.
6. Links between the buyer of the export goods and supplier of the countertrade goods.

The critical points, however, are who ships first (5) and funds flow management. We call the options 'advance compensation' and 'pre-financing' (5).

Compensation – the only way? (6)

The previous section is concerned with countertrade demands made by buyers, or governments in the country of those buyers. There will be cases, however, where countertrade is not demanded, but represents the only way to finance exports to a country. That country may have no experience in such matters, or may even have had bad experience.

If no foreign exchange, and no lines of credit or commercial credit are available, a compensation deal could represent one solution to the problem of financing an export sale. Such an arrangement differs from compensation demanded as a government policy, in that the concept must be *sold* to the buyer and/or his government.

Structuring a countertrade proposal for submission to a foreign buyer is not complex – indeed, its very simplicity is a vital feature. The construction of a proposal is described on pages 38–41.

The sales team

Armed with a good understanding of countertrade and its relevance to the foreign market, the company is ready to send its team or individual to commence negotiations. But who should it send? The traditional salesperson may have insufficient knowledge of countertrade. To send additional staff solely for the countertrade side could mean unnecessary expense. The local agent may not have the right connections and would, in any event, probably need educating in countertrade matters.

There is no easy answer to the question of who to send. A good background briefing for the salesperson may be sufficient in the first instance. Thereafter, additional personnel can be sent if the situation so demands. Certainly, many companies have found that it is not easy to combine the two functions of selling and negotiating countertrade in one person. A realistic view of the countertrade problem is necessary, and a salesperson may ignore the problem or make light of it, in the interests of showing his or her ability to make a sale. Consideration could be given to recruiting a consultant for negotiating the countertrade aspect, if the size of the transaction justifies the expense.

Negotiations

Armed with a good knowledge of the likely demands, or the techniques to be employed, the negotiators are ready to discuss the export sale and the countertrade arrangements. Where there is a formal policy and procedure in the buyer's country there may be little, if any, room for manoeuvre. Other countries, though, approach countertrade in an *ad hoc* fashion, and it is important here to try to impose the company's ideas. This goes back to the drafting of a countertrade proposal (see below).

Bearing in mind that there may be several different agreements to negotiate, with several parties, it is more sensible to attempt broad agreement on the various issues, finally signing a framework agreement (7) to bring together the points agreed upon in these early discussions. In the view of many people experienced in countertrade, a framework agreement is the key document. What is likely to be included in such a document? Before we examine a typical agreement, let us go back to the start of the negotiations, and the proposal to be tabled as a working paper/discussion document.

The countertrade proposal

To reiterate, the purpose of the proposal is to set out guidelines, terms and conditions on which the company would like to see the countertrade handled, in the absence of formal procedures and documentation from the buyer. In preparing the paper, the following are key points to remember:

1. Keep it simple.

2. If your language is not widely understood in the country of the buyer, translate the proposal.
3. Avoid jargon – remember the lack of agreement on terminology (see Chapter 3).
4. Try to present a complete picture – do not assume knowledge on the part of the buyer.
5. Consider who may be reading the proposal, e.g. the buyer, government officials, central bankers.

A typical proposal would be divided into the following sections:

1. The intentions of the parties.
2. Profiles of the parties.
3. Summary of the sales contract.
4. Summary of the countertrade goods purchase arrangements.
5. The management of the funds flow.
6. A diagram of the whole transaction.
7. Summary and proposals for future negotiation.

The first section represents a plain-language, uncomplicated 'executive summary' of what the transaction sets out to achieve. It will also stress the benefits of the scheme, the security offered by the system proposed and the integrity of the parties.

In profiling the various parties, the intention is to show the buyer and the buyer's government that they can have confidence in the commercial ability of the parties, and in their integrity. Bearing in mind that the government and its central bank may need to see the proposal, profiles of all parties should be included, as follows:

1. Exporter.
2. Buyer (importer).
3. Countertrade goods supplier.
4. Countertrade goods buyer.
5. Local bank.
6. Overseas bank.

Only a summary of the sales contract needs to be included, as the final document will, in many cases, be lengthy and technical. One would expect to see certain basic clauses included, mostly of a commercial nature, relating to validity of offer, payment terms and so on.

In setting out the arrangements for the purchase of countertrade goods, unless the type of goods are known the conditions can only be of a general nature. Nevertheless, these conditions are in themselves critical, and could well pre-empt the imposition of onerous conditions by the supplier of the countertrade goods or their government. This section of the proposal will form the basis of the framework agreement, which is one of the subjects of Chapter 7.

When dealing with compensation transactions in particular, and developing countries in general, it must be recognised that foreign exchange – or the lack of it – is the central issue. Great care must be exercised in describing how the foreign exchange flow will be handled. It would, for example, be disastrous to describe what in essence is a safe system thus:

> We will take your goods and sell them, and keep the money until we send you our goods.

As a simple way of describing how advance compensation works, that sentence may well help in understanding the way things will be done, but would be unacceptable to an exchange control department in a central bank. Within the 'management of the funds flow' section, reference will also be made to security, if required. Guarantees, performance bonds or standby letters of credit are examples. Once again, the points made in this section will be incorporated in the framework agreement.

To draw a picture of a transaction may seem to some people an exercise in over-simplification. It should be remembered, however, that readers of the proposal will be coming to it 'cold'. The writer will have such an intimate knowledge of the way the transaction should be structured, it would be easy to assume understanding on the part of the reader. Later in this book, Figs. 6.4, 6.5, 6.8 and 8.1 provide examples of transaction structures in an easily understood form.

The proposal is designed to sell the countertrade idea to the buyer and any relevant authority in the buyer's country. It should conclude with a suggestion as to what the next step should be – usually negotiations followed by the signing of a framework agreement.

Having prepared the proposal, it will be submitted for consideration. There is no simple answer in deciding to whom it should be sent. Some countries without formal rules have indicated which area of government will consider proposals. Zimbabwe would be a good example, where a Special Trading Arrangements Committee exists, whose members are drawn from various government ministries. The Committee's role is to consider proposals, but the criteria for approval and manner of submission are not widely known.

As controllers of a country's foreign exchange reserves, the central bank will almost certainly have a role to play, as will any import licensing authority. Copies may be sent to these bodies for comment.

It is vital that the approval for the countertrade deal comes from the right levels of government. Care should be taken when dealing with regional or local government, who may – in their enthusiasm or desperation – overstep their authority. When negotiating the deal, it is a good idea to record minutes of all meetings, summarising the discussions and agreements reached, in exchanges of letters with the other attendees. Bear in mind that government personnel (and governments!) change quite rapidly, and verbal agreements may not hold.

The overall purpose of the framework agreement is to set out the parameters within which the sales contract and countertrade contract will be structured. Its terms should be based on the exporter's own ideas, wherever possible, and the best way to have these ideas brought to the buyer's attention is through the countertrade proposal.

CHAPTER 6

Putting a deal together: 2

The previous chapter followed a logical – almost chronological – path, leading up to the point where the exporting company is ready to discuss specifics. At this point several things happen simultaneously or in an order determined by the facts of each case.

Let us assume that a compensation transaction is demanded, or represents the only way to finance the deal.

Compensation

Figure 6.1 shows a compensation transaction in simplistic form. We can build on this diagram to show the various parties involved, their relationships and the goods and funds flows. It will also help us to identify areas of risk. In so doing, the most common scenario will be described, with brief notes on variations.

The exporter's principal relationship will be with the importer of his goods. He will want to enter into a commercial supply contract which will follow his standard format in every respect except payment. For reasons which are explained in greater detail in the next chapter, the supply contract must be kept separate from the countertrade contract. The framework agreement is the bridge between the two, and is the reference document for the terms and conditions within which the two contracts will be drawn up.

The exporter is to derive payment for his export from the sale of goods made available to him in the country to which he is selling. 'Made available' is a term chosen deliberately, as it is unlikely that the countertrade goods emanate from the buyer of the principal export goods. The availability and saleability of goods offered in countertrade are the key issues in structuring a successful deal. (Chapter 10 goes into the question of countertrade goods, and Chapter 14 examines the very special situation that exists in Eastern Europe.)

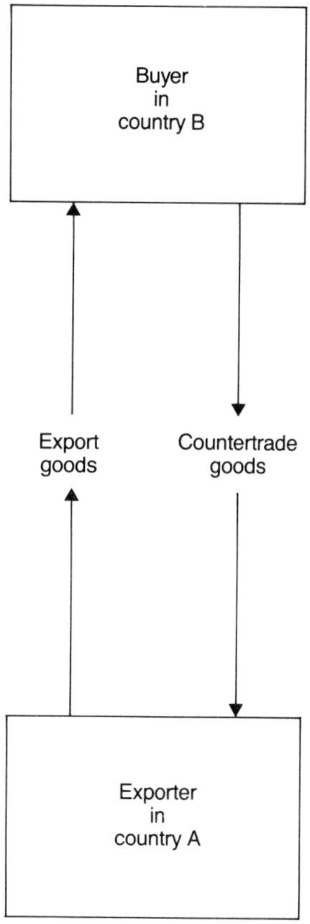

Fig. 6.1 Compensation deals (1)

Once approval has been given to a countertrade, the next step is to examine how the countertrade leg of the deal can be organised.

The options are as follows:

1. Identify goods for use within the exporter's own company or group.
2. Identify goods and then find a buyer.
3. Identify a trading house knowledgeable in that particular market, and ask them to seek suitable goods.

The first option is rather unusual and for now we can ignore it. Whichever of the other options is chosen, the relationships and implications remain the same.

At this stage, we reach one of the most important features of countertrade: the 'disagio'. Almost without exception, if a country could sell its goods for cash, at an acceptable price, it would do so. When goods are made available for countertrade, it is safe to assume that they are 'defective' in some way, or conditions are imposed which will make their sale difficult or expensive. Overcoming the problems will, therefore, cost money. With the countertrade contract assigned to a trading house, it is the trader who will need to suffer the financial burdens associated with selling the countertrade goods. This expenditure, coupled with the trader's profit, is charged to the exporter in the form of a composite fee – called a disagio. (Chapter 10 explains how the disagio is built up.) Minimising the disagio is of considerable importance to the exporter, as it will ultimately affect his profitability or competitiveness. The exporter, in seeking a trader (or end-user) to manage the countertrade aspect of the transaction must, therefore, not only seek the most capable trader, but also the cheapest in terms of disagio demanded.

Figure 6.2 shows where we stand now. The exporter has struck his contract with the foreign buyer, and the trader has struck a bargain with the supplier. But the two need to be tied together as regards the flow of money. Although such deals are often called barter, we can see that there must be a flow of cash at some stage. We must remember too that the country buying the exporter's goods has imposed, or is forced to use, compensation, owing to a lack of foreign exchange. That will also in many cases indicate a lack of creditworthiness. For the exporter, the implication will probably be that confirmations on letters of credit will not be available. We have the situation, therefore, that the exporter is relying on the sale of countertrade goods *not yet delivered.*

The exporter may take a view on the likelihood of the countertrade goods being delivered, but there is no guarantee that the funds generated from the sale will be delivered to the exporter. The reverse side of the deal sees the same difficulty – linking the importer of the principal export goods to the exporter of the countertrade goods. Individual agreements must be struck between the parties setting out the mechanism for payment of the various sales proceeds; Fig. 6.3 illustrates the point.

Agreements struck in this way are, unfortunately, not always as strong as prudence would dictate. The support of letters of credit may be necessary, and in any event highly desirable. Many people seem to think that because the purchase of goods is taking place in a countertrade deal, the usual commercial precautions are abandoned. Letters of

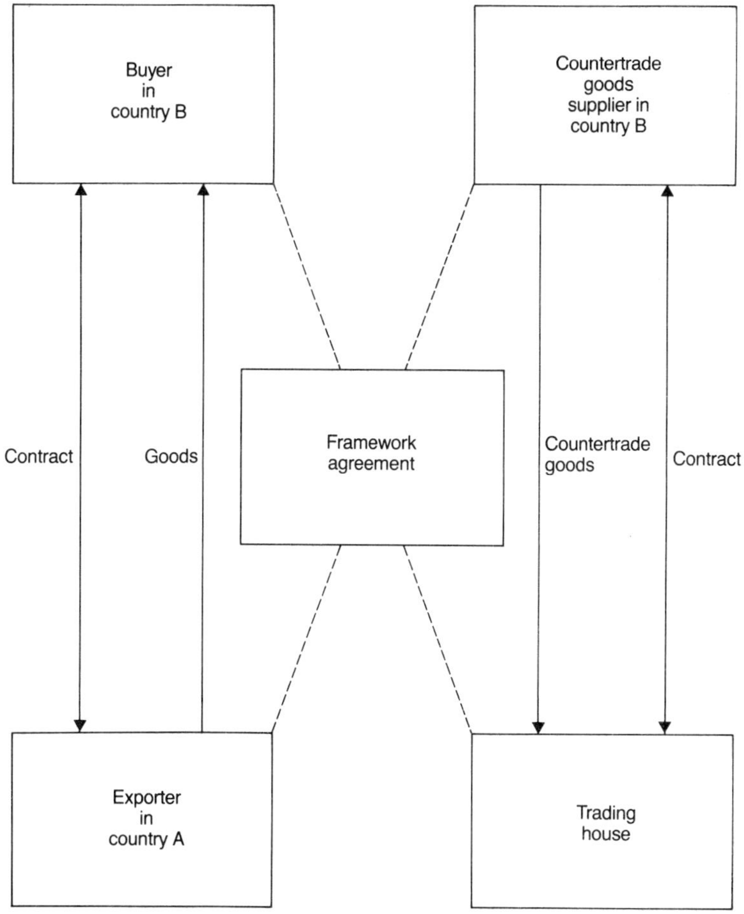

Fig. 6.2 Compensation deals (2)

credit provide a great deal of protection to buyer and seller. Even if the letter of credit from the foreign buyer cannot be confirmed, it will still be a useful link in the chain. The letters of credit will be claused so that a drawing on the 'hard' credit will provide the funds for the drawing on the 'soft' credit. This can only be handled efficiently when both letters of credit are dealt with by the same bank. ('Soft letter of credit' refers to those established by a foreign buyer, where confirmation of the letter of credit has been impossible to arrange. 'Hard letter of credit' refers to the letter of credit for the purchase of countertrade goods, where confirmation would be available if required.) The agreement between the

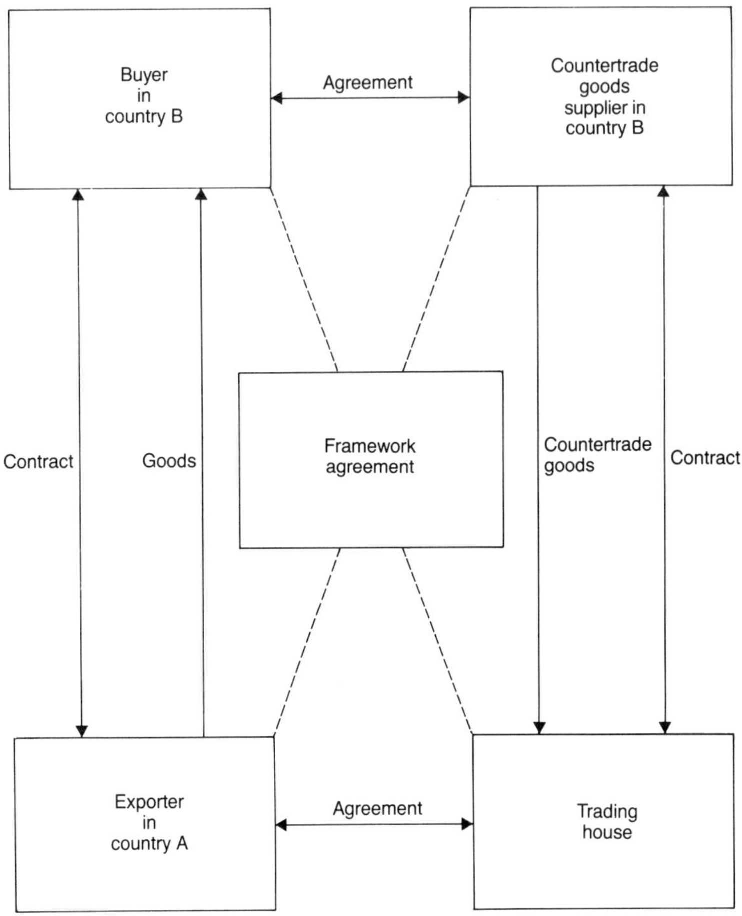

Fig. 6.3 Compensation deals (3)

exporter and the trader will also describe how the disagio will be paid.

Figure 6.4 shows the transaction as it looks when completed, with notes on the sequence of events after signing the framework agreement.

Within this arrangement there are several documents peculiar to countertrade:

1. Framework agreement.
2. Agreement with trading house.
3. Specially claused letters of credit.

These documents are dealt with in more detail in Chapter 7.

Note: The sales contract and countertrade goods purchase contract should not differ to any great extent from normal sales/purchase contracts.

The additional costs unique to countertrade have been mentioned already, but there are also risks inherent in transactions of this kind. We can examine the transaction step by step, identify areas of risk, assess the implications and then suggest ways of overcoming those risks.

From this analysis, two obvious solutions are presented to cover several of the problems. Each will be described in greater detail later on:

1. Insurance (Chapter 9, on countertrade insurance).
2. Timing (Chapter 8, on advance compensation).

In the transaction described in Figure 6.4, it has been assumed that the trading house will act as the principal in buying the countertrade goods. In some situations it may not be possible to achieve such an arrangement. Either the trading house or the supplier of the countertrade goods may not wish to see the trader as principal, but will insist that the exporter is also the buyer of the countertrade goods.

Unless the countertrade goods are to be used within the exporter's company, the exporter should *not* consider buying such goods on an 'open' basis, i.e. without the benefit of a buyer, already committed to the purchase of the goods.

Figure 6.5 shows how the arrangement would look diagrammatically if the exporter had to act as buyer of the countertrade goods.

The arrangement shown cannot be recommended. There are risks additional to those described above, such as product liability risks. Foremost, however, are the problems relating to the back-to-back contracts and letters of credit. Exactly matching terms may be used, but any ambiguity could be seen as a source of dispute. The exporter may be faced with the problem of honouring a commitment to buy and to pay only to find that the trading company's 'mirror' obligations are avoidable for some reason. Transferable letters of credit are to be preferred, rather than back-to-back, if the arrangement described is unavoidable. Chapter 7 on documentation mentions the various types of letters of credit.

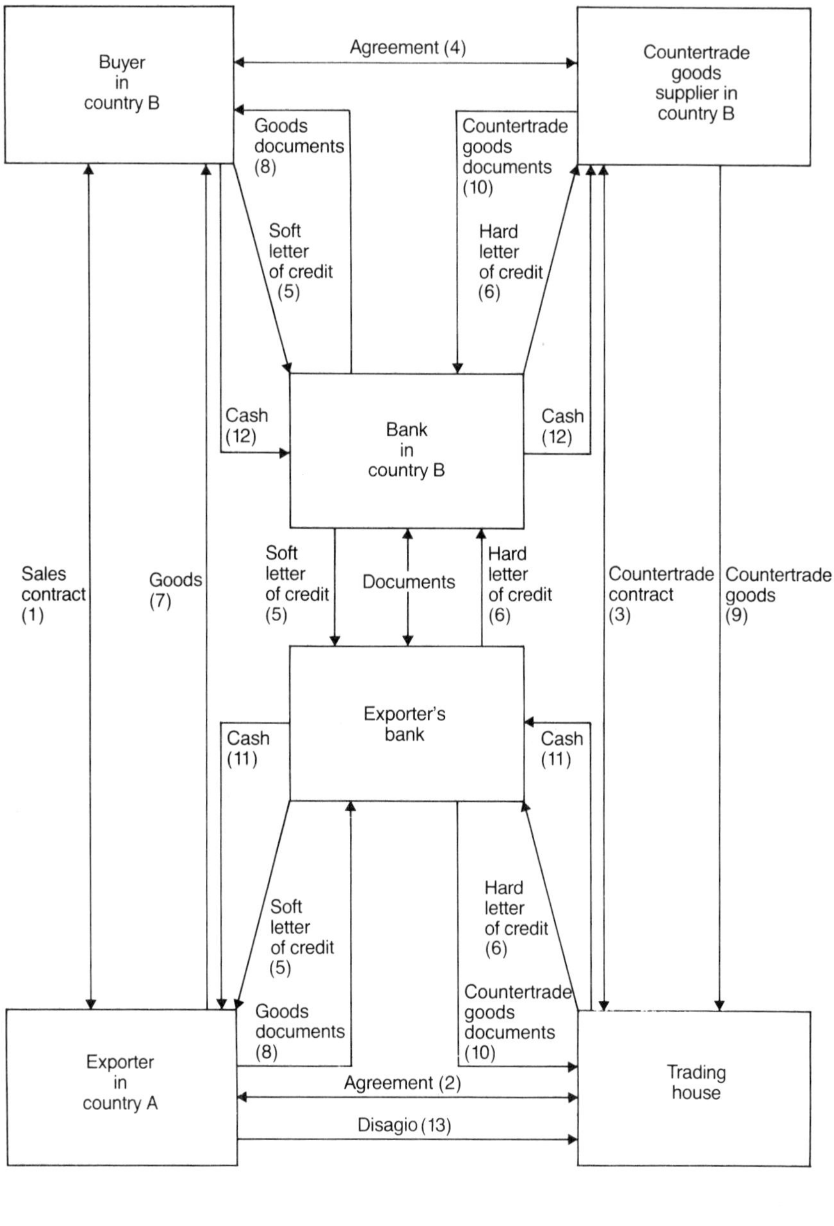
Buyer in country B
Agreement (4)
Countertrade goods supplier in country B
Goods documents (8)
Countertrade goods documents (10)
Soft letter of credit (5)
Hard letter of credit (6)
Cash (12)
Bank in country B
Cash (12)
Sales contract (1)
Goods (7)
Soft letter of credit (5)
Documents
Hard letter of credit (6)
Countertrade contract (3)
Countertrade goods (9)
Exporter's bank
Cash (11)
Cash (11)
Soft letter of credit (5)
Hard letter of credit (6)
Goods documents (8)
Countertrade goods documents (10)
Exporter in country A
Agreement (2)
Trading house
Disagio (13)

Summary of process in compensation deals (4)

(1) The exporter signs a sales contract with the foreign buyer, which makes no reference to the countertrade leg.
(2) An agreement is signed between the exporter and the trading company on how the funds will be handled, how the disagio will be paid, etc. (see Chapter 7).
(3) The trading house will contract with the supplier of the countertrade goods; this contract also describes how the funds will be paid.
(4) In the importing country, the importer will reach an understanding or sign an agreement which will, in many ways, mirror the agreement described in (2) above.
(5) The importer will arrange to establish a letter of credit (probably without benefit of confirmation) in favour of the exporter, claused to direct payment thereunder from the proceeds of the letter of credit described in (6).
(6) The trading house will establish a letter of credit in favour of the countertrade goods supplier, possibly confirmed, but claused as regards reimbursement.
(7) Goods are shipped by the exporter.
(8) Shipping documents as called for under the letter of credit are presented to the bank.
(9) Perhaps simultaneously with or before (7), countertrade goods are shipped to the trading house.
(10) The countertrade goods shipping documents are presented as called for under the letter of credit.
(11) The payment due from the trading house under the countertrade goods letter of credit will cover the drawing on the letter of credit in favour of the principal exporter.
(12) The reverse happens in the other country.
(13) The exporter pays the trading house the agreed disagio.

Fig. 6.4 Compensation deals (4)

Counterpurchase

Figure 6.6 shows a counterpurchase transaction in simplistic form. Once again we can build on it to show the various parties involved, their relationships, and the goods and funds flows.

To reiterate, the difference between compensation and counterpurchase lies in the flow of funds. Whereas the sale of the countertrade goods in the former provides the hard currency to pay for the export, in the latter each leg of the transaction is separate as regards payments.

A framework agreement may exist, setting out the counterpurchase obligation of the exporter to buy goods to an agreed value. The options available to the exporter faced with a compensation problem are equally applicable here:

1. Identify goods for use within the exporter's own company or group.
2. Identify goods and then find a buyer.

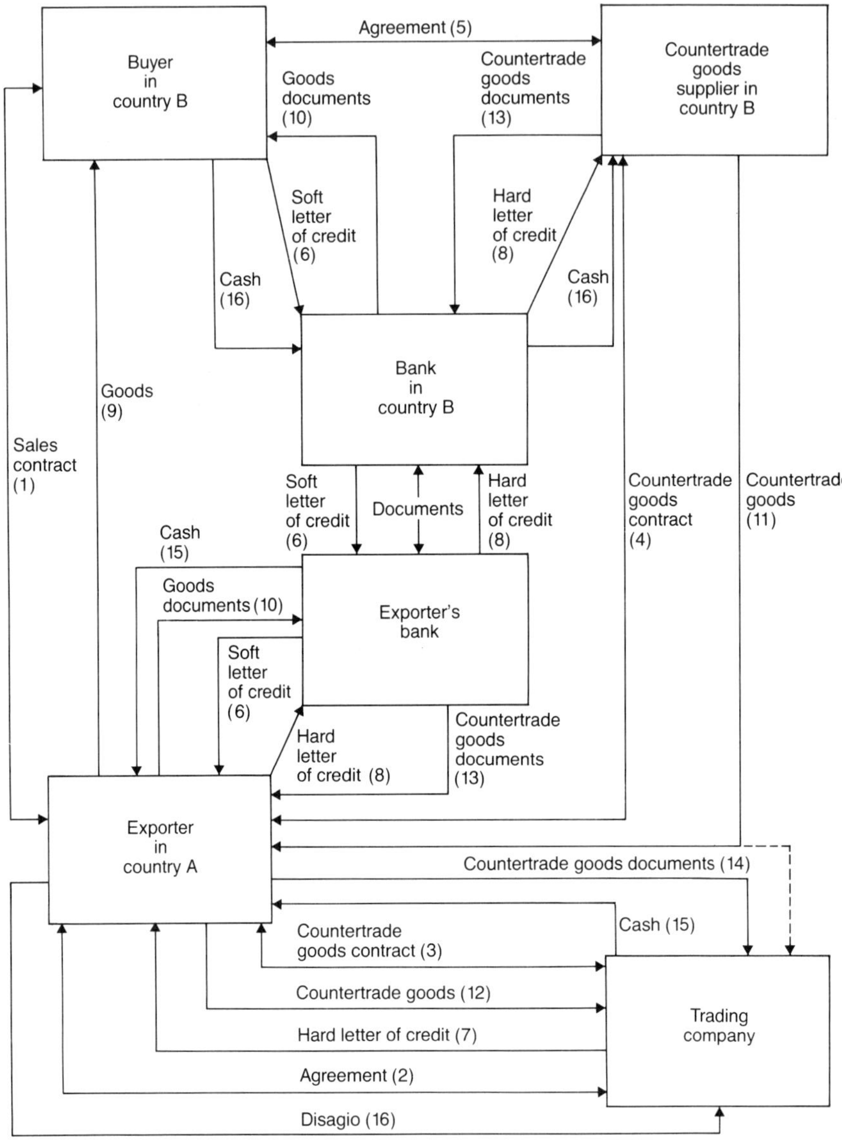
Buyer in country B
Agreement (5)
Countertrade goods supplier in country B
Goods documents (10)
Countertrade goods documents (13)
Soft letter of credit (6)
Hard letter of credit (8)
Cash (16)
Cash (16)
Bank in country B
Goods (9)
Sales contract (1)
Soft letter of credit (6)
Documents
Hard letter of credit (8)
Countertrade goods contract (4)
Countertrade goods (11)
Cash (15)
Goods documents (10)
Exporter's bank
Soft letter of credit (6)
Hard letter of credit (8)
Countertrade goods documents (13)
Exporter in country A
Countertrade goods documents (14)
Cash (15)
Countertrade goods contract (3)
Countertrade goods (12)
Hard letter of credit (7)
Agreement (2)
Disagio (16)
Trading company

Figure 6.4 shows how a countertrade obligation would be discharged if a trading company acted as principal in the purchase of countertrade goods. Figure 6.5 shows how the transaction would look if the exporter acted as principal, *back to back* with a trading company.

(1) Exporter in country A signs a contract with the buyer in country B.
(2) In terms of a separate framework agreement, exporter A has to undertake a counterpurchase of goods from a supplier in country B, and recruits a trading company to take delivery of the goods, the trading company *not* acting as principal.
(3) When specific countertrade goods have been identified, the exporter negotiates the conditions on which the trading company will buy the countertrade goods, and signs a contract.
(4) The exporter signs a contract in the same terms, with the countertrade goods supplier in country B.
(5) The buyer and the supplier in country B reach an agreement on how the payment of local funds between them will be organised.
(6) The buyer in country B establishes a soft letter of credit in favour of the exporter.
(7) The trading company *may* be asked to establish a letter of credit in favour of the exporter in support of the contract.
(8) The exporter establishes a letter of credit in favour of the countertrade goods supplier in country B, claused to divert the proceeds to settlement of the soft letter of credit (see point (6) above).
(9) The exporter ships goods to the buyer in country B.
(10) Shipping documents as called for in the soft letter of credit are presented to the bank.
(11) At approximately the same time as (9), countertrade goods are shipped, possibly to the ultimate buyer.
(12) If the goods have *not* been delivered direct to the ultimate buyer, the trading company, they will now.
(13) Documents evidencing the shipment of the countertrade goods will be presented under the terms of the hard letter of credit.
(14) The documents will be presented under the letter of credit from the trading company (if established—if not, the documents will be presented for payment direct).
(15) Hard currency will be paid by the trading company to the exporter's bank, who will use it to meet the drawing on the soft letter of credit by paying the exporter.
(16) In country B, settlement will be made by payments in local currency by the buyer to the countertrade goods supplier. The exporter will now have to pay the agreed disagio to the trading company.

Fig. 6.5 Compensation deals (5)

3. Identify a trading house knowledgeable in that particular market, and ask them to seek suitable goods.

In compensation transactions, timing is critical – the exporter would not wish to be left waiting for a long period after shipment of his goods before countertrade goods are found and sold. With counterpurchase, the timing is not so critical. Provided the exporter was reasonably certain that a particular product or products of an acceptable quality

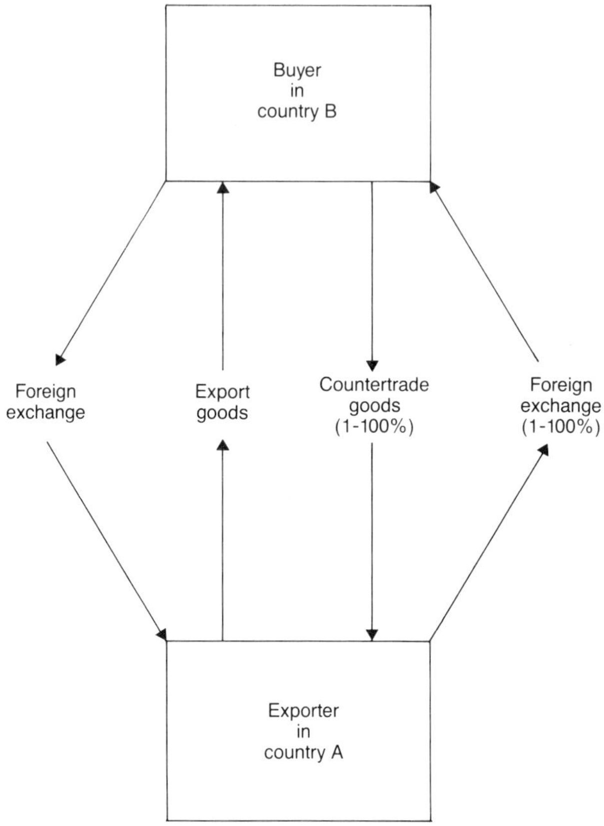

Fig. 6.6 Counterpurchase (1)

would be available at some stage, then choosing goods for in-house use would be a viable option.

Most often, however, options (2) or (3) would be chosen and the comments in the section on compensation relating to disagio (page 44) would still apply. The exporter must strike a relationship with the trader – usually a somewhat simpler matter than compensation deals due to the subsequent independence of the two legs. Equally, the relationship between importer and supplier of the countertrade goods will be a very simple one – indeed there may be no contact whatsoever. If a country has a countertrade policy based on the principle of counterpurchase, then the administration of the policy will be in the hands of a central body which will provide the link.

Counterpurchase transactions are of only limited and occasional use in commercial transactions not involving governments. There is no incentive for a private importer to demand that the exporter buys goods in counterpurchase from a supplier unconnected with the importer. Naturally, if the importer saw some benefit in having the exporter buy the importer's own products, then counterpurchase could be applied. Figure 6.7 shows the very separate nature of the two legs in the transaction – linked only by the framework agreement.

It is appropriate at this point to highlight another golden rule:

> Countertrade may be an answer to the problem of foreign exchange shortages, but is not an answer to a need for credit.

Compensation is essentially a cash generation system, and it is very

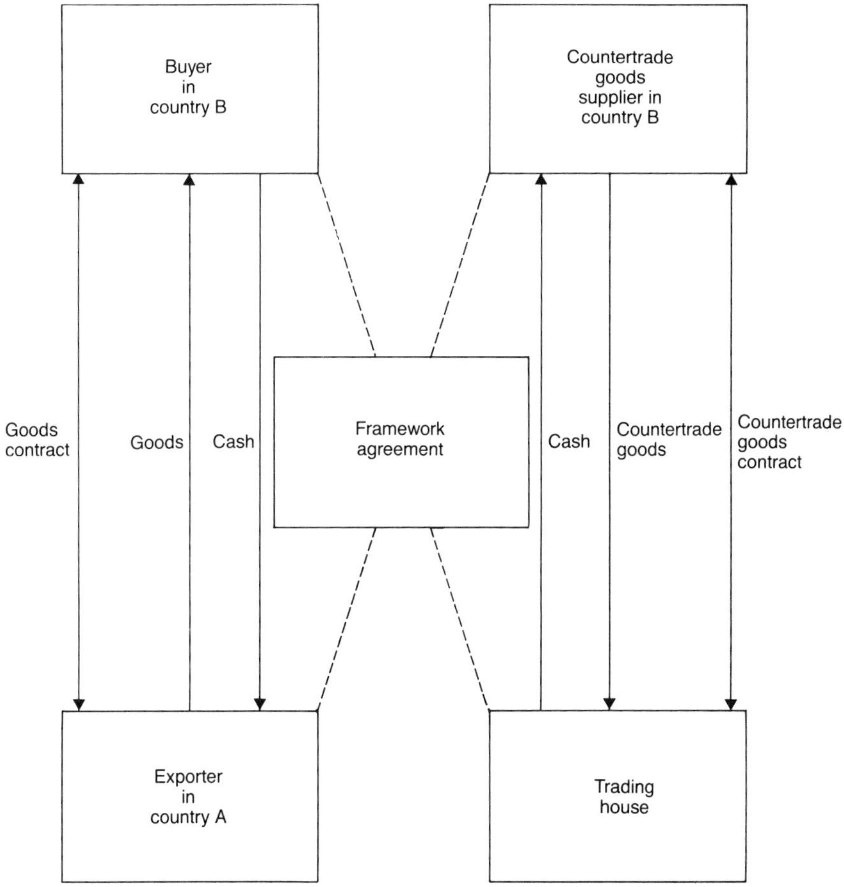

Fig. 6.7 Counterpurchase (2)

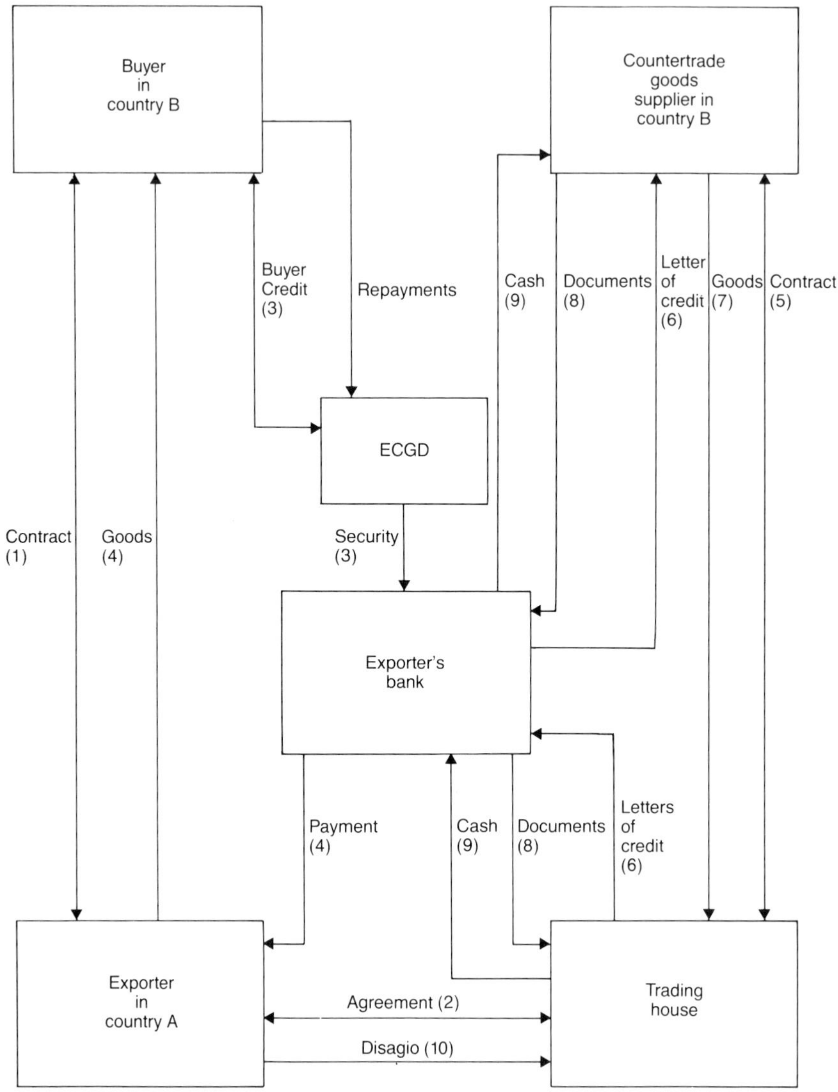

Buyer in country B
Countertrade goods supplier in country B
Buyer Credit (3)
Repayments
Cash (9)
Documents (8)
Letter of credit (6)
Goods (7)
Contract (5)
ECGD
Contract (1)
Goods (4)
Security (3)
Exporter's bank
Payment (4)
Cash (9)
Documents (8)
Letters of credit (6)
Exporter in country A
Trading house
Agreement (2)
Disagio (10)

Under the terms of a framework agreement, the buyer in country B will buy goods from exporter A, if a counterpurchase is undertaken.

(1) The exporter signs a sales contract with the foreign buyer, which makes no reference to the countertrade leg.
(2) An agreement is signed between the exporter and the trading company whereby the trading company undertakes to discharge the counterpurchase obligation against payment of a disagio.
(3) The exporter may arrange for a medium-term credit facility, with (say) ECGD support through a commercial bank, so that the exporter receives cash on shipment.
(4) The exporter will ship the goods and receive payment.
(5) In the meantime, the trading house will sign a contract for the purchase of countertrade goods.
(6) In support of the contract, letters of credit may be established.
(7) The countertrade goods will be delivered.
(8) Documents evidencing the despatch of the countertrade goods will be presented under the terms of the letter of credit.
(9) Payment will be made under the terms of the letter of credit.
(10) On successful completion (or partial completion) of the countertrade leg, the exporter will pay the disagio (pro rata) to the trading house.

Note For the sake of simplicity, the bank in country B has been omitted from the diagram.

Fig. 6.8 Counterpurchase (3)

difficult to introduce a system of credit. The same is not true of counterpurchase. As both legs are financially independent, there could be a credit facility available for the principal export. As mentioned earlier, the export credit agencies such as ECGD will provide support for counterpurchase deals because payment for the export will be in cash, not goods. We could therefore see a transaction structured on the basis of Fig. 6.8.

It is obvious that the risks associated with counterpurchase are considerably less than those in compensation deals. The analyses in Tables 6.1 and 6.2 illustrate the point, but first a further comment on penalty guarantees (see also Chapter 7). Many countries using counterpurchase as a technique are not happy to accept 'best efforts' undertakings to discharge obligations. They will require a formal undertaking, supported by a performance bond – often called a penalty guarantee. If the counterpurchase is not undertaken, the guarantee will be called up. Under compensation deals, there will be no penalty guarantee, of course – non-performance of the countertrade leg is penalty enough, as no hard currency will be generated. The question of non-performance is considered in the risk analyses shown in Tables 6.1 and 6.2.

Table 6.1 Compensation: an analysis of the risks

Risks	Implications	Solution
* Numbers refers to the numbered stages set out in Fig. 6.4		
(1) A Repudiation/cancellation of export contract or insolvency of buyer, *before* establishment of soft letter of credit.	A 1. Loss of profit. 2. Pre-delivery costs. 3. If countertrade goods already shipped, disagio will still be payable.	1. Insurance. 2. Insurance. 3. Insurance.
B As (A) but *after* establishment of soft letter of credit.	B Exporter should be protected by letter of credit.	Insurance.
(2) A Repudiation/cancellation of agreement with trading company.	A Recruitment of replacement trading company may involve higher disagio.	Choose trader carefully or ask for performance bond.
B Insolvency of trading company, and subsequent failure to complete contract.	B If hard letter of credit has been established, no risk to exporter. If letter of credit has not been established, the implication is the same as in (2) A.	Have performance bond issued by bank or insurance company, to cover trader's non-performance.
(3) Repudiation/cancellation of contract to supply countertrade goods by, or insolvency of, supplier.	No goods will be supplied, and therefore new goods/suppliers must be found. Delay may be costly, a new trader may need to be found, and disagio may be higher.	Insurance. Performance bond.
(4) Disruption/cancellation or frustration of agreement between importer of principal export goods and countertrade goods supplier.	No implications for the exporter, other than that identified in (3) above.	—
(5) A Soft letter of credit may not contain the right clauses re drawings.	The linkage of the soft letter of credit to the hard letter of credit may not be possible, and exporter will not receive funds.	Use one bank, experienced in countertrade matters.
B Soft letter of credit expires before principal export goods shipped and drawing made.	Disagio could be payable if the countertrade leg has been completed.	Soft letter of credit to have longer expiry date than hard letter of credit.

Table 6.1 *Cont.*

Risks	Implications	Solution
(6) Hard letter of credit expires before countertrade goods shipped.	Countertrade goods not shipped and sold, therefore no hard currency available to pay for exports.	Set realistic expiry dates for letter of credit. Do not ship exports until countertrade goods shipped.
(7) Goods shipped but countertrade goods are not.	As (6) above.	Insurance. Do not ship exports until countertrade goods are shipped.
(8) Shipping documents do not conform to soft letter of credit requirements.	Subsequent drawing in hard currency may not be possible. (*Note*: this risk exists in normal letter of credit based transactions.)	Subsequent ratification – no special preventative measures.
(9) A Countertrade goods shipped, but export contract cancelled, repudiated or importer fails through insolvency.	A Export may not take place, but disagio will still be payable.	A Countertrade goods not to be shipped until soft letter of credit established. Insurance.
B Countertrade goods shipped, but prove to be unacceptable to trading company.	B Trading company may not be able to sell the goods.	B This is a problem for the trading company – the letter of credit drawing will be paid provided the documents are in order.
C Countertrade goods not shipped, but export goods have been.	As (6) above.	Insurance. Do not ship exports until countertrade goods are shipped.
(10) Shipping documents do not conform to hard letter of credit requirements.	Drawing in hard currency may not be possible so no funds available to meet drawings under the soft letter of credit. (*Note*: this risk exists in normal letter of credit based transactions.)	Subsequent ratification – no special preventative measures.

Once the two sets of documents are in the hands of the bank, and both conform to their respective letters of credit, the banks will effect steps 11 and 12. On satisfactory conclusion of the countertrade leg, the disagio will be payable – step 13.

Table 6.2 Counterpurchase: an analysis of the risks

Risks	Implications	Solution
* Numbers refer to the numbered stages set out in Fig. 6.7		
(1) Contract for export goods cancelled or buyer insolvent.	A Pre-delivery expenses. B Loss if any fee paid to trading house.	A Insurance. B Insurance. Avoid signing agreement with trading house incurring commitment fees, etc.
	C Insistence on execution of counterpurchase by trading house, and therefore payment of disagio.	C As (1) B.
(2) Export contract fulfilled, but agreement with trading house not honoured.	Exporter will not have honoured countertrade obligation, thus incurring any penalties which may be in the framework agreement.	Performance bond from trader. Have trader assume the penalty as principal.
(7) A Non-availability of countertrade goods.	A Non-performance of countertrade obligation and therefore loss of fees paid to trader plus payment of penalty fees.	Insurance. Ensure alternative choice of goods permitted in framework agreement.
B Non-delivery of countertrade goods.	As (7) A.	Insurance.

It is obvious that the risks involved are considerably less in counterpurchase than in compensation. A careful choice of trading house partner, a well-negotiated framework agreement and a wide choice of countertrade goods will overcome most of the underlying risks.

CHAPTER 7

Documentation

Where countries have a formal practice for countertrade, the contracts and agreements may be non-negotiable. Acceptance thereof is a matter for the company to decide. The notes which follow will not apply in those cases, but may form a useful guide to what is the most desirable situation. Such a comparison may enable the company to determine the risks involved in accepting contracts and agreements which do not contain the recommended clauses.

At the same time it is not suggested that the ideas set out here are tailor-made for every situation, or complete. New ideas will emerge as countertrade grows in sophistication.

Separate contracts

A crucial point in structuring countertrade transactions as a whole is the necessity to keep export and countertrade contracts separate. The principal reasons are as follows:

1. Export credit agencies will only insure export contracts where payment is in cash (even though payment may be through an escrow account or through linked letters of credit).
2. Different time-scales may be applied to each leg of the deal.
3. The export contract details will remain secret, and will not be seen by third-party traders.
4. Each contract stands alone as a separate legal instrument.
5. Cross-default is not as likely to be applied.
6. It is easier to have the countertrade obligation signed by a third party as principal, than to introduce a third party to the export contract.
7. The buyer of the export goods may not be the supplier of the countertrade goods and therefore should not be a party to the countertrade leg of the deal (and vice versa).

Not only would one seek to have the two contracts kept separate, but there should be no cross-referencing. The framework agreement, or its equivalent, will act as the link.

Having decided that separate agreements are necessary, what form would the agreements take?

Sales contract

As has been mentioned before, the sales contract should not differ to any great extent from normal sales contracts.

Framework agreement

Linking the sales contract with the contract to purchase selected countertrade goods will be some form of framework agreement, protocol or undertaking. The actual goods to be bought may or may not be detailed therein. It is vital that certain clauses be inserted to overcome some of the risks set out in the risk analyses in Chapter 6 (Tables 6.1 and 6.2). The notes below cover the main points which should be included in the agreement.

Recital

This should be a plain-language acknowledgement of the obligation, setting out the general intentions of the parties.

Definitions

For the sake of clarity, the parties to the agreement should be defined.

Effectiveness

The countertrade obligation should not become effective until the principal export contract is signed and ratified. This overcomes one risk that an exporter would be left with the countertrade obligation and the attendant risks and costs even if the principal contract was not ratified.

Time-scales

The basic principle is to negotiate long and discharge short, allowing time to undertake further research in the event of non-availability of suitable goods. Although the date for completion of the countertrade leg may be linked to expiry of the principal contract, allowance should be made for extensions to the completion date in case events occur which cause delay in securing countertrade goods. Avoid having the shipments of countertrade goods phased equally over a period; or if this is insisted on, the ability to accelerate deliveries must be sought. The time-scales for completion of the countertrade obligation should refer to the date by which orders must be placed rather than goods delivered.

Value

There are two major considerations here – the basis of the commitment and the currency. If the transaction is of the compensation type then the value of the countertrade leg will naturally be at least equal to the value of the export leg. To allow for charges, shrinkage (i.e. rejected goods) and the uncertain final value of some types of goods (e.g. the pricing basis for certain ores is only fixed after receipt), the value of the countertrade leg should be slightly in excess of the export leg. Care should be taken not to have too great a margin of excess as this will incur unnecessary disagio payments. In most cases it will be possible to phrase the value in general terms with specific values only applied in the countertrade contract itself. The currency in which the compensation contracts must be expressed should be the same as the currency used in the principal export contract, to avoid shortfalls caused by currency movements.

On the question of counterpurchase, however, the aim must always be to reduce the obligation to the lowest acceptable level (see Chapter 5). Many countries insist on the counterpurchase being expressed as a percentage of the principal contract. Where the contract price is fixed and final, obligations expressed in terms of a percentage should not cause too much of a problem. Difficulties could arise, however, when the contract value is increased (through inflation?) or extended (further work?). The increased counterpurchase commitment which would arise may be assignable to a third party only at a higher rate of disagio than has been allowed for in the export contract price. Also, if a percentage commitment is called for, the underlying value on which the commitment is based must be clearly stated. Options would be as follows:

1. The foreign exchange content of the export contract.
2. The export contract value, less local costs, and less any aid content.

3. F.o.b./c. & f./c.i.f value of the export goods.
4. The whole contract value.

A more acceptable commitment from the exporter's point of view would be a fixed value, which may in itself represent a percentage of the original contract, but which would at least be fixed.

As regards currency, the commitment should be phrased in the currency of the principal export contract (or other hard currency), *not* the local currency. Exchange rate fluctuations could create enormous problems, by inflating the volume of goods to be taken to satisfy the commitment. (The level of commitment could be fixed by the countertrade policy of the buyer or his government or could be determined by the degree of priority of the imports. High-priority purchases would attract lower levels of demand for countertrade and vice versa.)

Pricing

Where the goods to be used in countertrade have already been determined, the basis of pricing can be fixed according to the facts of the case, or according to any normal pricing formula. An example would be a metal traded on the London Metal Exchange, where the price could be related to quoted prices.

If the countertrade goods are to be selected from a basket of commodities or are still to be identified by the trader, the basis of pricing cannot be so explicit. To ensure that the prices to be applied are not widely variant to the market price, the framework agreement pricing clauses must contain general conditions. Such clauses can be useful later in proving that the countertrade contract is unworkable when overpriced goods are offered, and that the foreign parties are in breach.

Typical clauses would refer to the supply of goods at international market prices, or internationally competitive prices. Wherever possible, however, a pricing formula should be applied which makes it easy to determine *actual* prices and which removes the possibility of dispute. Avoid quoting fixed prices in the framework agreement unless there is no alternative, or some special benefit accrues.

Payment terms

In compensation deals, the method of payment will be determined by the agreed funds flow, i.e. linked letters of credit or escrow accounts (see Chapter 8). Counterpurchase presents a different set of problems.

The trading company may wish to extract from the supplier of the countertrade goods a period of credit to give time for the goods to be moved on to an end user. Early warning of this requirement should be given by making reference to it in the framework agreement.

Choice of goods

Unless the countertrade goods to be taken are quite obvious, the goods clause in the framework agreement should be worded in non-specific terms to provide the greatest degree of flexibility. The risks relating to non-availability and non-delivery of goods have been listed in Chapter 6. Although in counterpurchase contracts such occurrences would constitute breach (see later in this chapter), in compensation real problems could be created, as the sale of such goods would have provided payment for the export goods.

The overriding criterion is 'freedom of choice'. Although lists of countertrade goods may be supplied, the availability of such goods may be questionable. The list may change without advice or warning. Selection of the goods should be the preserve of the exporter and/or his trading house partner. In addition the source of the goods should be at the exporter's or trader's discretion.

Where the buyer of the export goods is different from the supplier of the countertrade goods, we call the relationship 'linkage'. It represents the hardest relationship to structure, unless there is a firm policy permitting linkage. Linkage, therefore, is what we must seek to achieve in every deal. References to 'subject to approval' should be avoided when discussing linkage – freedom of choice is the goal.

Included in this clause could be a stipulation that the exporter reserves the right to inspect the goods before shipment by a neutral surveyor.

Marketing limitations

Following on from the idea of 'freedom of choice' and realistic pricing is the idea that there should be no restriction on where the countertrade goods can be sold. The seller will be looking for protection in his traditional markets by imposing restrictions. Indeed one of the rationales for countertrade is to break into new markets by passing the marketing obligations to companies more able to tap such markets. It may be necessary to make concessions here by offering to try to sell the goods into new markets on a 'best efforts' basis. There may be advantages in the exporter/trading house seeking an undertaking of exclusivity in new markets identified by the export trader.

One final restriction which the suppliers of the countertrade goods may seek to impose is that of price – they may insist that the goods are sold without subsidy. As this represents the most favoured technique for the disposal of countertrade goods, such restrictions are to be avoided.

Transferability

Throughout this book reference has been made to the involvement of third parties in the buying of countertrade goods. This may not be what the foreign buyer/supplier has in mind. They may wish to see a direct purchase by the exporter. To be safe, specific reference must be made to the right of the exporter to transfer or assign the countertrade to a third party. Any suggestion that the third party *must* be in the exporter's country should be resisted.

Discharge/measurement of fulfilment

The system for monitoring or measuring fulfilment of the countertrade obligation must be clearly defined. Topics to be covered in these clauses would be as follows:

1. Document required to evidence value of shipment.
2. Officer or official responsible for certifying acceptance of a purchase of goods as part settlement of a countertrade obligation.
3. Review meetings to discuss progress or problems.
4. Credit to be given for appropriate purchases of countertrade goods which had been made prior to the execution of the contract under discussion.
5. Inclusion of local purchases of services as partial settlement of the obligation.

Special mention should be made that if orders for countertrade goods are placed but not fulfilled by the supplier, the value of the order should be credited to the obligation (counterpurchase only). Final settlement of the countertrade obligation should be evidenced by the issuance of a certificate of completion or discharge.

Performance bonds, etc.

There could well be a call for background security from both sides. The exporter should seek security – if the facts of the case so suggest – if delivery of the countertrade goods is in doubt. This could take the form of a suitably worded performance bond, confirmed or re-issued by a bank in a hard-currency area, or a standby letter of credit (to be discussed later in this chapter). Acts of default to be covered would include failure to ship, shipping inferior goods or late delivery.

The 'reverse' performance bond – often called a penalty guarantee – is a far more serious affair. Many countries demanding counterpurchase require a form of security that the counterpurchase of goods will actually take place. The level of the bond varies from country to country, but could be for as much as 100 per cent of the principal contract value. It is obviously in the exporter's interest to minimise the amount of the bond/guarantee, for two reasons: firstly, the guarantee may be called; secondly, the higher the value, the higher the bank fee for its issue. In practice, many such bonds or guarantees are issued by the trader as principal, or back to back with one issued by the exporter. Penalty guarantees are described in greater detail below.

*Breach/arbitration/*force majeure

The final clauses will cover the legal remedies for breach, their consideration by arbitration in the event of dispute, and the application of *force majeure*. On the subject of arbitration specifically, the court should be one which sits outside the country of the buyer. As a concession, a third country could be chosen, and Austria, France and Switzerland are commonly selected.

The above suggestions are of a general nature and will not all apply to both compensation *and* counterpurchase. Each point should be considered during the negotiation process to determine whether it is applicable to that particular transaction.

Countertrade contracts

If the obligation to purchase countertrade goods has been assigned to a third party, that party will be responsible for the negotiation and signature of the purchase contract. There should be no significant difference between a purchase contract struck within a countertrade transaction and a normal commercial deal, except as influenced by terms in the framework agreement. On the basis that the goods will be unattractively priced, the trading house buyer may be buying at a price which is higher than that which will ultimately be realised. In such cases, the principal exporter will have undertaken to pay a disagio to the trader, but no mention of this fact will be made in the countertrade contract.

Just as in the framework agreement one would refer to the fact that the countertrade obligation only comes into effect if the principal contract does, a similar reference could be made in the countertrade contract. There are no hard and fast rules, as a great deal will depend on the relationship between the buyer of the principal export goods and the supplier of the countertrade goods. In some cases, the third-party buyer of the countertrade goods may insist that the countertrade contract is effective notwithstanding, as he may be relying on delivery of the goods.

A constraint on the time-scale for completion of the countertrade will probably have been imposed within the terms of the framework agreement. The exporter should ensure that the countertrade contract is to be performed by the expiry date.

The value of the contract may not be the same as the amount of the countertrade obligation as determined by the framework agreement. The contract may be one of a series or the trader may have parcelled the obligation with several others. The currency of the contract may be different from that of the principal export but this need not be a consideration for the exporter as long as the agreement between exporter and trader is in the right currency for the exporter's purposes. This would be particularly important in the case of a compensation transaction. There would be a problem if the currencies were different, as losses could arise from exchange rate fluctuations when the trader pays the countertrade goods value to the exporter. In terms of counterpurchase a different currency to the countertrade obligation could mean that if the exchange rate varies, more countertrade goods would need to be bought to satisfy the obligation.

Particular mention must be made of two important considerations:

1. *Counterpurchase*
   As and when goods are supplied under the countertrade contract, credit should be given for the value of the purchases, against the total obligation of the exporter. Reference must be made to this in the contract.

2. *Compensation*
   The trading house will not pay the value of the countertrade goods to the supplier but will account for them in the way described in the framework agreement. Reference should be made to the funds flow in the countertrade contract unless the letters of credit associated with the purchase cover the requirement adequately.

The complexities associated with the purchase of some commodities, such as oil and ores, should be enough to suggest to the exporter that contracts to purchase such material are best left to experts. In some situations where the exporter is obliged to buy as principal, the ultimate buyer of the countertrade goods should set out the terms and conditions of the purchase so that the exporter is acting back to back, with his contracts, letters of credit, etc., mirroring those of the ultimate buyer.

Agreements with third parties

With the growing sophistication of the participants in countertrade, considerable refinement has taken place in the structuring of the relationships with third parties. Many of the trading companies active in countertrade have model agreements setting out the basis on which the company will assume countertrade obligations. Naturally, the agreements will seek to impose the trading company's conditions and exporters should not sign without careful consideration. Much will depend on how the transaction is structured, but the following options could apply:

1. Trader acts as agent or principal.
2. Trader contracts direct or back to back.
3. Trader is buying known goods or is yet to choose.

Agent or principal

The trader could contract in his own name or act as agent for the exporter, in the countertrade contract. The former is preferable for obvious reasons.

Contract direct or back to back

If the exporter undertakes the countertrade contract direct as principal, the trading company must act back to back with the exporter. If the trading company contracts direct, the note above is applicable.

Firm or best efforts

An exporter should try to pass the obligation to a third party totally and without recourse. In some situations, however, the best that might be achieved would be for a trader to offer to undertake the countertrade obligation on a 'best efforts' basis. In a compensation deal, such an arrangement could be satisfactory provided the exporter is not obliged to deliver until a firm countertrade contract is struck. Generally, however, a firm undertaking should be sought, for a fixed disagio, rather than 'best efforts'.

Undertaking contractual or otherwise

The form of the agreement between exporter and third party could vary enormously. As mentioned in the introduction to this section, standard agreements are produced by some trading companies. They tend to be contractual in form (see Appendix 4 for examples). Simple statements of intent should be avoided.

Penalty guarantee issued by third party or otherwise

If the framework agreement or government rules call for a penalty guarantee, ideally it should be issued by the third-party trader. If this is impossible or impractical, an indemnity should be taken wherever possible from the third party, to cover the exporter's guarantee. There is a cost implication here in that if the exporter issues the guarantee, the cost would be borne by the exporter.

Where the third party issues the guarantee, the fee will be paid by that third party in the first instance (although probably recovered from the exporter in the form of an increased disagio).

There are so many ways of structuring the relationship between the parties, that a complete picture could not easily be given. Apart from the facts of the case, what could also determine the way the relationship is set up will be the financial strength, commercial ability or integrity of the third party. Exporters are encouraged to investigate third parties thoroughly before committing to a contract.

Finally, unless the third party is happy that the agreement itself provides sufficient security (i.e. he is satisfied that the exporter would honour the undertaking to pay a disagio) the third party may call for a form of security, e.g. a guarantee or letter of credit. As both may cost money (such as bank fees) they are best avoided.

Penalty guarantees

Failure to complete the countertrade leg of a compensation transaction is a penalty in itself. If sale of the countertrade goods is to provide the hard currency to pay for the principal export, non-performance means non-payment.

With counterpurchase, however, there is no link between the two sides of the transaction as far as finance is concerned. Many countries using counterpurchase recognise the dangers of non-performance. Although they may have legal recourse under the framework agreement for breach of contract, further protection is often sought in the form of a penalty guarantee. This could be called a performance bond or reverse performance bond.

If the countertrade obligation has been passed to a third party, every effort should be made to have the guarantee issued by the third party or their bankers. Second best is to have the third party indemnify the exporter against claims made under the guarantee issued by the exporter direct.

It is as important to have the guarantee drafted correctly as the sales contract or framework agreement. The notes that follow cover the main points with regard to the issue and construction of such guarantees.

Value

The guarantee should be linked to the value of the countertrade obligation, usually by quoting the extent of the maximum liability as a percentage. Care should be taken to ensure that the guarantee is linked to the value of the countertrade obligation and not to the value of the principal export contract. The value should decrease progressively, with the gradual performance of the countertrade obligation. A clause must be inserted to this effect, although if the guarantee is issued by a financial institution, it may require a fair degree of negotiation to get a clause acceptable to both sides.

Issue

At one time, guarantees of performance would be issued by the exporting company, but it is increasingly common for buyers and/or their governments to demand guarantees from financial institutions. Experience has shown that banks, for example, with international reputations to protect, will respond to calls under the guarantee more readily, provided of course that the call is in terms of the guarantee.

Many banks dislike guarantees where the call is anything other than 'first demand', so exporters will be unable to depend on their banks resisting the call. In contrast, the company issuing its own guarantee could defer payment under a call so that the courts can adjudicate on the fairness, or otherwise, of the call. From the exporter's point of view, the cost of the guarantee, if issued by a financial institution, must be allowed for in calculating the extra cost of countertrade.

Calling of guarantee

It must be remembered that for many countries performance of the countertrade is more important than receiving payment under a penalty guarantee. For this reason, some countries insist that payment under the guarantee does not constitute discharge of the obligation. Remedy for performance or damages could still exist in the countertrade contract or framework agreement. (The Greek system follows this idea; see Appendix 1.) Exporters should try to have the penalty guarantee section of their agreement – if any – worded in such a way that payment under the guarantee constitutes discharge of the obligation.

A fairly common practice among exporters to Eastern Europe a few years ago was merely to pay up under their penalty guarantees rather than attempt to perform their countertrade obligations. They saw such payments as the ultimate cost of countertrade. This had two results. The level of penalty guarantee was increased to a more punitive figure and some countries introduced a form of blacklisting. Delinquent exporters were either shut out of future sales opportunities, or were faced with higher levels of demand for countertrade.

In the above section on value, mention was made of the manner in which guarantees can be called if issued by a bank. There can often be a conflict between the bank's obligation to pay and the exporter's wish to delay payment whilst proof of performance is considered by the relevant authorities. Although the bank may have to respond to a simple demand, the penalty guarantee should contain a clause to the effect that payment will be made three months after 'simple demand'. During this time, the exporter can pursue the proof of performance needed to avoid payment under the guarantee.

The apparent ease with which calls can be made underlines an important point which was discussed under 'Framework agreements'.

The manner in which performance is measured and monitored is critical. Details of meetings, oral exchanges, etc., should be committed to paper. Regular statements of amounts fulfilled and amounts outstanding should be agreed by both sides. Similarly, attempts to find suitable countertrade goods should be recorded, as should failures to deliver. Such evidence could be useful in having the guarantee extended rather than called. Calls under the guarantee should only be permitted after the expiry of the principal contract, unless partial performance is called for during the currency of the contract. When calls are made, although in the form of a simple demand, supporting documents should be called for to evidence *why* the call has been made. If claims are to be made under insurance policies (see Chapter 9 on Countertrade insurance), then such papers could be valuable evidence.

If possible, payment should be linked to the value of any arbitration award, rather than to a simple demand from the overseas party. This will ensure that the exporter has had an opportunity to prove performance, if there is some doubt about the validity of the claim. In such an arrangement, payment would be against the arbitration court claim or statement of findings.

Finally, one practice to be avoided is where the buyer has the ability to deduct the amount of any penalty from the principal export proceeds.

Examples of penalty guarantees are given in Appendix 3.

Letters of credit

Before we look at types of letters of credit used in countertrade transactions, a few words on letters of credit generally. The overriding principle relating to the use of letters of credit in commerce is their independence of the contract and goods to which they relate. This independence provides parties to a transaction with a good degree of security.

The types of credit which may be seen in countertrade deals are as described below.

Standby letters of credit

United States and English legal systems do not recognise 'penalties' in contracts. A liquidated damages clause which awards an innocent party a sum in excess of their actual loss, is considered to be a penalty. One way around the problem is to have a standby letter of credit, where the debtor pays the creditor on simple demand.

In compensation transactions, where the countertrade goods are to be delivered *after* the principal export, a standby letter of credit could provide a measure of security for the exporter. It is a fall-back source of funds in the event that the countertrade goods are subsequently not delivered. The main problem here lies in the acceptability of the letter of credit. As compensation is a system used to overcome lack of foreign exchange or credit, which can indicate uncreditworthiness, it may be impossible to have the letter of credit confirmed. Its strength as a form of security may, therefore, be diminished.

Transferable letters of credit

Many banks prefer to see these credits to those established in a back-to-back arrangement.

Transferable letters of credit are used fairly widely by traders and entrepreneurs who perhaps lack the resources to finance a 'trade' between a supplier and the ultimate buyer. The ultimate buyer would establish a transferable letter of credit in favour of the trader. On receipt, the trader will ask the advising bank to transfer all or part of the credit to the supplier or suppliers of the goods. When the goods have been despatched, the supplier presents his documents to the advising bank in his country and receives payment. The documents are sent to the trader who substitutes his own invoice – grossed up to include his margin – and then draws the balance of the letter of credit, i.e. his own profit. In countertrade, transferable letters of credit would be useful where an exporter was obliged to act as principal in a transaction to buy countertrade goods. He would not (or at least should not) do so without the benefit of a buyer behind him (see Fig. 6.8).

The ultimate buyer would issue a transferable letter of credit in favour of the exporter who would arrange for it to be transferred to the supplier of the countertrade goods.

Back-to-back credit

If a transferable letter of credit cannot be arranged, an alternative would be to have two letters of credit, lying back to back. The ultimate buyer of the goods would establish a letter of credit in favour of the trader, who would then arrange for the issue of a second letter of credit in favour of the goods supplier. This second credit has to be set up in such a way that the documents called for mirror those of the original credit. The expiry dates must also be linked. In countertrade situations, back-to-back letters of credit could be used where the exporter acts as principal in the purchase of countertrade goods. Back to back with his letter of credit would be another letter of credit from the trader or end-user recruited to handle the countertrade goods. Two problems could arise in the use of back-to-back letters of credit: firstly, the documents presented and accepted under the first letter of credit could prove unacceptable under the second; secondly, a third party may attempt to seize the money due under the first credit if he is a creditor of the beneficiary.

Back-to-back arrangements are less than satisfactory, and should be avoided if alternative arrangements can be established.

Assignment

Although the procedures for assigning debts may differ from country to country, the assignment of proceeds under a letter of credit can be used successfully in countertrade deals.

In a compensation transaction, the exporter may be the assignee of a credit established by a trader. A second use of assignment would occur when a trader was due to receive a subsidy (disagio) from a transaction but required some form of security. A portion of the value of a letter of credit could be assigned to cover the amount of the disagio due. As a drawing was made, a portion thereof – pro rata with the value of the assignment – would be paid to the trader.

Summary

Again it must be emphasised that countertrade is not a science. The documents, and their construction, described in this chapter are examples of what could occur in a transaction. What is important is that the clauses described herein should be included or, at best, considered if any of the documents described in this chapter are used in a countertrade transaction.

CHAPTER 8

Advance compensation/escrow accounts

Advance compensation

In Chapter 6, the risk analysis for compensation deals (Table 6.1) highlights the problems associated with non-delivery of the countertrade goods. For example, if an exporter in country A is exporting to country B and is to be 'paid' through the supply of goods from country B, the exporter's fear will be that once he has supplied his goods, the countersupply of goods from country B will not take place. One answer to this problem is for country B to supply its goods first. Country B may object to this on the basis that the exporter in country A may not perform under *his* contract, or that the funds generated from the sale of country B's goods will be used for some other, unauthorised, purpose. A technique exists which – if properly structured – will overcome both sets of fears. It involves the use of escrow accounts, and is called 'advance compensation'.

Methodology

For the sake of clarity, we will continue to refer to country A as the exporting country and country B as the supplier of the countertrade goods. Figure 8.1 shows the structure of the transaction and these notes refer to the numbered steps:

A. An exporter in country A arranges to sell his goods to country B, and in payment is offered, for example, tobacco.
B. It is agreed that country B will make its goods available first.
C. The exporter in country A has no use for the tobacco directly but recruits a trader/end-user to buy the tobacco – this buyer *could* be in a third country (C).
D. The transaction then proceeds as follows:
  (1) Country A goods exporter signs an agreement or contract with the tobacco buyer in country C.

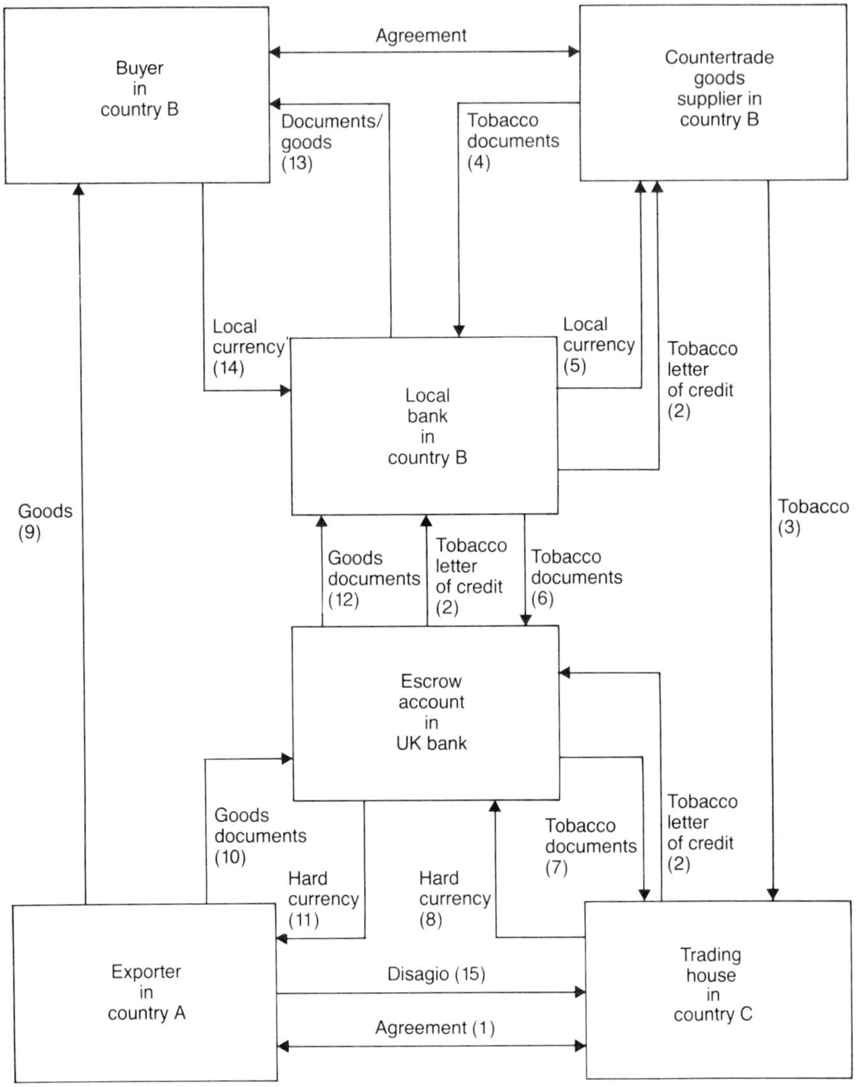

Fig. 8.1 Advance compensation

(2) The buyer in country C establishes a letter of credit in favour of the supplier of the tobacco in country B (who will often *not* be the importer of the goods from country A). This letter of credit is claused to direct funds from the letter of credit to an escrow account in (say) the United Kingdom.

(3) The tobacco supplier ships the tobacco.

(4) He then presents the shipping documents to a bank in country B.

(5) The local bank in country B provides local currency to the tobacco supplier at an agreed rate of exchange, usually the rate ruling on the date of despatch. As security for this payment, the local bank could ask for a cash deposit from the eventual local importer (in country B), or an inland letter of credit, a guarantee or some similar facility.

(6) Documents in respect of the tobacco shipment are sent to the escrow bank, in terms of the tobacco letter of credit, by the local bank.

(7) In turn the documents will be presented under the letter of credit by the escrow bank.

(8) Sterling (or other hard currency) will be drawn, and credited to the escrow account. This account represents the means of safeguarding the interest of *all the parties* to the transaction. (It is discussed in greater detail in the next section.)

(9) The exporter in country A will be notified that there are funds available in the escrow account, and he will be told that if he ships the goods described in the escrow agreement before an agreed date, he will be able to draw the funds – the exporter then ships the goods to country B.

(10) Documents – as called for in the escrow agreement – will be delivered to the escrow bank.

(11) The documents will be checked to see that they conform to the requirements of the escrow account, and, if in order, the exporter will be paid.

(12) The escrow bank will forward the documents to the local bank in country B.

(13) In turn, the documents will be presented to the importer in country B.

(14) Unless local currency has already been paid in advance, the importer will now pay the local bank in country B.

(15) At some stage after arrival of the funds in the escrow account, the agreed disagio will be paid by the exporter to the tobacco buyer.

Note: The exchange rate governing the export of the tobacco and the import of the goods will be the same, despite different dates of shipment. This ensures that both sides of the transaction are valued the same in hard *and* in local currencies.

An alternative arrangement to that described in (9) above would be to have a letter of credit issued by the buyer in country B in favour of the exporter. The bank holding the escrow account will confirm the letter of credit, if the letter of credit is claused to allow for reimbursement from the escrow account. Such an arrangement also overcomes the (albeit slight) risk that the escrow account could be blocked.

Escrow accounts

The concept of escrow accounts is new to many people. A simple analogy would be with trust accounts – funds held in another right or on behalf of another party. In the context of a countertrade transaction, the escrow account is the vehicle for the funds flow management, and for this reason it is crucial that the agreement governing operation of the account be constructed with great care. Generally speaking the account will be in the name of a bank from the country of the buyer. The location of the account is, quite naturally, absolutely critical. It should be held in a hard currency country, in a bank of international standing. If the account is held in the buyer's country, there is a much greater danger of interference with the funds.

The escrow agreement should be looked upon as the mandate for operating the account. It should cover the rights and obligations of the exporter, the account-holding bank and the bank in whose name the account is held. The emphasis must be on total protection for *all* the parties to the transaction. Wording of the agreement is subject to negotiation, and the facts of each case, but the following notes describe, point by point, the clauses which should appear in one form or another.

1. *Recital of general intentions in the underlying contract*
   A plain language description of the transaction.

2. *Access of information by all parties on the balance of escrow account*
   It is important that all parties to the transaction should have access to information on the balance of the escrow account. In the case of the bank in whose name the account is held, regular reconciliations may be necessary. Statements will be required periodically, together with supporting documentation. The account-holding bank may be required to advise all the parties of the balance on the account, or merely respond to requests.

3. *The manner in which deposits are to be made*
   Clauses and sub-clauses will cover the currency of deposits, whether they are made by mail or telegraphic transfer, or by drawings on a letter of credit.

4. *The allocation and payment of interest*
   In most cases, the account will be interest-bearing. How the interest rate is to be determined (e.g. linked to bank deposit rate) and who receives the benefit of the interest, will be set out in the agreement. Although it would be of obvious benefit to the exporter if interest could be taken to off-set the disagio cost, rarely is this possible. Most often, the interest is returned to the bank in whose name the account is held.

5. *The manner of drawing from the account*
   In particular:
   (a) a schedule of supporting documents;
   (b) amount to be drawn (e.g. face value of invoice); and
   (c) whether part-drawings are allowed.

   This is the key clause. Drawings can be effected by presenting a series of documents, details of which will appear in an appendix to the agreement. There is no reason why the documents should not follow those which one would expect to see in a letter of credit. Before allowing the drawing, the escrow holding bank would scrutinise the documents for accuracy. An alternative would be to have drawings on the account made through a presentation of a letter of credit drawing. From the exporter's point of view this is preferable. His shipping documents will be considered in light of the letter of credit conditions, not the escrow agreement.

   Unless the letter of credit route is chosen, care must be taken to ensure that the basis of establishing the value of the drawing is clear. Is it to be f.o.b., c.&f., c.i.f.? Can any additional fees be included? Attention must also be paid to the question of part-drawings. If insufficient funds are available in the escrow account, can the exporter claim the amount that is there, and go back later for the balance?

6. *Time limit for execution of transaction*
   Setting an expiry date for the escrow agreement requires careful consideration. The key issue is that there must be sufficient time available between arrival of the escrow monies and expiry of the

agreement to allow the exporter to (manufacture? and) ship the goods.

One solution which offers the exporter the greatest protection is to have expiry fixed at a certain number of days *after* arrival of the funds in the account. This interval will be decided on by establishing the length of time needed by the exporter to prepare goods for despatch and to present the documents to the bank *plus* a number of days for contingencies such as dock strikes.

7. *Disposal of residual balance*
The manner in which some products are priced or valued could result in a yield in hard currency which does not equal the amount of the export contract. A residual balance could be left on the account, and disposal procedures must be set out in the escrow agreement. In the unfortunate event that the export does not take place, the funds in the escrow account would have to be sent back to the bank in country B. The system for repatriation would need to be determined.

8. *Restriction on use of account*
At the start of this section, the comment was made that escrow accounts should provide protection to all the parties. The clause referring to the use to which the escrow funds can be put is an example of how such protection can be provided. With a restriction on the use of the funds to financing the export described, the central bank in the buyer's country will take comfort that there is less chance of malpractice. Such a clause will also give a measure of protection to the exporter as it will further block any attempt to divert the funds to a use other than financing his export.

9. *The responsibilities and obligations of the bank*
Just as with letters of credit, banks will deal in documents not goods. They will seek protection from claims of negligence by restricting their role to an examination of the documents for regularity of form; that is, if the documents say that X goods have been shipped, it is not the responsibility of the bank to find out whether the goods were actually despatched.

10. *Jurisdiction, governing law and procedures for communication*
Efforts to have the jurisdiction of the buyer imposed on the contract and the escrow account should be resisted. At best, the

exporter's country's jurisdiction should apply; at worst, that of a friendly neutral country. The same applies of course to the seat of arbitration. Because of the vagaries of international communications systems, the method of conveying information and instructions should be clearly stated. Telex is the most common if speed is necessary; otherwise recorded or registered letters. Addresses, telexes and telephone numbers should be detailed.

11. *Protection of the balance against blocking orders*
Although in a perfect world it would be comforting to have a clause in the agreement which would overcome any attempts to block the account, it is not entirely possible. Clauses can be inserted, however, which clearly state that the funds are held on behalf of another person or in respect of a claim yet to be made. The precise wording will depend on individual legal opinion. There has been no test of such clauses in courts, but on the basis that nothing will be lost by including a suitable form of words, an attempt should be made.

12. *Details of the authorised parties*
This provides a summary of who can operate the account or issue instructions. If the account can only be varied by joint agreement, mention should be made of the names of the authorising officials.

There are as many variations as there have been agreements, but the above notes present a structure around which an agreement should be built. Escrow accounts and advance compensation present a technique which is not widely appreciated, but which has benefits for all the parties to a transaction.

CHAPTER 9

Countertrade insurance

Background

The risk analyses in Chapter 6 (Tables 6.1 and 6.2) mention the use of insurance as a way of mitigating some of the risks involved in counterpurchase and compensation transactions. This category of insurance is usually referred to as 'political risk'. Obviously there will always be a need for insurance against the physical risks – damage, fire, theft, etc. – but political risk insurance covers political interference with the performance of a contract.

A useful definition of a political risk is used by the commercial insurance market:

An act or omission of a Foreign Government
which is – damaging to a Corporation
– arbitrary and discriminatory
– in defiance of generally accepted principles of international law.

Traditionally, cover against such risks has been provided by the national export credit agencies such as ECGD (UK), SACE (Italy) and COFACE (France). There are two problems associated with such schemes in the context of countertrade:

1. Availability: cover is often not available for the type of country which uses countertrade.
2. Applicability: national export credit agencies will not cover compensation deals.

In addition to these problems are the fundamental ones that national agencies often want to cover whole turnover rather than selected transactions, and the extent of the cover offered is not as comprehensive if the exported goods come from several countries.

The private (or commercial) political risks market represents, in some cases, an alternative to the national agencies, but often represents the *only* option. Before we look at the types of risk covered, an examination of the structure of the market may be useful.

The private market

The market has grown significantly over the last 15 years. It differs in one principal respect from the national agencies: it is governed by market forces and commercial judgement, not by such things as 'national interest'. Although the market is dominated by Lloyds, there are other insurers.

Lloyds

This is the oldest and largest insurance market in the world. It is a collection of individuals (about 28,000), divided into some 450 syndicates ranging from a few to a few thousand. These individuals have pledged their personal wealth to secure insurance contracts. (The security pledged amounts to £1.5 billion in cash in the United Kingdom, $5 billion in the United States, with a further £2 billion of proven assets.) In its 300 years of existence, Lloyds has pioneered many new types of insurance cover.

Its entry into political risk cover was a natural development of its involvement in cover for trade generally, e.g. marine and cargo risks. Cover is only available against insolvency and payment default risks associated with publicly owned bodies. Cover for private buyers is limited to political risks only.

The United States

The American-based insurance companies provide various forms of credit insurance cover (including political risk) in the United States. Their London operations provide packages of political risk cover, ranging from 'one-off' for specific countries to blanket arrangements for total export turnover. One of the leaders in this market is the American Insurance Group (AIG). Assets of the Group exceed $12 billion, and it has been in existence since 1919. Unlike Lloyds of London, AIG is able to cover insolvency or credit risk on privately owned buyers.

Others

There are several other sources of insurance, among them Pan Financial, and Black Sea and Baltic. The former is a recent creation, owned by Continental Corporation, Skandia International and Yasuda Fire and Marine. The latter, formed in 1925, is owned by the Russian State Insurance Company (Ingostrak). It specialises in exports to Comecon. Table 9.1 lists the market leaders and comments on the features of the risks each will cover.

Insurance brokers

Access to the various sources of insurance is through an insurance broker. In the case of Lloyds, for example, only the 260 Lloyds brokers are allowed access. The brokers' role is not only to find the best source of insurance, but also to prepare the case for submission to the insurers. (A typical pre-quotation questionnaire is presented in Appendix 5.) The aim of the broker is to collect together sufficient information to prepare a case which will sell the proposal to the insurer whilst at the same time providing all the necessary information.

The choice of a broker could be governed by two factors: firstly, is there an obvious 'horse for the course'; secondly, does the company have its own appointed broker?

Risks covered

When examining the risks coverable by the private market, we should first of all identify what constitutes a government or public buyer:

1. Central government itself.
2. A ministry, department or agency thereof.
3. A regional or local authority.
4. A nationalised undertaking, utility or public corporation, including a state trading corporation, provided government exercises full financial responsibility, and is committed to the continued existence of the entity.

Note: The private market is unlikely to recognise an entity as 'government- or public-' owned, where an expatriate company operating in a foreign country is obliged to have 51 per cent local or national ownership.

Turning to the risks actually covered, these fall into several categories: countertrade goods supply risks, export risks, disposal risks, bonding risks and funding risks.

Countertrade goods supply risks

These risks relate to the supply of countertrade goods, and will include the following:

1. Insolvency of supplier.
2. Default of supplier – this could be brought about by crop failure or sheer unavailability of goods. Obviously such risks cannot be covered. Default would arise where, say, goods were available, but the supplier refuses to supply them.
3. Repudiation of contract by supplier.
4. Cancellation or non-renewal of export licence.
5. Restrictions on exports not subject to licence.
6. War, civil war, revolution, etc.
7. Loss of advance payments.

In addition, Lloyds offer a contract frustration-supply interruption policy. This covers loss of profit due to non-supply caused by the following:

1. Law, decree, etc., preventing the production, processing, sale or export of the contract matter.
2. Conditions in the selling country whereby lack of law and order prevents the export of the contract matter.

The ratio of loss of profit is defined in the policy and applied to the reduction in turnover or additional expense caused by the non-delivery.

Export risks

Contract frustration – where political or *force majeure* events outside the control of the buyer or exporter prevent performance.

Import restrictions – cancellation of an import licence or the implementation of a law which prevents the import of goods.

Export restrictions – the cancellation or non-renewal of an export licence or the implementation of a law which prevents the export of the goods.

Table 9.1 Private market insurers

Name/entry into market	Owned by/fronting for	Cover/policies	Market comments
American International	US insurance companies	Political and/or commercial, one-off and whole turnover; contract repudiations, unfair calling of bonds. Amount of cover flexible, to 90 per cent. Max. term 3 yrs political risks, 5–7 yrs export credits. No financial guarantees.	Market leader. New management in New York, re-insurance problems now resolved. Cutting back in some areas. Shift of underwriting philosophy to more one-off business. Willing to work with national schemes (US, Sweden, especially). Limits $50m per policy. $70m (max. probable loss) per country.
Black Sea and Baltic/1925	USSR government	Political. Comecon only; one-offs, max. term up to 5 yrs.	Tending to expensive. Policies not easy to raise finance against as considered East European risk. Off cover for North Korea, Poland, Romania, Yugoslavia. Will cover Albania, Cuba.
Cigna/1981	US public company	Commercial, some political but very restrictive. Now concentrating on US, OECD credit risks only.	Strictly market follower. Top staff gone, loss of political risks reinsurance treaty cost CIGNA dear. Problems symptomatic of industry. Limit around $7m per country/buyer.
Lloyds	Syndicate members	Political only; one-offs, contract repudiation, non-payment. Financial guarantees unlikely. Amount of cover flexible up to 90.95 per cent. Average max. term 3 yrs but can go longer. All insurance tailor-made.	Market leader, key role in political risks. Solid core of 50 underwriters, best known are Merrett and Thompson. Retrenchment in last year, underwriters now more professional. Market not especially competitive. Large exporters preferred. Can go up to $100m per risk.

Table 9.1 *cont.*

Name/entry into market	Owned by/fronting for	Cover/policies	Market comments
Pan Financial/1985	Continental Corporation, Skandia International, Yasuda Fire and Marine.	Political, non-payment, repudiation, bonding. Up to 95 per cent, max. term 3yrs. Commercial cover of 100 per cent available above large first loss; policy aimed at large companies.	Most promising newcomer; professional management, powerful backers. Initial stance cautious, may be difficult to meet high level of expectation. Reinsurance satisfactory, max. £3m per risk.
Trade Credit Underwriters/1985	Private shareholders, Merill Lynch, The Aetna	Political/commercial, one-offs limited whole turnover. But needs 50 per cent reins per case. Up to 95 per cent cover, max. terms 5 yrs for political risks. High min. premium, flexible repayment periods.	Disappointed market so far, still viewed as having potential, but little chance of success without reinsurance. Limits \$50m per sovereign buyer, \$5m private subject to 50 per cent reinsurance.
Trade Indemnity/1918	Public company, 70 per cent owned by insurance companies	Political/commercial, whole turnover, one-offs. OECD policy-holders, mostly OECD risks. Also catastrophe cover. Normal cover 85–100 per cent.	Sleeping giant. Now working hard to change image, become more flexible, market oriented.
Universal Investment Consultants (UIC) 1985	Private partnership with Arthur J. Gallaher (insurance broker) and Johnson Matthey Bankers/ North River Insurance Company	Political only, non-payment, confiscation, 3 yrs cover max. amount 75–100 per cent. Will co-insure.	Newcomer acts as underwriting agent. US based, but half business comes from Europe. Max. amount for non-payment \$5m (\$8m with facultative reins), \$25m for confiscation.

Source: *Euromoney Trade Finance Report*

Repudiation or termination of contract by buyer

Refusal to honour arbitration award

Contract non-satisfaction

Cover is normally for an exporter's accounts receivable, out-of-pocket expenses or profit forgone if the contract is frustrated for reasons beyond the exporter's control. The maximum possible exposure is the contract value itself.

Disposal risks

These are basically the same risks as described above, both in terms of export and import interruption, but referring specifically to the countertrade goods.

Bonding risks

Unfair bond/guarantee calling – where a bond or guarantee has been 'called' by the buyer without cause.

'Fair' bond/guarantee calling – where the bond or guarantee has been 'called' in circumstances where the exporter is prevented from fulfilling the contract through no fault of his own.

Funding risks

Exchange transfer/currency inconvertibility – where a law in the buyer's country prevents or delays the transfer of funds to the exporter.
Note: the non-payment of hard currency due to a chronic shortage thereof is *not* covered, unless separately negotiated – often a difficult and expensive process. Insolvency risks are not covered by Lloyds, but can be covered by AIG. Naturally, currency fluctuations are also not coverable by insurance but other facilities exist such as forward contracts.

The underwriters' approach

The insurance broker will, as described above, assemble a case for submission to the underwriters. In turn, the underwriters will examine the proposal on the basis of certain criteria:

1. Status and solvency of the buyer.
2. Status of the exporter.
3. Priority and 'logic' of the contract.
4. Political stability of the buyer's country.
5. Previous trading experience.
6. Contract quality.
7. Security for payments and transfers.
8. Period and amount at risk.
9. Underwriters' claims experience in the country of risk.
10. Basis for pricing the countertrade goods.

In determining the *premium* to be charged, the underwriter will need to make a judgement based on the degree of risk as assessed by reference to the above criteria, plus the following:

1. The capacity within overall country exposure limits.
2. Volume of business placed by exporters and loss experience.
3. The period for which insurance will be needed.
4. The extent of cover required.
5. Exposure to loss – often less than the total contract value.

Note: the underwriter will normally limit the liability to 90 per cent of the exposure to loss.

Limitations, loss settlements and waiting periods

Underwriters will pay to the exporter the insured amount of the *ascertained net loss* as soon as practicable after such net loss has been ascertained and assessed. The delay – the waiting period – will be between the date of the occurrence of the incident giving rise to the claim, and when the claim is paid. It is unlikely the delay will be less than 180 days, and it could be as long as 720 days. In settling the claim, the premium paid is deemed not to be an expense in assessment of any claim. There are, of course, limitations:

1. *Period* – the private market will not normally cover risks beyond 36 months in duration.
2. *Financial guarantees* – the private market will not, in general, allow banks to be the named insured on any policy. (This problem can be overcome by, for example, having the bank named as loss payee.)
3. *Private buyers* – although AIG *may* cover private buyer risks, this will only be done selectively.

4. *War* – all policies exclude risks associated with war between the countries of the exporter and the buyer.

The advantages

The private market must be seen as a complement to the national export credit agencies, and only marginally as a competitor. There are features of the private market which give it certain advantages:

1. *Selectivity* – where cover is only wanted for certain buyers or contracts in certain countries.
2. *Specific risks* – areas of risk in a contract can be isolated and insured.
3. *Multi-sourcing* – where goods or services are being supplied from various countries or where subcontractors come from a variety of countries.
4. *Risk sharing* – where cover from the 'ground up' is either not necessary or not desirable – an exporter can take a proportion of the risk in return for a lower premium cost.
5. *Speed of response* – the private market is able to quote more quickly and an indication of the availability of cover can be sought early on in contract negotiations.
6. *Flexibility* – policy wordings will be custom-built for each case, particularly important in countertrade cases.
7. *Premium calculation* – based on exposure, rather than total contract value.
8. *Security for advances* – banks may accept a policy as collateral.

Summary

'Insurance is a planned expense to cover against an unplanned loss.' (Bert Edwards, formerly Head of Political Risk Insurance at Jardine Insurance Brokers)

It is important to recognise that insurance will not rescue a bad piece of contracting. Risks can be minimised or avoided in several other – cheaper – ways, as shown in the risk analyses in Chapter 6 (Tables 6.1 and 6.2).

The private market is growing, both in the range of risks covered, and in the markets coverable. It is not without its limitations, however, and certainly its appetite for difficult markets will be as restricted as national export credit agencies. An early approach to a good broker could be very useful in determining the prospects for insurance, and the experience gained by the insurers in looking at other countertrade deals could be an important contribution to the exporter's success.

CHAPTER 10

Countertrade goods

A few years ago an adjective was used to describe typical countertrade goods: 'distressed'. Although more often used to describe cargoes of goods which are unsold or unclaimed, in the context of countertrade the word implies that there are defects in the goods, or problems associated with marketing. A golden rule in exporting is

If goods could be sold for hard currency at an acceptable price, they would be.

The principle behind this statement is that countertrade is an inefficient trading system, and apart from those cases where countertrade is used as a way of deliberately diverting funds away from central control, sales for cash must be preferable.

In this chapter we will examine the types of goods commonly used in countertrade, the problems associated with them, and the impact on the exporter.

Types of goods

Most people involved in countertrade would prefer to see transactions involving bulk commodities of the type widely traded in the major trading centres. This would have the benefit that the manner in which such goods are bought and sold would be subject to the 'rule' of the market, or at least to a well-established procedure. In addition, the existence of such well-ordered markets often provides a basis for pricing the goods.

Unfortunately, the goods found in countertrade are either of the non-traded variety, or carry restrictions which move them outside the scope of the market's operations. Appendix 1 lists the goods known to have been used in countertrade. It is fair to say that apart from oil, most of the commercial transactions (i.e. not government to government), involve goods from outside the range of traded commodities.

In selecting goods for use in countertrade, the exporter or his trading house partner should obviously seek out the goods which can be sold with the smallest subsidy, yet relatively easily. A balance must be achieved between the payment of the subsidy and the need to sell the goods quickly, especially in compensation transactions.

Here we may run into a conflict between the wishes of the trading house and those of the exporter. It is possible that the trader will look for the easiest goods to sell, irrespective of the level of subsidy needed. The exporter could therefore pay a higher level of subsidy than is necessary, merely because the trader does not choose to try to buy other goods which may be harder to on-sell but which attract a lower subsidy. There is no easy answer to this problem, other than to exercise care in selecting a trading house partner.

In crude terms, the following list prioritises countertrade goods, but it is only a guide:

1. Traded commodities (e.g. metals, grains, oil, cotton).
2. Non-traded commodities (e.g. ores, minerals, coal).
3. Bulk chemicals.
4. Bulk foodstuffs/timber.
5. Bulk raw materials/low value-added, semi-processed goods.
6. Processed foodstuffs.
7. Manufactured consumables.
8. Machinery, equipment, high-technology goods.

Somewhere in this list one could include services; shipping, air freight, road transport, hotel accommodation, professional services and tourism would be examples of services which could be used to discharge countertrade obligations, subject to the prior approval of the relevant countertrade authority.

Likely countertrade products

The opening paragraph of this chapter described countertrade goods as 'distressed'. What causes goods to be so described, and what are the implications for the exporter? If the golden rule quoted in the first paragraph is true, then countertrade goods must be those goods which cannot be sold by the supplier in hard currency at the right price. In order to make them saleable, extra expenses/costs will be incurred and here we have the reason for the payment of the disagio referred to in earlier chapters. A short definition of disagio would be as follows:

A disagio is the amount required to be spent to make countertrade goods saleable.

It will also include an element of profit for the trading house. To understand the problem more fully, it might be useful to examine what defects exist in typical countertrade goods, and how the disagio overcomes some of those problems (see Table 10.1).

Table 10.1 Use of disagio to overcome defects in countertrade goods

Problem	Use of disagio
Goods over-priced The supplier may not wish to discount the goods on-hand to avoid demands from existing buyers for discounts on normal sales. There may also be price cartel considerations (e.g. oil), or fears of charges of dumping.	The trading house will arrange to buy the goods at the price asked, on-selling the goods more cheaply. The supplier is able to demonstrate that a sale has taken place at 'full value'. In turn the trading house will use most of the disagio to cover the discount on the price charged, the balance being profit.
Poor quality Low-grade primary goods or badly made manufactured goods offered at unrealistic prices, will cause problems. Some goods which are of good quality in themselves may be technologically inferior.	The obvious answer is to offer the ultimate buyer a discount, but this may not be feasible in the case of manufactured goods. Cases have been recorded where the disagio represents the cost of *improving* the goods to make them more saleable. For example, the money could be spent in sending experts to the supplier's factory to give advice on quality control, new designs or more modern technology. Equipment could be provided to improve quality or the buyer of the countertrade goods could arrange for the goods to be improved by a third party. (See also the notes below on marketing and credit.)
Presentation Goods of an acceptable quality could be packaged poorly. This is particularly true when the goods have been produced initially for unsophisticated domestic markets. In many countries, consumer goods and foodstuffs are of limited supply in domestic markets, and there is less need to present them in attractive packaging. Other problems could include: (a) use of local language on labels and books of instruction; (b) insufficient detail on contents, e.g. nutritional data; (c) non-international sizing; (d) insecure packaging.	Improvements to the way goods are presented can be effected, either at source (preferably) or after purchase. Consumers in more developed countries will be influenced by such matters, often notwithstanding the underlying quality of the product. Spending money on improvements in presentation could be a less expensive way of making the goods saleable than a straightforward discount.

Table 10.1 *Cont.*

Problem	Use of disagio
Marketing Developing and newly industrialising countries may be producing goods for export for the first time. Despite being of good quality and well presented, the goods may not sell in other markets if no marketing structure exists. To break into new markets and to maintain sales often requires considerable expenditure on market research, local representation, after-sales service, advertising and so on. Without the basis of an infrastructure geared to providing free help – such as embassies – it is extremely difficult for new exporters to succeed.	As a basic rationale for countertrade is to develop new markets for goods, the expenditure referred to in column 1 will be the responsibility of the exporter and/or his trading house partner. Money will be spent on contacting potential buyers or sending samples. In one famous example, an exporter's in-house trading unit produced a catalogue of available countertrade goods. The preparation thereof cost the company money, but less than a full marketing programme. One incentive which could be offered to a potential buyer is a period of credit. There would be a cost involved in funding this period of credit.
Delivery The lack of infrastructure can cause problems in the actual delivery of countertrade goods. Vehicles to bring goods from areas of production to the port of loading may not be available.	A rather radical but effective answer would be to provide transport. Supplying trucks could serve as an inducement to a producer to make available goods which in themselves are of good quality and marketable.
Quota restriction Of the various types of non-tariff barriers to trade, quotas are the most significant. Consumer countries and regional groupings such as the EEC may impose import quotas on certain types of goods to protect home-based producers. Such quotas restrict the marketability of some categories of goods.	To find alternative markets, the trader will need to transport the goods further, or further subsidise them to make them price-attractive in what could be an over-supplied, non-quota restricted market. Good examples of quotas which affect countertrade goods would be the International Coffee Organisation coffee quotas and the Multi-fibre Agreement.

Pricing

As mentioned above, the types of goods chosen will often determine the basis of pricing. 'Official' government prices will often be used, and these should be compared with international prices. There will be occasions when price lists will be supplied. These should be treated with caution. In some cases special prices will be applied purely because the goods are being supplied as part of a countertrade agreement.

It is worth while repeating one important point: the basis of valuation must be determined at the outset, i.e: f.o.b., c.i.f., etc.

Marketing

In addition to the problems associated with geographic marketing restrictions, there are also the difficulties which could arise if an agent already exists in a chosen market. Commissions may need to be paid to that agent, to overcome his claims of market exclusivity.

It matters not how clever a transaction is, if suitable goods are not available and/or cannot be sold without punitive levels of subsidy. Even when goods have been identified, problems could still exist in the execution of the transaction. Recruiting the right trader or buyer to negotiate the purchase of the goods is vital and Chapter 12 explains the make-up of the countertrade service industry.

Remember the word 'distressed' when considering countertrade goods, and you will remember the reason why you are being offered those goods.

Part II

CHAPTER 11

Review

The story so far

In this chapter the points set out in preceding chapters are summarised and the key issues identified.

1. Trading conditions world-wide have changed. There are fewer creditworthy countries now than at any time over the last 30 years. The few creditworthy countries are reducing in number as crisis follows crisis.
2. The modern resurgence of countertrade came in two waves: after the Second World War out of Eastern Europe, and in the 1970s and 1980s out of the Debt Crisis. The figures quoted for the extent of countertrade can largely be discounted. There are no maximum or minimum transaction sizes. Over 80 countries have been known to use countertrade.
3. There are four basic reasons for its use:
   (a) lack of foreign exchange;
   (b) export market/product development;
   (c) exploiting buyer's market;
   (d) political policy.
   Its use spreads from the developed countries, through the newly industrialising countries, to the lesser developed countries.
4. There are many words in use, and no common agreement. The main terms used in countertrade are compensation (barter), counterpurchase (parallel contracts) and off-set (a disturbing development, with the growing insistence of developed countries on 'reciprocity'; exploiting their position as cash or creditworthy borrowers they are able to demand additional concessions from suppliers – a sales package could now include concessions on production-sharing, technology transfer and agreements to buy back goods from the buyer's country). Care must be exercised in communications and negotiations to ensure everyone agrees on the techniques to be employed.

5. Exporters should adopt a logical approach to the countertrade negotiation. Advice should be sought at the earliest time. The type of countertrade demanded must be established. Assistance will be needed from outside advisers or consultants if no in-house expertise is available and if there is no government policy.
6. Compensation is a barter-like procedure, with the sale of the countertrade goods providing the hard currency to pay for the export. The overriding risk is that the countertrade goods may not be delivered. Counterpurchase involves the exporter in a parallel obligation to buy countertrade goods. Both the export and the countertrade transaction will be settled independently in hard currency. In both types of countertrade, extra costs are involved – principal among them is the disagio, the amount to be spent to make the countertrade goods saleable.
7. In addition to the principal export sales contract, there are several other agreements to be negotiated, many peculiar to countertrade. Expert advice is needed.
8. One way to overcome the risk of non-delivery in compensation is to organise the purchase of the countertrade goods first, before the export goods are shipped. This technique involves the use of escrow accounts.
9. Another means of protecting against losses is insurance. The growth of the private political risks market has been significant.
10. Countertrade goods are generally 'defective' in some way – whoever handles the purchase of the goods will require an inducement. This payment may be used to discount the goods, or improve them. The fee paid to the buyer of the goods is called a 'disagio'.

Countertrade is not a science, and the preceding chapters describe the most common practices. An attempt has been made to set out the *best position*, but in reality some concession will be needed. To what extent the exporter can make such concessions will depend on commercial judgement and the importance of making the export sale.

In the following chapters we will examine several other aspects of countertrade, and related practices.

CHAPTER 12

The countertrade service industry

As trade developed, so specialist entities were created to provide support services. Freight forwarding, clearing, warehousing, insurance and banking are just a few of the areas dominated by specialist firms today. Exporters rarely provide such services in-house, relying instead on their knowledge of where to go for the appropriate help.

Until just a few years ago, countertrade services, and the number of companies providing such services, were limited. The trading companies and banks of Austria and Switzerland were skilled in the handling of East European countertrade, but it was difficult for exporters facing countertrade for the first time to find these organisations. Many companies set up skilled in-house units to handle countertrade matters, but such an idea was beyond the resources of many smaller companies.

The growth in countertrade activity attracted the attention of traders, bankers, trade consultants and the insurance industry. With the introduction of magazines devoted to trade and countertrade and with the growing attention paid to countertrade in the financial press, the service industry was at last able to advertise its existence.

Although the notes which follow describe the activities of the various 'players', and despite the obvious overlap in some areas, it should be remembered that the services provided are often complementary. It is the assembly of the right team which can often determine how successful a transaction can be.

Countertrade consultants

In negotiating a contract in an overseas market where countertrade may be requested, it may be appropriate for a company to employ a consultant. It is unlikely that a consultant would have the right skills for every case, given the wide range of countries and techniques involved.

The consultant is more likely to specialise, in one or more of the following ways.

Geographically

The unique trading arrangements found in most East European countries require many years to learn, and it could prove costly if the necessary skills are acquired only in the course of negotiations on a specific contract. Recognising this, individuals with knowledge of East European countries, together with good language capabilities, set up as consultants. They have an encyclopaedic knowledge of how the foreign trade organisations conduct their business and have personal contacts in these countries. More recently, we have seen individuals or firms set up to offer similar services for South America, Africa and South East Asia.

Care must be exercised in dealing with small firms or 'one-man bands' claiming to have global countertrade skills. Countertrade experience is not easily transferred from one country to another, or indeed from one case to another.

By commodity

Just as some traders may deal in only a limited range of goods, so may a consultant. Many such people have a trading-house background, and offer consultancy services in the products with which they are most familiar. Oil would be a classic example. A good knowledge of the workings of the oil trade is brought to bear, with access to market knowledge likely to affect the pricing of the product. As with a consultant specialising geographically, the negotiating skills of a product consultant could be critical.

By industry

Perhaps the most common industry specialisations are aviation and defence. The consultant has industry knowledge, probably gained first-hand, coupled with knowledge of the special problems that countertrade demands are likely to impose. The specialist consultant can play an important role in the negotiation of a contract. Whether his skills lie in the market, product or industry, he can fill a gap in the exporter's negotiating team.

But what about weaknesses?

It is very difficult to find the consultants in the first place. In the last two years, specialist magazines have been produced in which consultants have advertised. In the United Kingdom the government has included a few names in its countertrade manual. But it remains very difficult to find the right consultant at the right time.

There is also the question of track-records. A few consultants have made quite extraordinary claims as to their capabilities and successful cases. The secrecy which seems to surround countertrade does not make it easy to test these claims.

One must also be sure that the consultant has adequate resources – both in terms of time (personnel) and finance – to support a lengthy negotiation process. Most would work on the basis of a non-refundable up-front fee, full cost recovery, a per diem and possibly a percentage on successful completion of the transaction.

Finally, it is important to remember that the consultant will not take title to countertrade goods. It will be necessary to find a trader or end-user to take the countertrade goods although the consultant should include such a task in the services he offers.

Banks

The role of banks with trading company subsidiaries is examined in the next chapter. But what of the other banks that claim a countertrade expertise?

In the early 1980s it became apparent to many banks that there was a growing demand for advice on countertrade matters from exporters. Until that time, the banks' responses had varied from declining to help in any way, to offering a list of names and addresses of potential sources of help.

When, in 1982, Indonesia published its countertrade policy, many banks realised that they could no longer ignore the subject. Exporters, traditionally supported by a sophisticated infrastructure of export-oriented services, continued to look to the banking community for help. Those banks *without* a countertrade capability were in danger of losing traditional export finance business to the banks *with* the expertise. A bank's options were as follows.

1. *Do nothing*
   Although cheap and risk-free, it was quite obviously not the right response.

2. *Establish a trading company or trading department*
   This would involve considerable investment in specialist staff, whose salary structures would not be compatible with those of their banking colleagues. There could be a problem in identifying which speciality products should be covered, as most traders specialise in a limited range of products. There was also the problem to be faced of what would happen if countertrade died away, where the bank would be left with specialist staff whose use to the bank would also disappear.

3. *Buy a majority/minority stake in a trading company*
   This would be a rapid, if expensive, way to acquire expertise. The same problems of product specialisation would arise, and many felt that the risk management techniques of trading companies were not compatible with those of banking.

4. *Establish an advisory unit*
   The vast majority of banks, therefore, ended up with advisory units. The image portrayed by the expression 'advisory' is not entirely accurate. A great deal of very active assistance is available. There is now a trend for banks to try to structure their own deals.

Although the range of services is still evolving, the list which follows covers the main areas of activity.

Bank advisory units

Concept/terminology

The units provide a basic educational role, advising exporters addressing countertrade for the first time of the implications, basic techniques and risks.

Country practices

Most banks will keep a close watch on countertrade activity worldwide, and should be able to advise on countertrade laws, procedures or attitudes in foreign markets.

Transaction structures

By bringing to bear the experience gained from other cases, banks can help in structuring a transaction, advising on how to submit a proposal to an overseas government, how to manage the flow of goods and control the flow of funds.

Documentation

Initial drafting of some of the countertrade documentation can be done by the bank, or at least advice on the wording can be given. This is particularly true of penalty guarantees, letters of credit and escrow agreements.

Insurance

Where risks are identified which can only be covered by insurance, banks can approach brokers – sometimes their own subsidiaries – for quotes on insurance cover.

Countertrade goods

Advice on the identification of suitable countertrade goods can often be given through the benefit of previous experience, or through contact with branches in the country in question, or by reference to the country/trade economists which most banks employ.

Disposal of goods

Earlier in this chapter it was suggested that the purchase of goods by a bank acting as principal did not represent the benefit which seems apparent at first sight. Bank advisory units will maintain data on likely buyers of a wide variety of goods. By contacting several for each enquiry, competitive offers can be sought – in confidence – and the best option chosen. The trader or end-user selected should be the one willing to take over the obligation in its entirety, without recourse, and to include issuance of the penalty guarantee.

Finance

Finally, as has been observed in Chapters 5 and 6, countertrade *does* involve a flow of funds. Where finance is required, banks can examine, advise on and perhaps provide the appropriate kind of finance. A typical example would be the blending of forfait with countertrade. (See Appendix 6 for an explanation of Forfaiting.)

The competition

The basic dilemma facing bankers is whether to trade, i.e. to act as principal, or not to trade. It may be worth while looking at how a trading bank would operate. Generally speaking, a trading bank imposes contract limits below which it declines to help. This is to ensure that the bank's personnel are not tied up with potentially unprofitable business. They may not take open positions, i.e. they may not buy countertrade products without having another buyer back to back. They will earn their fee in a number of ways, including building-in price differentials between their purchase and onward sale prices. This contrasts with the attitudes of non-trading banks, which will also seek out end-users or traders prepared to buy the goods but without the bank interposing itself as a principal. The bank would look to receive introductory commissions from the trader/end-user. The trading bank's position as principal is often another complication, and another cost element. Naturally, this is not true of all banks with trading subsidiaries. Some will take over countertrade obligations 'blind', and this could be an enormous benefit to the exporter.

The dilemma facing the exporter is in deciding whether a trading bank is interested in a contract from its own viewpoint as a principal, or from the exporter's view. Whose interests are the bank protecting? Will a bank as principal be considered an impartial intermediary by the third party?

There is also the question of whether a bank's trading house clients will in any way be aggrieved by finding its bank acting in a trading role. Traders pass confidential information to their banks and they may not be too keen on finding the very same bank possibly competing for trading business.

Trading companies

The following notes suggest that traders have strengths *and* weaknesses.

Strengths

Many trading houses bring a great depth of knowledge on their products, and the marketing thereof. They may belong to commodity markets, where appropriate, and will be bound by any rules relating thereto.

Care should be taken in the selection of a trader to ensure that the company is financially sound. Once this has been done, the exporter is usually able to rely on the traders' credit lines to finance the countertrade leg of the transaction.

The peculiarities of the commodities sector as regards financing contracts will be understood by the trader's bankers, whereas the exporter may have more difficulty in persuading his bankers to finance the countertrade transaction.

The trading houses are able to assume – for a price – forward delivery risks, i.e. they will commit to buy a fixed quantity of goods at a fixed price at a fixed point of time in the future. This does not mean that the trader will *always* be able to do so, but where it is possible, then the exporter is relieved of the risks involved.

It may be possible for traders to use their existing trade with a country to facilitate countertrade deals there.

Weaknesses

The strength of specialisation is also a weakness. In some transactions, the goods may be drawn from a basket of commodities and goods. It may be difficult to find one trader able and willing to deal in *all* of these different products. If more than one trader is employed, there are very obvious complexities.

If the countertrade leg of a transaction is small, or if it is broken down into a series of contracts based on small quantities of different goods, it may be unattractive to traders used to dealing with larger contract 'lots'.

Some people have detected a sense of frustration on the part of some traders, due to the low success rate and the long time-scales involved in countertrade deals. It is vital, therefore, to pick a trader with a firm commitment to countertrade.

Some traders are not prepared to back up their offers to take over countertrade obligations with an undertaking to pay penalties for non-performance (see Chapter 7).

Many of the comments made relate to deals involving commodities.

Others, however, involve 'goods' for which there is no structured market, such as manufactured goods, ores, wine and even services. It is harder to find traders willing to take on such products.

Finally, it is becoming quite common for trading houses to initiate deals, rather than just react to demands from third parties. A classic example would be the establishment in 1985 of bilateral trading arrangements between Pakistan and major foreign trading houses.

The next chapter explores in greater depth the role played by trading companies and draws the distinction between the activities of the traders of the United States, Japan and Europe.

Insurance brokers

Chapter 9 looked at the use of insurance in countertrade. Naturally the experience and knowledge gained by the brokers, underwriters and insurance companies represent a valuable resource. Although no two transactions will be identical, the lessons learned from one can often be transferred to another.

Insurance brokers are an important source of help and advice on countertrade. The underwriting of the actual insurance itself may well be done by only a limited number of underwriters or companies, but there is no doubt that some brokers are more skilled in the evaluation of proposals than others. Selecting the right one is therefore important. The brokers have to 'sell' the case to the underwriter and can only do so if they have a firm grasp of the facts.

Rather than try to identify the risks and ask the broker to investigate the availability of cover, it is preferable to give the broker full details of the transaction, including copy contracts, so that *they* can identify the risks. The pre-quotation questionnaire presented in Appendix 5 will form part of the evaluation and risk identification process.

Government/national organisations

France

The official government line is that countertrade is contrary to French international commitments to a multilateral trading system. At the same time, the government recognises the need to assist French exporters, particularly if they are to remain competitive in foreign markets where countertrade features.

For many years, the Direction des Relations Economiques Exterieures (DREE) has performed an advisory function, and is known to have actively assisted French exporters in the discharge of countertrade obligations. One such case involved increasing an import quota to permit the sale in France of countertrade goods.

French banks have a longer history in countertrade than their British rivals. Credit Lyonnais has a joint venture with the Merban Group (Continental Grain) – Greficomex. Sogepec is the countertrade division of Sogexport, the trading company in the Société Générale Group, while the same bank has a share in a trading house called Secopa, which handles East-West trade.

Many large French companies have their own trading subsidiaries or departments. For example, Renault has a 100 per cent owned subsidiary called Sorimex. Their rival, Peugeot-Citroën, has split the function between Sogedac, which endeavours to link Peugeot purchases with subsequent sales, and a second company which helps with the disposal of countertrade goods unwanted by the Peugeot companies.

Although most of the major banks have their own in-house countertrade departments, they were also founder-members of the countertrade association, ACECO (Association pour la Compensation des Exchanges Commerciaux). It was set up in 1977, following a proposal by M. Raymond Barre, at that time Minister of Foreign Trade. It is an independent non-profit association which seeks to help French exporters with countertrade problems, particularly small- to medium-sized companies with no in-house expertise. In addition to the major banks, other founder-members were:

(a) The Paris Chamber of Commerce;
(b) The Confederation of French Industry;
(c) The National Federation of Trading Companies;
(d) National Industrial Federation.

ACECO is funded in part by the annual subscriptions of its 200 plus members, but it also receives contributions from the five founding banks and various government departments.

ACECO operates rather like a clearing house where information on countertrade experiences, problems and opportunities are exchanged. The countertrade practices of countries are monitored and reports on country techniques are published. Help is offered to exporters in structuring countertrade transactions and identifying countertrade goods. Through a database, help is offered in matching the countertrade obligations of exporters with the buying opportunities of importers. (ACECO can be found at 28 Avenue Hoche, 75008 Paris Tel.: 563–01–00 Telex: 640192.)

The French government has established a trading company Sodicomex, as a vehicle to leverage French exports against its own imports. It is not known how successful the venture has been, but the idea is interesting, and reveals a great deal about French government thinking.

Sweden

The Swedes have an organisation, similar in origin to ACECO, called Sukab. Formed in 1940, it seeks to assist Swedish exporters with countertrade and other special trading arrangements. It operates on a non-profit-making basis, with its shares held by a wide range of Swedish companies (e.g. Alfa-Laval, Asea, Atlas Copco, Bofors, Handels, Incentive, Axel Johnson & Co., Saab-Scania, and Volvo). These companies are from both the public and private sectors, and include a number of trading companies. The shareholders receive no dividend, nor do they receive preferential treatment when using Sukab's services which are available to all Swedish exporters/importers. Sukab co-operates with Swedish foreign trade authorities and leading banks/financial institutions. Operations are financed through a small charge on the actual export transaction.

Although there is a government involvement through its ownership of several member companies and the government contributes to the Sukab budget, it is an independent organisation. It must be said, though, that the government involvement does give Sukab an edge when negotiating with foreign governments.

In the early days of its formation, it concentrated mainly on European countries, principally France, Italy and Spain. As European trade stabilised after the Second World War, the emphasis shifted to state trading countries (Comecon – Council for Mutual Economic Assistance) as well as developing countries in Asia and Africa. Attention is now being paid to Central and South American countries.

Sukab's operations range from single transactions on behalf of an exporting company to the negotiation and administration of bilateral trade agreements. It has negotiated such agreements in Algeria, Bangladesh, Egypt, Iran, Mozambique, North Korea, Pakistan, the Philippines, Syria, Tanzania and the USSR. The oldest of these goes back to 1967. Trading under these framework agreements reached 500 million Swedish kronor in each direction in 1985.

Assistance is given to Swedish exporters in the disposal of countertrade goods with Sukab able to use the experience it has gained over many years of trade and countertrade activity. Although many leading Swedish companies have an involvement with Sukab, there are a number of such companies with their own trading subsidiaries (e.g. Mercator is a joint venture between Axel Johnson & Co. – a major trader – and the Wallenberg industries such as Saab-Scania, Atlas Copco and Electrolux. Inter-Export Gmbh is the countertrade company in the Novo Steel Group). These trading companies look after the special needs of their parents.

Austria

Although the Austrian equivalent of Sukab was founded much later – in 1968 – it has the same background. It is a private, independent, non-profit-making association of exporters, countertraders, trading houses and banks, and is called Evidenzburo. Based in Vienna, it also has offices in several East European countries.

A membership fee is charged, and full reimbursement of costs is expected when the association is involved in a specific case. As with Sukab, Evidenzburo is partly funded by the government. The Ministry of Trade was a founder member, together with the Austrian Federal Chamber of Commerce and the Austrian Association of Industrialists.

The principal objective of the Evidenzburo is to provide a variety of services to its members when they are faced with countertrade demands. It will act as an intermediary between its members and foreign buyers, and will assist in the identification and disposal of countertrade goods.

United Kingdom

There is no centralised body or association of the type found in some European countries. A great deal of discussion has taken place about whether the British government should take the initiative in establishing such an organisation. Many people mistakenly believe that Sukab, ACECO, and Evidenzburo are totally government-funded and organised, and that the British government should do the same.

In looking at the level of its involvement, the government faces a dilemma: to support exporters and ignore its obligations to the official bodies which are opposed to countertrade (e.g. GATT – General Agreement on Tariffs and Trade, EEC – European Economic Community, IMF – International Monetary Fund), or maintain its obligations internationally and leave exporters to manage alone, disadvantaged in comparison with their foreign competitors.

The government's solution is probably the best that can be achieved in the circumstances. An advisory unit was set up within the Projects and Export Policy section of the Department of Trade and Industry (DOTI). Its first task was to update the Department's booklet on countertrade. Until early 1984, the booklet was not particularly helpful, either in explaining what countertrade is, or in how and where exporters could get help. In an area where things were changing fairly rapidly, it was also out of date.

The advisory unit does not operate as a separate entity, however. Staff have countertrade work as part of their overall function, but do not work full-time on countertrade matters. They are there to monitor countertrade activity and can use their overseas embassies and high commissions to check on local practices. They also maintain a small directory of companies, firms and organisations able to provide countertrade services.

The present DOTI booklet is a very useful guide, particularly for those companies looking at countertrade for the first time. (Copies are available from DOTI, 1 Victoria Street, London SW1.)

Many chambers of commerce and trade associations have a countertrade capability. Often, though, these lack the depth and resources necessary to be of assistance in contract negotiations. Because there is a general lack of awareness about countertrade among UK exporters and in the absence of an 'association', Britain has seen numerous seminars on the subject over the past two years.

The following extracts are taken from an article written by Mr Michael Boxall for the magazine *Countertrade and Barter Quarterly*. At the time of writing this article the author was head of the DOTI Countertrade Unit.

> 'The British Government, along with most others, has remained agnostic in this debate, for several reasons.
>
> We have yet to see evidence that countertrade has developed beyond a marginal feature in UK trade; nor have we seen evidence that its effects to date have in practice damaged Western interests or those of the developing countries concerned.'

Mr Boxall suggests that there are practical constraints on the growth of countertrade, but any efforts by Western governments to discourage its use could slow the development of trade with less developed countries.

He comments that any attempt to control countertrade among Western traders would divert the trade of these less developed countries to the Eastern bloc, and he continues with a warning:

'If we are sceptical about some of the claims made for and against the global impact of countertrade, we certainly do not underestimate its importance when it does arise. Even if no more than 5% of UK exports involve countertrade, that still represents over £3 billion of business which might not otherwise have been won.

In this environment, the UK Government has sought an essentially pragmatic response to countertrade, aiming to balance appropriate support to UK exporters against the risks of encouraging the growth of countertrade demands or otherwise acting to undermine the open world trading system. We are certainly not hostile to countertrade, but neither do we advocate it as something to be sought for its own sake.

Our advice to exporters is to look first for simpler, more conventional alternatives before entering countertrade commitments. Countertrade is, after all, simply one set of the many different ways of financing or facilitating trading transactions.'

It is interesting that in the debate on whether there should be greater UK government involvement, many experienced companies are self-sufficient in their countertrade needs. As Mr Boxall says:

'For major companies with experiences in this area, who know their way around the alternatives in such situations, there is usually little part for government to play in helping them make their judgements on countertrade. For those newer to countertrade, we can offer some general guidance on countertrade requirements and experiences in particular markets, and on some of the points to consider. Much of this information is given in our Guidance Notes for Exporters.

We can in many instances back up this basic information with more detailed intelligence about particular markets obtained through our local Embassies or High Commission.'

The latter service is more significant than it may seem. A knowledge of countertrade practice in foreign markets is critical and exporters would be well advised to use diplomatic representatives as a source of information. Mr Boxall's view, however, is that help should be drawn from a variety of sources:

'. . . the most important part of the Guidance Notes, and in my view the most important guidance we in DTI can provide, is that which directs exporters towards the professional experts on countertrade – whether in trading houses, bankers, consultants, brokers, or general information services. A glance through the relevant pages of the Guidance Notes shows the depth and range of such services available in the City of London. The list is growing almost daily, indicating the strength of demand for such services and the responsiveness of the commercial services industry to that demand.

While comprehensive, this growth in countertrade services remains disparate, and some people have suggested that a greater focussing of national capabilities would be valuable.

Attention has been drawn, for example, to the national countertrade bodies established in France, Italy, Austria, Sweden and elsewhere, with suggestions that there should be something similar in the United Kingdom. Mr Paul Channon, the Minister for Trade, is on record as prepared to discuss this possibility, but has observed that all of these overseas bodies – ACECO, COGIS, Evidenzburo, SUKAB – are in fact primarily private sector organisations, funded by industry on a trade association basis, albeit each with some support and encouragement from their respective governments.

It has to be said that there has been very little response from UK industry to the Minister's invitation for proposals, which may lead one to conclude that those British exporters getting involved in countertrade are in fact obtaining sufficient support from the wide range of commercial specialists offering their services in this area.

To summarize, we regard the growth in countertrade in recent years as a real and significant development in world trade, though not as extensive as some have suggested. The UK Government has sought to respond to this development realistically and constructively, and has in particular extended the information and guidance services available to exporters. But ultimately, even more than "normal" international trade, countertrade is an essentially entrepreneurial activity – most appropriately, and most effectively, undertaken by private sector initiative.'

United States of America

Like many other countries, the United States government views countertrade as a practice which is inconsistent with the principles it supports in the area of free trade. It is particularly opposed to government-mandated countertrade but recognises that countertrade demands reflect market conditions.

Various studies have been undertaken within the US government:

Countertrade – Its Nature and Scope (John Wrecting, Bureau of Intelligence and Research, 1984).

Analysis of Recent Trends in US Countertrade (Ronald J. DeMarines, US Trade Commission, 1982).

Countertrade Practices in East Europe, the Soviet Union and China (P. Verzariou, US Department of Commerce, International Trade Administration).

The US government involvement in, and attitude to off-set as a countertrade device, is examined in more detail in Chapter 4.

Each October the President and Congress are informed of the level of countertrade activity experienced by US companies. State involvement in countertrade is at present limited to the laws which affect trade generally. For example, the Trade Act of 1974 gives the President power to impose quotas on imports which the International Trade Commission deem to be injurious to domestic industry. This Act makes specific reference to imports from Communist countries. Countertrade *could* be viewed as an unfair trade practice, according to the provisions of Section 301 of the Act (as yet untried).

Although goods imported to the United States under countertrade deals are not recorded as such, the same rules as regards dumping would be applied. Investigations were held into one of the most famous deals ever struck, to determine whether the countertrade goods were being dumped. Occidental Petroleum Corporation had constructed an ammonia factory in the USSR, and took payment in ammonia. The first enquiry found that the ammonia imports represented 'dumping', although this finding was overturned by President Carter. A subsequent enquiry found there was no market disruption.

It is interesting that there is legislation which actually encourages the use of countertrade by the US government. The Strategic and Critical Materials Stock Piling Act says

> 'The President shall encourage the use of barter in the acquisition of strategic and critical materials for, and the disposal of materials from, the stockpile when acquisition or disposal by barter is authorised by law and is practical and in the best interest of the United States.'

Other legislation has similar provisions.

The role of the US government is, as part of its export-support functions, to provide US exporters with advisory and market intelligence services. These services include counselling and information on countertrade practices in foreign markets.

Several attempts have been made to set up barter exchanges (e.g. Miami Barter Exchange) where buyers and sellers can be paired. There are also informal 'round tables' to discuss countertrade matters, but as yet there is no US equivalent of an ACECO or Evidenzburo. The size of the American economy would preclude the establishment of one such body, and we are more likely to see countertrade organisations emerge from industrial associations or chambers of commerce.

An important factor in US attitudes to countertrade is the great need to increase exports. The trade deficit in goods is likely to rise from the $69 billion in 1983 to $150 billion in 1985. (See the section on export trading companies in the United States, in Chapter 13, for one development in the fight against this deficit.)

Singapore

The Trade Development Board (TDB) has been active in the promotion of Singapore as a transit trade centre. Singapore middlemen and traders set up transactions between countries, either using Singapore as a physical transit centre, or merely using local skills and finance. A major aim of the TDB's Countertrade Unit is to promote Singapore exports through countertrade.

Australia

It is unclear whether it was the development of the Australian government's own countertrade (off-set) policy, or the experience of Australian companies which led to the formation of the Australian Countertrade Association, but there is obviously a very real interest in countertrade globally. Companies such as Elders are expanding internationally and may well find countertrade in trade which does not involve Australia at all. The basic function of the Association is to provide a clearing house for information.

Magazines, newspapers, seminars, etc.

Until 1983/4, most press comment on countertrade was limited to specialist journals on East-West trade. Since then there has been a small explosion in the incidence of media comment on countertrade. But how useful has it all been?

It must be said that much of what has been written is speculative, ill-informed and inaccurate. Many exporters have been misled as a result. When statistics are quoted showing the volume of countertrade transacted world-wide, exporters become concerned as to why *they* are not exporting, for example, 30 per cent of their goods on the basis of countertrade. Similarly, there has been a tendency to over-simplify the matter, and the casual use of the word 'barter' has conjured up pictures of a simple exchange of goods – rather like a spy-swap! Exporters have been disappointed when they finally learn of the complexities, often to the point where they shy away from all discussions on possible countertrade transactions.

Criticism can also be levelled at the seminars organised throughout the world over the last few years. Often badly structured, speakers are repetitive and not always relevant. Cynics say that the only people making money from countertrade are the conference organisers. Whilst not exactly true, it is a fact that their money is made more quickly and easily than exporters'.

Care should be exercised in choosing which journals are read, and which conferences are attended. On the basis that there is more than one way to skin a cat, a magazine such as *Euromoney Trade Finance Report* is a useful source of information on *all* trade finance topics. A list of journals relating to or commenting on countertrade appears in Appendix 7.

In choosing a seminar to attend, a great deal will depend on the level of knowledge already acquired. For the newcomer, the basic introductory seminar would provide a general understanding of countertrade theory. A good speaking panel would include a trader, a banker, a consultant, an insurance broker and an exporter with previous experience of countertrade practice. Later, attendance at a seminar concentrating on one practical aspect, e.g. off-set, or one area, e.g. Latin America, may be beneficial.

Finally, if a company maintains a subsidiary, associate or agent in a foreign market, use should be made of this facility to monitor countertrade attitudes, policies and opportunities.

CHAPTER 13

Trading companies

A successful countertrade depends ultimately on one's ability to dispose of the goods offered by the 'other' party. The sophistication of the transaction itself will count for nought if the goods to be taken are unsaleable, or at best are saleable only on payment of a significant subsidy.

This chapter describes the activity of the trading community. It has been split geographically, depending on location of the ultimate controlling parent company. The split is more natural than might be immediately obvious, as the structure of the trading community in each area is quite different. Not only does this reflect the background and development of the trading companies and the countries from which they operate, but it also suggests that in the face of intense competition, trading companies in all countries are developing characteristics which traditionally have been found in other countries. As it is widely believed that the Japanese Sogo Shosha could be the model for many traders in the future, particular emphasis has been made in the notes which follow on describing their activities. First, however, we cover the trading houses of Europe.

Trading houses, Europe

The specialisation referred to above is particularly true in Europe. There were many trading companies concentrating on limited areas geographically, sometimes with an emphasis on trading activity in a few product lines. This geographic specialisation grew out of relationships going back, in some cases, hundreds of years.

Britain's overseas empire established close trading links with Africa, the Middle East, the Indian subcontinent, Australasia and so on. The French had close ties with parts of Africa and the Far East, while Denmark's East Asiatic Company had the close trading connections that the name implies.

Today, this geographic specialisation is less pronounced, and it is more appropriate to divide the trading houses into two main categories.

(a) Bank/industry-owned

In the section on the export trading companies of the United States, we examine the rationale for the development of export trading companies within the framework of a banking/financial institution. The development of bank-owned traders can be traced back to Europe, however, where it is a fairly common feature today.

The best known of these trading house subsidiaries are to be found in Austria, where there has traditionally been a close link between the state, the banks and industry. Centro-Handelsbanken, for example, is owned by a collection of banks: Genossenschaftliche Zentralbank, Banco di Sicilia, Bank Handlowy W. Warszawie and Kleinwort Benson. Allegemeine Finanz und Warentreuhand Ag is a subsidiary of the Austrian state-owned bank Creditanstalt. These companies owe their existence to the special relationship between Austria and several of the countries of Eastern Europe. There are said to be over 700 companies in Austria active in transit trade, i.e. trading in goods which do not originate in Austria, or which will not be sold in Austria.

There is a great deal of expertise within these sorts of companies, built up over many years. Being subsidiaries of banks they have a very large captive market, and also have the benefit of being able to blend traditional bank trade-related services to the more trading-oriented needs of countertrade. Most take title to the countertrade goods, trading as principals directly with the overseas country, or back to back with the principal exporter if he is required to act as buyer of the countertrade goods. With the growth of countertrade world-wide, these companies have broadened their horizons. Whilst their East European business remains important, they now take on countertrade transactions in many other parts of the world.

In Belgium the Société Générale Group is an extremely diverse group, with shareholding in some 2,000 companies, including banks. In 1984, the group established GTS (General Trade Suppliers International n.v.) as a specialised countertrading company. The company was created as a profit centre; that is, not merely to service the needs of the Société Générale Group. Interestingly, although GTS does take title to goods, it only does so back to back with other trading houses/end-users.

Another celebrated trading company, also part of an industrial group, is Voest-Alpine Intertrading. It was created in 1978 as a subsidiary of the Austrian state-owned steel company Voest-Alpine. It has general trading responsibilities for the Voest-Alpine Group. Following spectacular losses in 1985/6, the trading company was restructured.

Almost certainly, the most prominent trading company linked to German industry is MG Services. Although based in the United States, the company was originally incorporated as a trading subsidiary of Metallgesellschaft. The company operates through offices in several centres, including New York, London and Hong Kong. Through the expertise of its parent, it is able to handle a wide variety of metals and ores, whilst its new co-shareholder – Louis Dreyfus & Company – brings considerable expertise in soft commodities.

Mention has already been made of some of the French companies with trading subsidiaries, and many more examples could be quoted, throughout Europe.

All of the above have parentage involved in banking or industry. But the second category of trader is the more traditional type of company, buying and selling a limited range of goods.

(b) Independent trading houses

It is outside the scope of this book to describe in detail the operation of the London commodity markets, although reference is made to them in Chapter 10. Suffice it to say here that the existence of the commodity terminal markets in various centres has concentrated expertise in the products concerned in those centres and in the hands of the members of the markets.

Trading companies will usually specialise in a limited number of commodities, only occasionally crossing into other disciplines. For example, whereas a grain trader may also trade coffee, cocoa or sugar, it is less likely that it will trade metals or minerals. Naturally there will be exceptions. One such is the world's largest commodities trader, Phibro, part of the Phibro-Salomon Group. This group combines the enormous trading expertise of Philipp Brothers with the financial services provided by Salomon Brothers. Another example would be Cargills, the US trading house. A separate company – Tradex – exists for handling countertrade deals.

The advantages in using such companies have already been listed, but it is worth emphasising that these companies represent the best possible expertise in the field of commodities. Their enormous product and market knowledge can be used to make a countertrade deal work, or alternatively to advise when a potential deal is unworkable. In so doing they could save an exporter a great deal of wasted time, effort and money.

Export trading companies, United States

When looking at international trade, it is worth remembering that the United States does not have a long history of external trade on the scale and geographic scope of Europe. With almost no overseas dependencies, no empire or colonies, the United States had no natural trading partners. The almost total self-sufficiency of the US economy has also contributed to the lack of growth in pure trading activity.

The imbalance in trade which became a minor problem in the early 1980s had to be corrected by encouraging domestic-oriented industries to seek overseas markets.

On 8 October 1982, President Reagan signed the Export Trading Company Act. Its main purposes were to promote exports, and to help small- and medium-sized businesses which had not previously exported, to do so through export trading companies.

The definition of an export trading company is as follows:

> A company doing business in the United States principally to export goods or services produced in the United States or to facilitate such exports by unaffiliated persons. It may be owned by foreigners and may import, barter and arrange sales between third countries, as well as export, so long as more than 50 per cent of revenues are export-related.

What made this legislation particularly exciting to the Americans was the concession it made to an involvement by banks. In recognising that a successful export trading company requires access to considerable capital funds, the Act permitted equity investments – including 100 per cent ownership – by bank holding companies, Edge Act or Agreement Act Corporations that are subsidiaries of bank holding companies, and bankers' banks. (A bank holding company is a holding company that owns at least 25 per cent of any bank subsidiary and that is registered with the Federal Reserve Board under the Bank Holding Company Act.) There are restrictions on the extent of a bank's investment in an export trading company, and on the amount it can loan to the export trading company.

The response to the passing of the Act ranged from the sceptical to the euphoric. Some banks thought the Act did not go far enough or was too restrictive. Others felt that although the Act gave them considerable freedom to engage in trade, it was not something to be rushed into. But many did. Millions of dollars were invested in export trading companies. Basically, three different approaches emerged:

1. Incorporate a new subsidiary and staff it from scratch.
2. Buy an existing export trading company.
3. Establish a new export trading company on a joint venture basis with an existing export trading house.

While some export trading companies concentrated on geographic areas, others focused on specific industries or products. Their success varied. Those that failed to achieve profitability early on blamed the restrictions imposed by the Export Trading Company Act, or bad trading experiences, or overheads in excess of income, where there had been overestimated potential volumes of business.

Specific problems encountered were as follows:

1. *Legal*
   (a) The 50 per cent test which demanded that at least 50 per cent of earnings came from exporting US goods over a two-year period. Countertrade and off-shore trading were not included as export transactions.
   (b) Restrictions on holding company investments in the export trading company.
   (c) Implied restrictions on position taking.
   (d) Restrictions on lending to the export trading company by affiliated banks.

2. *Operational*
   (a) Lack of trading experience among management. Difficulty in recruiting staff of right calibre.
   (b) Where an export trading company aimed to transact business globally, staff did not always have the appropriate product or market knowledge.
   (c) Over-concentration of activity.

What role can an export trading company play in an export transaction? There is no doubt that the blending of banking and trading is an interesting – even exciting – idea. The ability of an export trading company to take title to goods is often quoted as being of great importance to an exporter looking for help in the disposal of countertrade goods. Whilst a bank-owned export trading company presents a trustworthy and creditworthy principal, its involvement as a principal may not add a great deal to the transaction. If an exporter wants a trading partner to take over the responsibility for marketing the countertrade goods, an export trading company may undertake to do so. One thing to be remembered here, however, is that their ability to trade on an open position may be limited. The export trading company may need a confirmed buyer in place before entering into a commitment to buy the countertrade goods. As far as the original exporter is concerned, the export trading company's intervention in such cases has added another layer of cost and has distanced the exporter from the end-user, who may have been a useful contact.

In the United States, the Administration is disappointed that the export trading companies have not grown into the Sogo Shosha type of operation that they had wished. Many bank-owned export trading companies have cut back on their operations and there are few that are as bullish now as when they started.

Appendix 2 lists banks and their associated export trading companies that were still operating in mid-1985. It is believed that there will be further cutbacks in staff and a rethink in terms of strategy. There could be a concentration on what banks do best: trade finance.

Amidst all this upheaval, countertrade continues to receive a great deal of attention, and many banks which have cut back on their trading activities have retained a countertrade capability.

Perhaps the export 'lobby' in the United States will engineer the changes the export trading companies seek in the Export Trading Companies Act. There is a widespread belief that like Sogo Shosha, which are regarded so highly, the United States should harness its massive buying power to facilitate exports.

At the moment, for the non-American exporter faced with a countertrade demand, there may be scope for using an export trading company with the appropriate product or geographic knowledge, but it would be wise to compare costs with other traders before entering into a firm commitment.

Sogo Shosha, Japan

Much has been said about the great strengths of the Japanese Sogo Shosha. Companies such as C. Itoh and and Co. Ltd, Marubeni Corporation, Mitsubishi Corporation, Mitsui and Co. Ltd and Sumitomo Corporation are to be found competing all over the world for major projects. The way Japanese industries are organised is often quoted as being the reason why they are so much more competitive. The ability to field a negotiating team representing different disciplines (e.g.

engineering, commercial, trading and financial) all under the same flag, is seen as a great advantage.

But how true is this idea? Certainly, there is evidence in plenty to suggest that the Japanese have won a great deal of business through their well-organised approach to contract negotiations. The question is, though, at what cost has this business been won?

An examination of the profitability of Japanese trading houses shows a disturbing narrowing of profit margins. The statistics in Table 13.1 show the results of Japan's largest Sogo Shosha for 1984. Much of the pressure on profitability came from third country trade, which represented 18 per cent of the Sogo Shosha's annual turnover in 1984. Offshore trading is generally less profitable than import-export trade. (The growth in turnover can be attributed to the rapid growth in exports to the United States and China – particularly of automobiles which are obviously steel-product based – and the large third-country trade in high-value commodities like oil and grains. The depreciation of the yen in 1984 also helped to inflate the sales figures.)

In the context of countertrade, the great strengths of the Sogo Shosha lie in their world-wide network of trading offices and their ability to harness their buying power to generate sales. They are able to identify openings for the sale of countertrade goods, and through their involvement in the area of financial services can often finance the sale of the countertrade goods. The Sogo Shosha have skilled buyers, as well as sellers, negotiating contracts involving countertrade. The interplay between the price of the export sale and the cost of disposing of the countertrade goods can be more easily managed if it all takes place in-house. Establishing the relationships between the various parties to a complete countertrade deal is discussed in Chapter 7. The advantages in having the countertrade deal structured in-house, within one legal entity, are obvious.

All of the above comments refer to the activities of Japanese trading houses coping with countertrade where it affects their own sales. But what of their use to third parties? If there is a profit to be made, the Sogo Shosha will of course accept the business, and it is well worth approaching the major houses to discuss countertrade problems.

To summarise the foregoing points the following comments come from *East-West* (an excellent guide to trade with Comecon, published fortnightly; see Appendix 7). In reporting on the sale of video recorders to Hungary against 'payment' in Hungarian furniture, *East-West* made the following comments:

It has been recognised that several recent Japanese successes in Hungary were

Table 13.1 Results of Japan's largest Sogo Shosha fiscal 1984[1]

Company	Sales Yen (billion)	Operating profits (Yen billion)	Current profits (Yen billion)	Gross profit ratio (%)
Mitsubishi Corp.	16426.801 (9.3)[2]	36.549 (8.8)	51.716 (11.0)	1.23 (0.006)
Mitsui & Co.	14900.071 (6.7)	68.659 (13.2)	39.866 (17.6)	1.52 (0.01)
C. Itoh & Co.	14077.235 (8.4)	45.492 (14.9)	40.041 (29.3)	1.37 (0.03)
Marubeni Corp.	13563.875 (14.7)	41.729 (23.5)	37.761 (63.5)	1.2 (0.02)
Sumitomo Corp.	13164.753 (13.3)	44.681 (0.2)	45.502 (7.4)	1.3 (0.07)
Nissho Iwai Corp.	8552.413 (9.8)	24.733 (5.9)	19.130 (43.2)	1.39 (0.09)
Toyo Menka Kaisha	4503.311 (11.1)	19.403 (1.3)	7.697 (69.0)	1.53 (0.12)
Nichimen Corp.	3952.639 (19.9)	12.493 (50.6)	5.649 (40.6)	1.45 (0.15)
Kanematsu-Gosho	3750.895 (7.5)	16.313 (30.2)	6.809 (256.6)	1.43 (0.01)

Notes: 1. The figures are for the year-end March 1985.
2. Figures in parentheses indicate percentage change from previous year.
Source: Japan Foreign Trade Council, Inc.

due chiefly to the flexible approach regarding compensation by eight well known large Japanese trade houses. The trading houses are responsible for more than 90% of all Japanese exports to Hungary. Typically, the Japanese trading houses sell products from third countries to Hungary in addition to Japanese-made products. 1984 estimates indicate some 24–27% of their sales to Hungary were products from Western Europe.

In 1984 Japanese trading houses sold West European chemicals worth some $5 million to the Hungarian firm CHEMOLIMPEX. Again the Japanese were willing to accept compensation which West European chemical companies refused. The trading houses sell these chemicals to other COMECON countries as well.

East European sources claim that one of the reasons for the Japanese success is not just the prompt payment which accompanies the purchase order in Hungary but the granting of trade credits for the financing of Hungarian purchases of Japanese goods. Another reason is a perfect system of monitoring Hungarian manufacture lists, allowing early determination of eventual purchases and making those possibilities well known to their subsidiaries worldwide.

MARUBENI's spokesman pointed out that when they discover interesting new Hungarian products, they are sure that within several days there will be some favourable reactions to buy from at least some of their 74 commercial offices worldwide.

What are they?

Sogo Shosha: in Japanese the words mean 'general trading companies', but the operations of Japan's Sogo Shosha are far broader than this term conveys. These uniquely Japanese institutions are, therefore, now increasingly referred to around the world by the original Japanese term.

The Sogo Shosha are highly sophisticated corporations, varying in size but with similarly comprehensive trade and business-related activities. Employing over 81,000 persons world-wide, they are active in virtually every country of the world. Their total annual sales are equal to over one-third of Japan's gross national product.

They possess vast communications networks that span the world, collecting and transmitting comprehensive data on day-to-day commodity price fluctuations, markets, areas of surplus and shortage, and everything that bears on trade. One Sogo Shosha, for instance, lends an entire floor of a large office building to its communications centre. Its telex and facsimile machines and computer terminals link 187 offices across 77 countries. Another Sogo Shosha has over 3,500 employees reporting from around the world through exclusive computer-linked lines. Between Tokyo and New York alone it has eleven lines; between New York and London six. An average of 50,000 messages pass through the system each day.

The Sogo Shosha's expertise and experience extend from the trade and distribution of goods to finance, engineering and construction, transportation and natural resource development. As a result, they are uniquely equipped to assist other companies in selling and making products and expanding international operations in general.

The Sogo Shosha differ from other companies in that they are not necessarily user- or manufacturer-oriented. Rather, they are supply/demand-oriented and function as problem solvers. Recognising demand for goods or services, the Sogo Shosha immediately look for ways to supply it, either taking the intermediary role in trade deals between a number of parties or independently directing the flow of trade.

They differ from multinational corporations chiefly in that their wide-ranging investments are all directly connected with trade, with the broad aim of stimulating international business. As commercial interests, the Sogo Shosha are variously restricted in acquiring status in some developing countries in ways not applicable to corporations with many non-trade-related business investments.

They are further distinguished by their roots in the Japanese economy and society. Their domestic business base and background give them distinctive features, such as long-term employee loyalty and broad diversification, that inevitably affect their style of business. This domestic base and thorough understanding of the Japanese system gives them unparalleled capacities for helping foreign firms successfully penetrate the highly competitive Japanese market, at considerable savings of expense, time and effort.

Their efforts to open the Japanese market further to foreign manufacturers and services are one expression of their growing international orientation. With their vast world-wide information gathering and processing capabilities, their increasing presence in overseas locations and growing co-operation with foreign firms through joint ventures, the needs of foreign countries and clients are playing a greater role in their extensive long-term corporate planning.

In recent years many foreign governments and businessmen have shown particular interest in the Sogo Shosha, as a key to understanding the Japanese economy and also as a possible model for the establishment of comprehensive trading companies in their own countries. The Sogo Shosha have responded, sending senior executives abroad to lecture on their organisation and history, sponsoring seminars and lectures in Japan, and receiving foreigners into their own companies for intensive study programmes or long-term employment. Moreover, foreign staff are brought to Japanese head offices to train for responsible positions in Sogo Shosha offices in their own countries.

Historical development

The origins of the Sogo Shosha can be traced back to the Meiji Restoration of 1868, when, after almost two and a half centuries of isolation, the country began an intensive modernisation effort. The new government's industrialisation programme prescribed the promotion of Japanese trading companies in order to secure raw material supplies and develop markets, and particularly to win control of trade from foreign traders.

In the 1890s the demand for raw materials by Japan's burgeoning cotton-spinning industry stimulated the beginnings of some of today's largest trading firms. New business opportunities during the First World War also propelled the growth of trading houses. Between 1874 and 1918, the proportion of Japan's foreign trade handled by Japanese companies rose from 1 per cent to 80 per cent.

The trading companies began early to supplement their role as suppliers of raw materials by investing in manufacturing industries. They became trade and finance intermediaries in domestic industries and foreign trade. These early traders shared several characteristics with today's Sogo Shosha. They introduced new technology, provided information, operated private communications systems, set up overseas offices and owned independent sales outlets. However, most specialised in one type or group of commodities; only two of the predecessors of today's Sogo Shosha had developed into general trading companies before the Second World War. These two largest traders acted as the supply and marketing agents of 'zaibatsu' groups – large financial, industrial and trading combines which played a pivotal role in Japan's industrialisation. Because of ties with the military, they were broken up after the War into a large number of small companies, and the zaibatsu were prohibited by law.

The free competition between hundreds of trading companies that ensued created many opportunities for expansion and diversification for the older and more experienced firms. Though the former zaibatsu members later regrouped in a new and much looser form, the business environment had undergone radical change with the rise of non-zaibatsu groups centred around banks and other major enterprises.

It was in this environment, propelled by intense competition and the restructuring of Japanese industry following the Korean War, that the diversification of the largest trading companies led to the full-fledged development of the Sogo Shosha.

The economy's shift from concentration on textiles to the rapid development of heavy and chemical industries gave rise to the need for long-term, steady supply of raw materials. In response, the traders began to organise large joint investment and resource development ventures, while securing supplies of grains and other foods.

Conversely, with the support of the Ministry of International Trade and Industry, they became the advance guard of Japan's export drive. With such a crucial role in imports and exports, they served as catalysts of Japan's rapid economic growth in the 1960s, helping the nation overcome severe trade deficits and attain developed nation status by 1964.

While developing the earliest overseas marketing networks for automobiles and electrical appliances, they also took advantage of the growth of a mass domestic market to move into many new business areas in Japan. These included large urban development projects, housing and ocean development, as well as the fashion industry, distribution, market consulting and engineering. Supporting these activities by organising new companies and investing in established ones, they built a firm and stable alliance with domestic financial and manufacturing sectors.

Yet, though their sales volume grew precipitously during this period, this was not achieved without many struggles and adjustments of strategy. Challenged by intense competition, changes in the composition of trade, and the tendency of some manufacturers to eliminate intermediaries, they were forced to seek gowth through diversification. To keep prices and costs to a minimum they sought to gain greater control over supply and marketing through upstream and downstream integration, consolidation of affiliates and entry into consumer markets.

Through these efforts they made significant contributions to rationalising the production and distribution system in Japan, while assisting many small- and medium-sized firms. Meanwhile, the increasing competitiveness of Japan's industrial equipment industry and engineering technology opened up a new business file in the export of plants to developing nations.

Their activities

The Sogo Shosha are, quite obviously, most active in Japanese foreign trade, but in the context of countertrade one of the things which makes the Sogo Shosha interesting is their involvement in external trade. In addition they consistently import more than they export. There is, therefore, great scope for them to use their buying power to leverage exports. Purchases can be re-sourced, so that those purchases would discharge countertrade obligations.

Sogo Shosha v. Europe's traders It is interesting to compare the activities of the Sogo Shosha with the trading companies of the Western world. The preceding notes and the following description of their functions is taken from promotional literature issued by the Sogo Shosha Committee of the Japan Foreign Trade Council Inc.

Trade The role of trade intermediary is the core of Sogo Shosha business activity. About 50 per cent of Japan's exports and about 67 per cent of her imports pass through the Sogo Shosha, which also channel an increasing volume of offshore trade. Their global operating scale permits risk absorption, market expansion and co-ordination of suppliers and buyers for maximum mutual advantage.

Distribution The Sogo Shosha offer access to major international and domestic distribution networks and operate their own distribution centres for added efficiency. Their experience and familiarity with domestic business channels assure the successful marketing of foreign products in Japan.

Organising Long experience as commodity traders has propelled the Sogo Shosha into increasing activity as comprehensive business project organisers. Proven dexterity in complex trade transactions, supported by strong management resources, enables their smooth co-ordination of large multinational projects for governments and private interests.

Financing With large-scale business diversification, the Sogo Shosha have developed a vital role in arranging or providing the massive funding required for trade expansion. Backed by impeccable credit rating and an international network of financial and foreign exchange experts, they assist clients in procuring credit, loans, loan guarantees and venture capital.

Investment Acting as investment intermediaries, Sogo Shosha provide firms with information about most countries, helping to encourage and direct their overseas investments. They also foster business growth through direct investment in resource, trade and industrial development.

Joint ventures To further the stable development of trade, Sogo Shosha introduce manufacturers in one country to suppliers in another, often resulting in joint ventures in which they may hold equity. Such ventures frequently involve the relocation of production facilities to export markets, contributing to industrial development and employment overseas.

Resource development Historically, Sogo Shosha have handled the bulk of food, fuel and raw materials imports on which Japan's prosperity depends. This role has led them into organisation of major raw materials development projects to assure the stability of supply. Increasingly, processing is being shifted to nations where these resources are located.

Transportation The Sogo Shosha co-ordinate goods shipments from suppliers to final destinations in order to minimise costs and delivery time. They even check packing, supervise loading, and take care of documentation and customs clearance.

Research Successful trade promotion and project feasibility assessment depend on extensive and accurate knowledge of markets, technological developments, changes in the structure of industry and demand, and business and financial conditions throughout the world. Research in all these areas is an important part of Sogo Shosha activities.

Planning The Sogo Shosha bring the widest possible experience and perspective to large-scale project planning, drawing on comprehensive information resources and familiarity with regional conditions. Their far-ranging business orientation guarantees expert performance in every stage from conception through construction, supply of capital and equipment, transportation and creation of long-term markets.

Marketing Their world-wide presence, marketing expertise and information facilities make the services of the Sogo Shosha particularly attractive to companies lacking overseas marketing networks or seeking to enter small or unfamiliar markets.

Information The Sogo Shosha possess information-gathering and telecommunications facilities that rival those of the largest governments, enabling instant access for both domestic and foreign clients to the most up-to-date intelligence bearing on trade development, business opportunities and marketing.

Technology transfer The role of Sogo Shosha as importers of advanced technology to Japan continues in the tie-ups with foreign firms for development and marketing of high-tech products. Overseas, turn-key plant construction projects effect the transfer of Japanese technical and managerial know-how to developing countries.

Export trading company, Sogo Shosha or trading house – how to choose

There is no simple answer of which to choose to assist an exporter in discharging a countertrade obligation. The database referred to in Chapter 16 will help in seeking out the right partner. In some instances, the exporter will be spoiled for choice, and selecting a partner may come down to a question of cost; that is, which trader or buyer is going to charge the least for his involvement.

For countertrade obligations in Eastern Europe, the choice may not be quite so open, and it will be necessary to contact a wide range of potential partners to determine which is able to assume the obligation at that time. Special relationships *can* be established in some cases, where traders will take on difficult problems on the understanding that they are given any better quality deals which may occur.

Likely developments

Over the next few years we may see a growth in the number of traders such as MG Services (described on page 120). Certainly, non-Japanese exporting companies could be disadvantaged in competitive situations through not having in their negotiating team a trader able to respond to countertrade demands involving a wide range of goods. The Sogo Shosha could be a model for some Western traders, a move which should be welcomed by Western exporters.

We will also see the growth of trading companies from new areas, such as South Korea, Hong Kong, Singapore, Australia, Brazil, and so on. Names such as Golden Bell (South Korea), Hutchison (Hong Kong), Elders (Australia) and Cotia (Brazil) may become as familiar as C. Itoh, Phibro and Louis Dreyfus.

Structuring the exporter's relationship with the trading company is dealt with in Chapter 7. It is worth while repeating, however, that the choice of partner should be based on the following:

1. Their known expertise and experience.
2. Their business integrity.
3. Their financial stability.
4. The level of commitment they will offer.
5. The cost of their involvement.

CHAPTER 14

Countertrade in Eastern Europe

Introduction

The following story is quoted by Oswald Burstin, Managing Director of M. Golodetz (Overseas) Limited in *The Journal of the British Soviet Chamber of Commerce.*

'In 1553 in the reign of Mary, five years before Elizabeth I came to the throne, an English merchant expedition, under the command of Sir Hugh Willoughby, was seeking a northern sea route to India – one ship, the "Edward Bonaventure", captained by Richard Chancellor, arrived at the mouth of the Northern Dvina river near the town of Kholmogor; Chancellor was summoned to Moscow by Ivan IV (Gronzni – The Terrible), who granted the English the right to trade in Russia on favourable terms. . . A letter written in 1555 by Ivan IV to Queen Mary contains the words "Forasmuch as God hath planted all realms and dominions in the whole world with sundry commodities, so that the one hath need of the amity and commodities of the other". The letter also allows English merchants to "tarry, abide and sojourn and buy, sell, barter and change all kinds of merchandise" – (one item of trade between the two countries at that time was tallow).

. . . That letter, written by Ivan the Terrible to Queen Mary in the mid 16th century, is still perhaps the best description of the basic essentials of trade between our two countries – we certainly have great need of each other's "amity" as well as each other's goods. Also, that early reminder that trade is not a one-way affair never applied more than today. What has changed, of course, is the pattern of trade.'

Eastern Europe represents the single most important area of countertrade activity. Modern countertrade can be traced back to the trading systems employed after the Second World War. Because of the special nature of countertrade in Eastern Europe, this chapter has been devoted to the subject. There will be overlaps with other chapters, but for the sake of completeness, the full picture is described here.

It is important to understand the way East European countries organise their industries and foreign trade. From country to country there will be minor variations, but there are fundamental similarities. Industries are grouped, for the purposes of foreign trade, by activity or sector. Each group then has one or two foreign trade organisations responsible for conducting the import/export activities of its members. They may also be called foreign trade corporations or foreign trade associations. In some of the East European countries, selected enterprises may have the authority to engage in foreign trade (e.g. Hungary). In the German Democratic Republic, some of the *Kombinats* – industrial combines – may also have similar authority.

This unique feature presents certain problems, not only in the basic sales negotiation, but particularly in the area of countertrade. The following notes are designed to be general guidelines to negotiation of a countertrade contract, not a rigid strategy.

First considerations

1. The bureaucratic process in Eastern Europe means that decision-making is slow and unwieldy. Be prepared for long negotiations.
2. Frequent visits may be necessary, to keep interest alive, and to maintain relationships.
3. Consider how the sales team will be made up. It may be necessary to take a countertrade expert.
4. Note everything that is said, especially names.
5. Minute all meetings, discussions and phone conversations. Follow up with an exchange of letters if necessary.
6. East European contracts are performance-oriented.
7. All draft contracts and agreements should be dated page by page to avoid confusion.
8. All agreements should be signed by the *authorised* signatories of the foreign trade organisation.
9. The likelihood of encountering countertrade could be based on the degree of priority of imports. Categories of imports, for example, would be:
   (a) priority (e.g. goods which will generate foreign exchange);
   (b) planned;
   (c) extra-plan (goods needed because of poor initial planning);
   (d) non-planned.
10. No indication will be given, but research could be undertaken by reference to Five Year Plans.
11. Countertrade could be linked to the degree of competition.

12. Mode of payment should be discussed at the earliest time, to determine whether the deal is based on compensation or counterpurchase.
13. If countertrade is likely to be an issue, ask to speak to the foreign trade organisation countertrade expert.
14. If a trading house is to be used, do not mention its existence immediately. Consider taking one of its staff as a member of your team.

Negotiations

1. In compensation deals the foreign exchange generated from the sale of the countertrade goods will pay for the principal export.

2. In counterpurchase obligations, the percentage of countertrade demanded should be negotiated downwards.
3. The price for the exports should not be quoted until the extent, and therefore the cost, of the countertrade has been established.
4. If a price *must* be quoted early on, it should be inflated by the amount advised by the exporter's countertrade adviser, bank or trading house. There is always room for discounting the price later.
5. Contracts should be negotiated so that separate agreements exist for the underlying primary contract and the countertrade. This is usually done by having:
   (a) a sales contract;
   (b) a countertrade framework agreement;
   (c) an actual countertrade purchase contract.
6. The documents should:
   (a) not be cross-referenced;
   (b) be drawn with different time-scales for completion;
   (c) be independent legal instruments, so that objections to one will not interrupt the other.
7. The benefits of separate documents are:
   (a) insurance of export leg is possible (*Note*: ECGD role);
   (b) countertrade contract is more easily transferred;
   (c) the primary contract details will not be seen by other parties.
8. The countertrade contract will only be signed when suitable East European goods have been found and their specification, delivery dates and price fixed.

9. When negotiating the framework agreement, the following aspects must be considered:
   (a) The obligation should be expressed, wherever possible, as a specific figure, not as a percentage of sale.
   (b) The agreement should permit transferability (e.g. 'The company commits itself to buy or to have bought through a third party, goods for $X from the following foreign trade organisations:')
   (c) It should not contain marketing restrictions.
   (d) It should state how monitoring should take place on subsequent fulfilments of the obligations (e.g. 'In fulfilment of the commitment entered into by (The company) under its sales contract dossier No. x of (date) and countertrade commitment No. x of (date) with (The foreign trade organisation). (The third party company) herewith purchases. . . . . .').
   (e) Signatories must have the appropriate authority.
   (f) It should permit linkage; i.e. the source of countertrade goods should not be restricted to one foreign trade organisation or industrial enterprise. (*Note*: This could involve payment of commission locally.)
   (g) It should contain reference to the fact that the foreign trade organisation warrants that the countertrade leg only comes into effect on execution of the primary sales contract.
   (h) It should be based on as wide a choice of goods as possible.
   (i) The percentage commitment should be minimised.
   (j) A specific list of goods should be obtained if possible, but care is needed if old lists are provided.
   (k) The seat of arbitration court should be stipulated, but should be *outside* the buying country.
   (l) The foreign trade organisation should warrant countertrade goods as being of 'export' standard, offered at internationally competitive prices.
   (m) There should be a clause giving the exporter the right to choose a neutral surveyor, selected by both parties, to pass a binding judgement on the quality of the countertrade goods, if the exporter finds them unacceptable.
   (n) The exporter's obligation should be reduced or released unconditionally if countertrade goods are not available when contracted for.
   (o) The non-fulfilment penalty should be minimised, and it

should be stated that payment thereof discharges the obligation.

10. Careful attention is required when negotiating the time-scales for completion of the obligation, particularly under counterpurchase. As a general rule, the exporter should extend the fulfilment period as long as possible. Searching for suitable countertrade goods, buyers thereof and obtaining foreign trade organisation approval will all take time.
11. Penalty guarantees are almost always demanded (except for compensation deals where non-performance is a penalty in itself). The following is a general guide to the establishment of penalty guarantees:
    (a) The greater the choice of countertrade goods and the fewer the limitations, the higher the level of penalty.
    (b) Penalties are lower for raw materials and non-perishables than products with high labour content, and perishable goods.
    (c) Penalties will be higher for companies having previously failed in executing countertrade obligations.
    (d) Transferability may increase the percentage of penalty.
    (e) The legal obligation to fulfil the countertrade contract will rest with the exporter or trading house signatory to the contract. Non-signatories involved in the countertrade contract will be treated as correspondents, but the principals will be held responsible for the correspondent's non-performance.
    (f) As the exporter will be liable under most countertrade contracts, if a trading house is employed, a separate written agreement with the trading house must be signed defining how damages are to be handled should the trading house not perform.
    (g) It is not a good idea just to pay the penalty, rather than attempt to perform the countertrade contract.
    (h) The penalty should not be based on the Western company's export sales price.
    (i) The penalty should be payable on the unfulfilled portion.
    (j) Payment of the penalty should terminate the countertrade obligation, e.g. 'The payment of the stipulated penalty automatically releases (The exporter) once and forever from any further financial or any other claim by (The foreign trade organisation)'.

(k) The penalty guarantee should not be 'first demand' – add 30 days.
(l) If the trading house establishes the guarantee, the exporter may be asked to pay the fee.

Countertrade goods

1. The selection of countertrade goods will be limited by availability and through restrictions on possible sources. In order of likelihood, the exporter will be offered:
   (a) products from the buying foreign trade organisation;
   (b) products from several foreign trade organisations subordinate to the same industrial ministry as the importer;
   (c) products from several foreign trade organisations subordinate to several industrial ministries;
   (d) mixed deals – percentage proportion from a variety of foreign trade organisations;
   (e) any products (i.e. free choice).
   (This list represents a guide to the least-to-best alternatives.)
2. Marketing the countertrade goods may also be subject to restriction as to *destination* and price charged, by one of the following:
   (a) conditions imposed by the East European foreign trade organisation;
   (b) conditions imposed by EEC/UK government in the form of quotas;
   (c) the existence of an East European sales company in the proposed market.
3. In considering the disposal of goods, apart from the points mentioned above, other considerations are as follows:
   (a) If an *end-user* is identified, will he act as principal in the countertrade contract?
   (b) If so, will this prevent the use of future purchases by that end-user as countertrade?
   (c) It is more likely that a trading house will be used, but bear in mind its product/geographic specialisation.
   (d) References should be taken up to ensure that the trading house is reputable and financially sound.
   (e) The time-scale for completion of the obligation by the trader should be less than that set out in the framework agreement, if the trader is not a signatory to the contract.

(f) It is conceivable that the trader may pass the obligation to another trader.

(g) Trading houses which deal with Eastern Europe very often, may well have countertrade credits, thus making discharge of a new obligation easier.

(h) An early guide to the disagio must be obtained, but it is wise to get indicative quotes from several trading houses.

(i) The exporter may be asked to open a letter of credit for the disagio.

(j) It should be remembered that the disagio is a composite fee and subsidy.

(k) Once the countertrade obligation has been fulfilled, a letter of release should be obtained from the foreign trade organisation. If a trading house has been involved, it will have to secure the letter of release.

(l) The letter of release will be useful in arranging cancellation of the penalty guarantee.

CHAPTER 15

Bilateral trading/'umbrella' agreements

This chapter deals with systems of bilateral trading, set up by government entities or private sector trading companies, either for their own benefit or for use by other importers/exporters.

The terminology used in this chapter draws a distinction between the various techniques employed – there is no common agreement on what each system should be called.

Bilateral trading

There are three principal types of bilateral trading arrangement. The distinction between them is not always made clear in press comment on deals that have been done this way. The differences between the three types are extremely important, as it is the manner in which the exporter is paid that determines why each system is unique in construction.

Bilateral trading agreements

A bilateral trading agreement is usually an agreement reached between two governments, state-owned trading companies or private traders, often referred to as a trading protocol. Both parties agree to undertake a certain volume of trade, quite often stipulating which goods will be traded. Payment for each individual contract struck under the protocol will be paid for in the normal way; that is, by letter of credit, documentary bill or open account. There is *no link between the flows of funds* in each direction, but the individual transactions are recorded as having taken place under the protocol.

For the exporter such arrangements may be useful in overcoming problems associated with import licensing, but not so useful in solving shortages of foreign exchange. Figure 15.1 illustrates the flows of goods and funds.

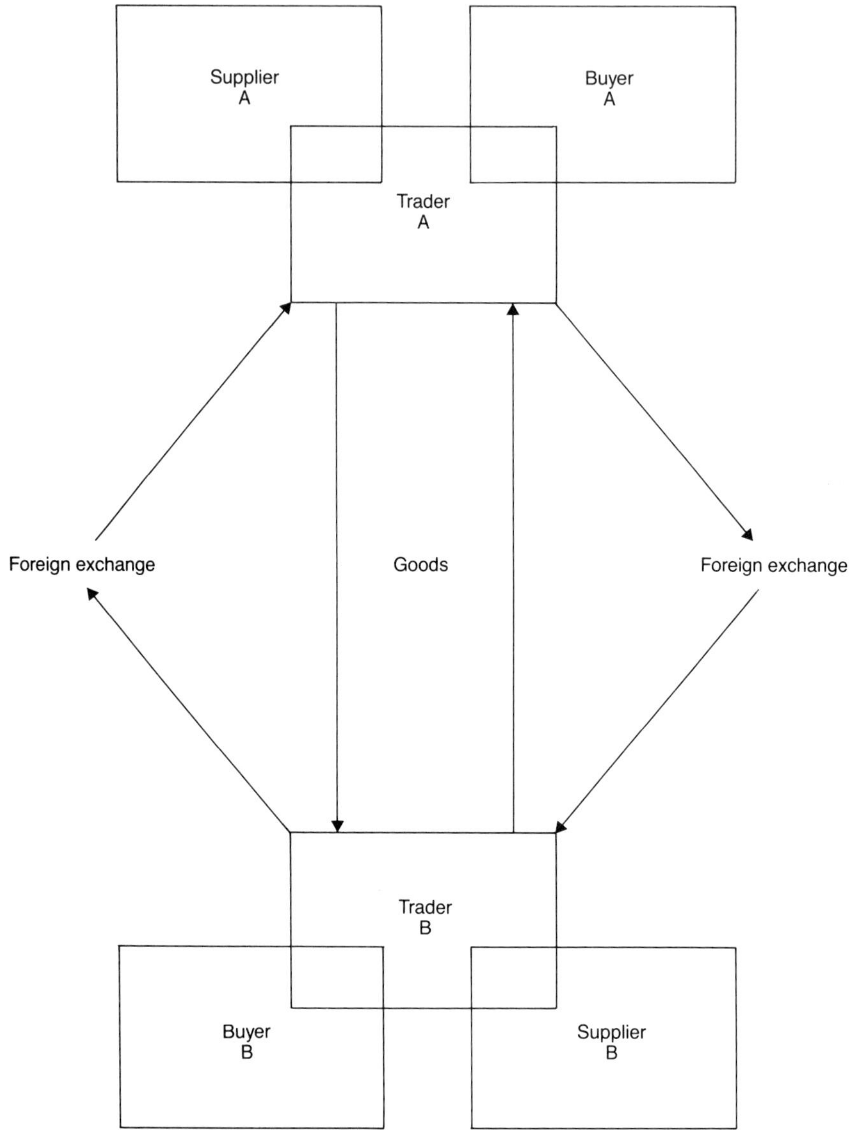

Fig. 15.1 Bilateral trading agreement

Bilateral payments agreements

Any bilateral payments agreement is probably set up on the same basis as a bilateral trading agreement, and is very often an extension thereof. An agreement governing the means of payment for the trade adds teeth to the underlying trading agreement. Figure 15.2 shows much the same sort of system as outlined in Fig. 15.1. The difference lies in the link which exists between the two flows of funds. The illustration refers to the use of letters of credit. An exporter may receive a letter of credit which has been established only because the trading company or state entity in the buying country has received a letter of credit for exports *from* that country. A link is established between the two flows of funds. In Chapter 6, countertrade deals on the basis of linked letters of credit were described. With bilateral payments arrangements we are concerned with a less formal linkage.

Obviously, if an exporter receives a letter of credit issued because of the establishment of a letter of credit in favour of the buyer or an entity in the buyer's country, it has not removed the credit risk. The letter of credit may still be unconfirmed. Because in most cases the linkage between the letters of credit is informal, Western banks will not confirm such letters of credit merely because a hard-currency-generating letter of credit exists in the other direction; they have no control over the funds generated by that letter of credit and therefore see no benefit in its existence.

The existence of the second letter of credit could, however, give comfort to an insurer who would be prepared to offer cover on the letter of credit in favour of the exporter. The underlying agreement that a bank in the buyer's country will 'look to' the proceeds of the second letter of credit to meet drawings on the first may be viewed as sufficient security to warrant covering the second letter of credit.

From the exporter's view, the existence of the bilateral payments agreement will mean that a letter of credit has been forthcoming *and* the letter of credit is insured against non-payment (for basically the same reasons as set out in Chapter 9). There are drawbacks, however. The cost of insurance must be taken into account – and this charge could exceed normal confirmation fees. Then there is the problem of residual risks. Insurers will not cover 100 per cent of the letter of credit, and the exporter is left with, say, 10 per cent of the risk exposed.

Bilateral payments agreements are negotiated by trading entities, but individual exporters may feed into them. Each sales contract is separate, and the exporter will not be involved in any way with the return leg of the arrangement. Ultimately the flows of goods must balance, or reach the previously agreed levels.

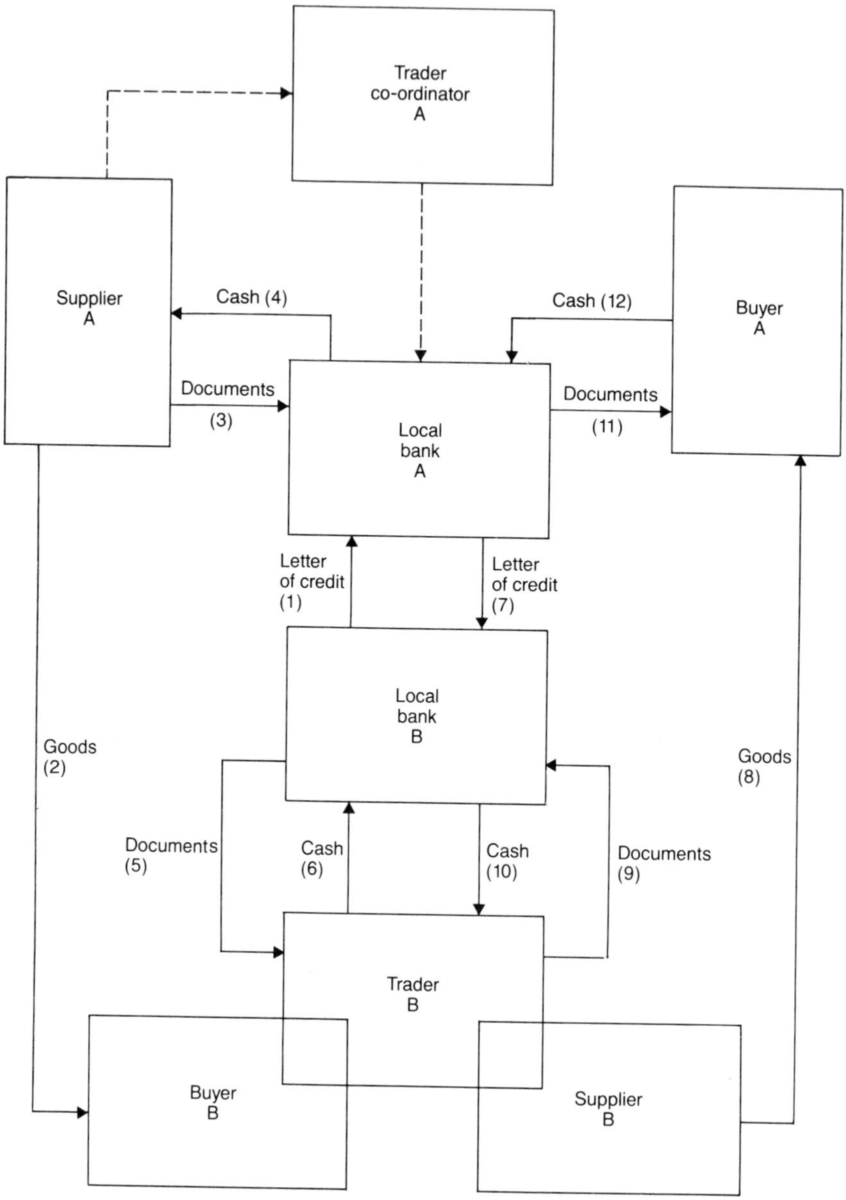
Trader
co-ordinator
A
Supplier
A
Buyer
A
Cash (4)
Cash (12)
Documents
(3)
Documents
(11)
Local
bank
A
Letter
of credit
(1)
Letter
of credit
(7)
Local
bank
B
Goods
(2)
Goods
(8)
Documents
(5)
Cash
(6)
Cash
(10)
Documents
(9)
Trader
B
Buyer
B
Supplier
B

Summary of a bilateral payments agreement

Figure 15.2 illustrates a bilateral payments agreement between a trading company in country A, acting as co-ordinator, and a trading company in country B, acting as principal, for subsidiaries or associates.

(1) Supplier A enters into a contract to sell goods to a foreign buyer trader B and receives a letter of credit from the buyer's bank.
(2) Supplier A ships the goods to buyer B.
(3) Supplier A presents documents to local bank A in terms of the letter of credit.
(4) Local bank A pays hard currency to supplier A.
(5) Local bank A sends documents to local bank B which presents them to the trader for payment.
(6) Trader B pays local currency to local bank B which will in due course settle with local bank A.
(7) Trader B enters into a contract to sell goods to the foreign buyer, buyer A, and receives a letter of credit from the buyer's bank.
(8) Supplier B ships the goods to buyer A.
(9) Trader B presents documents to local bank B in terms of the letter of credit.
(10) Local bank B pays local currency to trader B.
(11) Local bank B sends documents to local bank A which presents them to buyer A for payment.
(12) Buyer A pays hard currency to local bank A which will in due course settle with local bank B.

Local bank B will 'look to' the hard currency transfer referred to in (12) to meet its obligations under its own letter of credit as described in (6).

Fig. 15.2 Bilateral payments agreement

Bilateral clearing arrangements

A more complex system is in use which does not involve international transfers of funds, but which provides a great deal more security to the various parties. Accounts – called clearing accounts – are maintained in banks in each country. Local funds are debited and credited to these accounts. Figure 15.3 shows how the system operates and describes the manner in which payments are made.

Because it is impossible to balance the two-way flows of goods, the clearing accounts must allow for this by putting a limit on imbalances. The whole operation can be likened to a normal bank account on which an overdraft limit has been marked. Of course, the bank will not mark that limit for an uncreditworthy country any more readily than it will confirm a letter of credit. It is widely considered, however, that the system offers a good deal of security to the exporter.

Once again, these arrangements are usually negotiated by trading

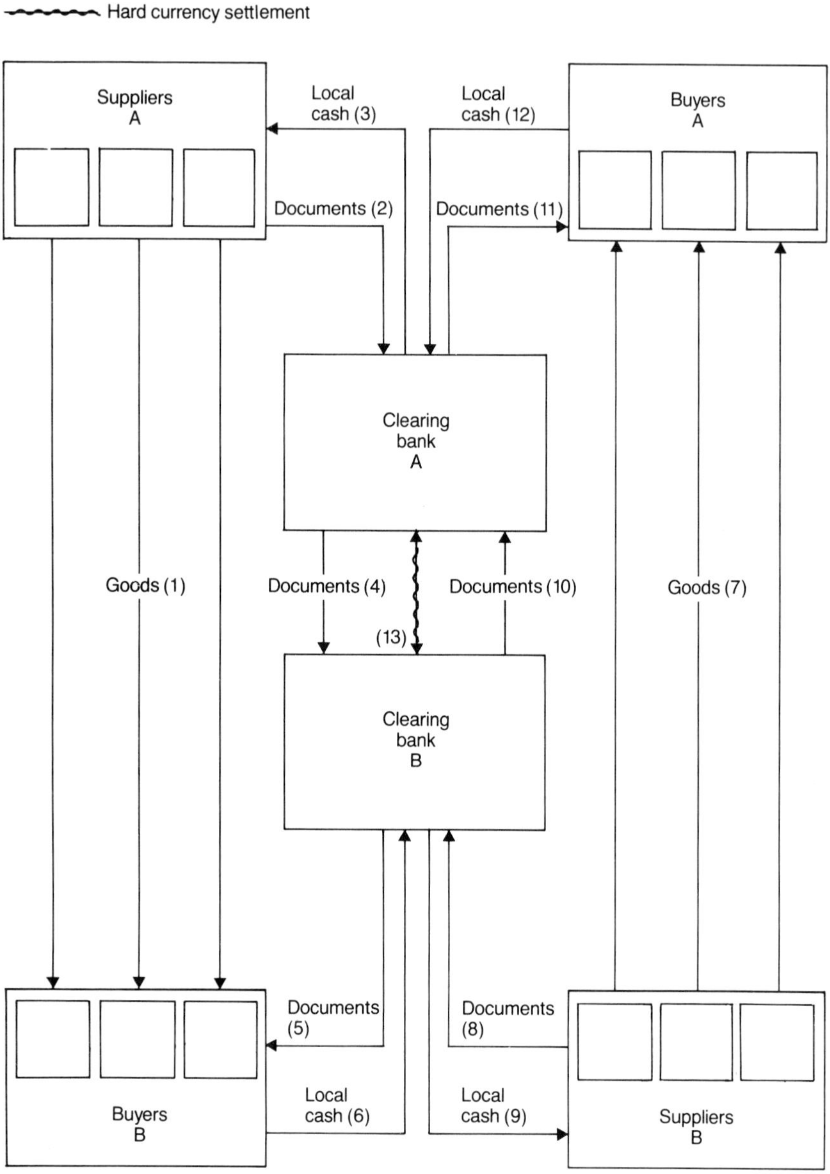
Hard currency settlement
Suppliers A
Local cash (3)
Local cash (12)
Buyers A
Documents (2)
Documents (11)
Clearing bank A
Goods (1)
Documents (4)
Documents (10)
Goods (7)
(13)
Clearing bank B
Documents (5)
Documents (8)
Local cash (6)
Local cash (9)
Buyers B
Suppliers B

Summary of a bilateral clearing agreement

In Figure 15.3, a clearing agreement is set up between two governments, trading entities or co-ordinating bodies. The system revolves around clearing accounts established in one bank in each country. The accounts operate like bank current accounts.

(1) Suppliers in country A contract to supply goods to buyers in country B. Authority is obtained for finance under the clearing agreement (backed in most cases by a letter of credit expressed in the 'currency' of the clearing account). The suppliers ship their goods to the buyers in country B.
(2) The suppliers in country A present documents evidencing despatch to the goods to the clearing account holding bank in country A.
(3) Clearing bank A pays an equivalent amount of local currency to suppliers A, *to the debit of a clearing account.*
(4) Clearing bank A sends the shipping documents to the clearing bank in country B.
(5) Clearing bank B presents the documents to the buyers.
(6) Buyers B pay local currency to clearing bank B which *credits the funds to a clearing account.*
Steps (7)-(12) show trade flowing in the opposite direction with funds passing in and out of the clearing accounts. As the accounts are both expressed in the same, 'clearing' currency, they will always balance.
(13) There is no flow of funds *between* clearing accounts, although the bilateral clearing agreement may allow for periodic settlements to correct any imbalances which may arise. These settlements would be in *hard currency.*

Fig. 15.3 Bilateral clearing agreement

companies or government entities, and the exporter will need to find a way to access the arrangement. Although there have been a number of clearing accounts set up with Western countries, to date most have involved East European countries. Chapter 3 describes switch dealing, which involves third party use of clearing systems, and Fig. 3.4 lists the main clearing arrangements known to exist.

'Umbrella' agreements

There is no commonly accepted term to describe these transactions. 'Basket', 'jumbo' and 'collective' are other terms used from time to time.

Umbrella agreements bring together the techniques of bilateral trading and escrow accounts. Usually established by trading companies, figures involved tend to be very large. Most of the more celebrated umbrella agreements in the 1980s have involved oil. For example, Iran entered into an agreement with Voest-Alpine Intertrading (VAIT) whereby VAIT would take large quantities of oil. The proceeds from the

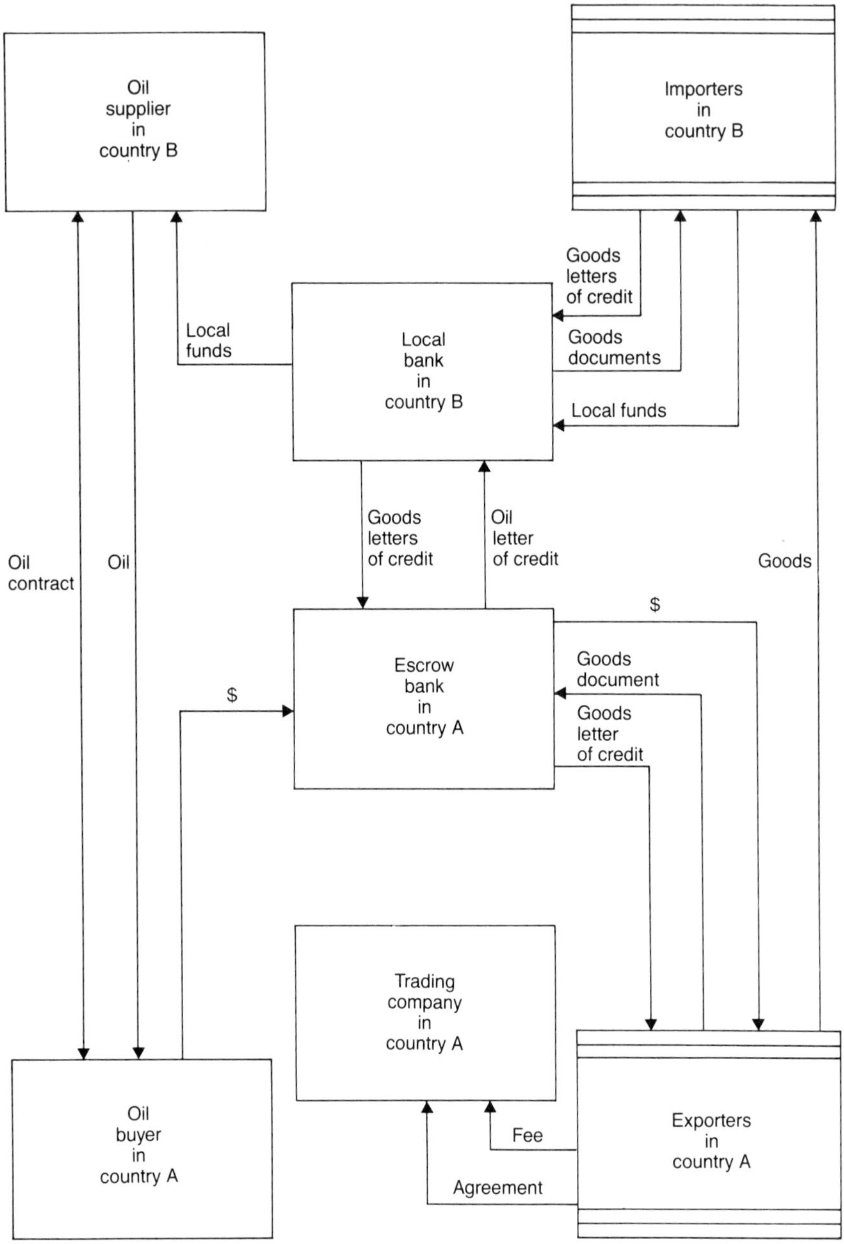

Fig. 15.4 'Umbrella' agreements

oil sale would be used to finance the sale of a wide variety of goods to Iran. The vehicle used to facilitate payments was an escrow account. Funds therein were used as security for the bank involved to pay drawings on letters of credit in favour of suppliers of goods to Iran.

Figure 15.4 describes the operation of such accounts. For the sake of clarity, what is not shown is the way in which the disagio is handled. Both the VAIT transaction and the equally famous Cotia Trading deal with Nigeria involved payments of a disagio. This payment represented a subsidy on the oil price which had been made available by both countries at prices above market rates. The disagio took the form of a subsidy paid to the oil company buying the oil. Subsequently, of course, it is recovered from exporters using the umbrella agreement as a way of financing their exports to the country in question. To many exporters, unaware of the need to subsidise the oil price, the fee demanded by the co-ordinating trader seems excessive. At one stage, the VAIT composite fee charged to exporters using the system for financing exports to Iran exceeded 15 per cent.

Exporters using such systems need to be cautious in their dealings with organisers of umbrella trading agreements. The level of commitment offered by the trading co-ordinator may be less than fully secure. Conditional letters of credit may be offered, which confirm payment will be made *only* if funds are available in the escrow account. This involves obvious risks. Advice should be sought on whether the risk can be covered in some way.

Gaining access to such facilities is usually dictated by buyers in the country supplying the countertrade goods. As they will be responsible for establishing letters of credit claused to claim reimbursement from the escrow account, their co-operation is, obviously, critical. In turn, the buyers may be subject to control from – in the case of Iran, for example – the Bilateral Transactions Committee. Nigeria controlled use of its facility with Cotia of Brazil through the use of special import licences.

Summary

Whether the system used is a bilateral trading arrangement of some sort, or is an umbrella type of arrangement set up by third parties, use thereof is usually fairly costly. The negotiations to set up facilities like these can often be protracted and the additional administration costs, together with whatever disagio is needed, will be passed on to users of the facility.

CHAPTER 16

Managing countertrade

Managing countertrade in-house

The following comments were made by Michael Cosgrove in a paper entitled 'How one company manages countertrade', delivered to a conference on the subject in Vienna in September 1984.

'General Electric has developed its worldwide capabilities for over a century. In recent years, however, international business has moved from the periphery of our company activities to the vital center. International business – exports, overseas manufacturing subsidiaries, licensing, and joint ventures – now accounts for more than a third of total GE revenues.

As we grew internationally, we developed a broad range of distribution, service, engineering and financing resources. During the 1970s, in response to the sharp growth in Countertrade and offset demands, we added valuable trading capabilities. More recently, we have added barter capabilities to respond to customer needs caused by dislocations in the world financial scene.

Our trade development activity has evolved from the Countertrade/offset requirements placed on GE, and now involves barter, worldwide sourcing, and third country trading. We provide our Countertrade service to all General Electric businesses and selectively to associated exporters. These businesses, divided into about 40 strategic business units, representing roughly 200 manufacturing plants worldwide, are responsible for marketing and selling their products worldwide. In a nut shell – General Electric Trading Company is responsible for helping them sell their products by handling the Countertrade obligations often required to make their sales.'

Cosgrove also quoted a few statistics saying that between 1974 and 1984, an acceptance of Countertrade had enabled General Electric to 'generate' about 3 billion dollars in military and civilian export business.

'The level of Countertrade obligation had been increasing. In the 1960s, the level of obligation averaged about 35% of the value of the related sale. In the 1970s, the figure increased to 50% or more and in the mid 1980s, over 80%.'

General Electric (GE) saw countertrade as an opportunity rather than a problem or liability, as it helped to increase GE's world-wide sales. A close working relationship with the buying government was sought, so that the efforts of General Electric Trading Company (GETC) were directed to the right goals.

An important company principle was that GE should never over-commit *and* it should discharge whatever it had pledged to do. These are important lessons – particularly the point that today, some countries will hesitate in awarding a contract to a company in default in its prior countertrade obligations.

GETC operated on the basis of maximising the buying power of GE, and directing countertrade goods to GE's suppliers. In the same conference paper referred to above, Michael Cosgrove said that the GETC system worked as follows:

> 'Working closely with our customers, we identify their needs and possible targets for sourcing.
>
> We search out and evaluate suppliers.
>
> We evaluate customer requests for quotations, obtain quotes from selected vendors, and review the quotes with purchasing people.
>
> We negotiate contracts and place the orders.
>
> We handle complete expediting procedures – reviewing production, providing samples and so on. We manage the export-import transactions, and coordinate installation, start-up, and service, where needed.'

Great emphasis was placed on the establishment of long-term trading relationships. Offices were opened in Bucharest, Toronto, Riyadh and São Paulo with others planned.

Most significantly GETC looked to expand its third-country and even third-party trading. In summarising GETC's attitudes to countertrade, Michael Cosgrove made the points that

- GETC's trading skills support the parent company's exports in difficult markets abroad;
- *additional* exports can be generated;
- the trading company aims to make a profit from its activities;
- the research undertaken gives GE access to new sources of products, components and materials;
- GETC's activities create a favourable climate for future business opportunities for the whole GE group.

Here we have a company taking an aggressive and progressive attitude to countertrade. It shows a positive corporate policy, obviously supported at a senior level.

The lessons

To what extent is the GE approach a model of corporate response to countertrade? What lessons can be drawn from its approach and its experiences?

It is neither within the power nor the resources of most companies to follow the GE route. The establishment of a trading subsidiary requires a commitment which many companies could not contemplate. Most of all, however, the exporting company would need evidence that the subsidiary would indeed fulfil its basic function – whether that is to earn a profit in its own right, or to generate profitable business for the parent, which might otherwise *not* have taken place.

A trading operation such as GETC requires a wide variety of skills. The countries and products involved will be diverse. Staff recruited for one set of skills may be faced with other situations which they are unfamiliar with. An obvious example would be a skilled grain trader faced with an oil countertrade. Specialist countertrade staff should, therefore, have a wide variety of skills and experiences. If they are capable people, with a good track record, *they will not be cheap*. Add this cost to the outgoings involved in maintaining a separate establishment (e.g. offices in several centres), and you have an expensive countertrade or trading company. This in itself could be problematical. Management of such a company could feel under pressure to 'justify' its budget by negotiating deals which are potentially very rewarding, but with levels of risks which would normally be considered unacceptable.

A few years ago, a case could have been made for setting up either a separate company, or a separate department to actually *trade*. The general level of countertrade support services was low, and many companies had to manage alone. The increase in countertrade awareness, and the growth of the countertrade services industry, were probably responsible for the fact that some companies withdrew from physical trading. Others, coming into countertrade for the first time, adopted a different approach. Responsibility for countertrade was passed to a 'dedicated' team or individual. Their role would be to help in negotiating contracts where countertrade was either necessary or had been demanded. They were self-contained, often having to operate with limited resources. Typically staff would be drawn from within the company itself. Their background could be commercial, technical, sales or financial.

In the secretive world of countertrade, gaining the necessary knowledge and skills will be a long and difficult process. The amount of time spent meeting bankers, traders and lawyers, trying to set up deals, trying to obtain permission to set up deals, trying to explain deals, locating counter products and trying to find someone to buy the offered counter products, is quite prodigious and, at least in the early days, greatly out of proportion with the returns.

Another significant point in looking at how a company responds to countertrade is to consider how the company can exploit its own strengths as a buyer. Its ability to consume goods could enable it to solve the countertrade problem in-house. There is often, however, a problem in the communication link between the selling or countertrade department and the purchasing department. Equally, a company could suggest to its suppliers that it will only continue to buy if the supplier buys goods in return, or helps to solve a countertrade problem by assisting in the disposal of countertrade goods.

This brings us back to GE and its own approach. If countertrade is based on demands for reciprocity, it cuts both ways.

Starting from scratch

What would be the best approach today? Without a doubt, the two most significant developments over the last few years have been the growth in the *use* of countertrade, and the increase in the number of support services available to exporters faced with the problem. Against the need to develop some sort of capability, therefore, we have the counterbalance of the availability of external support. Probably the most sensible approach for an exporting company would be to undertake a study, to cover the following areas:

1. The incidence of countertrade in traditional markets.
2. The markets which could become available if a countertrade capability exists within the company.
3. The abilities within competitor companies to accept/use countertrade.
4. The proactive use of countertrade to gain a competitive edge.
5. The company's experience to date.
6. The knowledge which exists within the company (or group).

7. The cost implications of accepting or using countertrade – what is the company's attitude to charging out costs to other subsidiaries?
8. The specialist services available to the company from the financial and trading communities.
9. The extent to which such support is appropriate for the company's activities (e.g. defence industries face off-set demands which are not always transferable).
10. The level and type of capability required within the company to cope with likely countertrade demands.
11. The 'structure' of the capability, i.e. a separate company, new department, or an individual.
12. The management line within which the capability would be sited, i.e. sales, commercial or financial.
13. The approvals necessary, within the company, for the creation of the capability.
14. The budget to be allocated – will a separate salary structure be necessary if a specialist is recruited?
15. The staffing of the function – to decide whether to recruit or to delegate responsibility to an existing member of staff.
16. The mandate of the new function
    (a) to trade;
    (b) to advise;
    (c) to seek new business;
    (d) to act as a staff function;
    (e) to act for third parties.
17. If a new company is to be formed, is it wise to trade under the parent's name?

A few golden rules

Whatever decision is reached on the company's involvement in countertrade, certain fundamental ground rules apply. It is possible to apply some of these rules to any area of corporate activity; like so many things they are based on prudence and commonsense.

1. Never get involved in a countertrade unless it is absolutely necessary.
2. Countertrade is costly in terms of executive time and out-of-pocket cost. There has to be an acceptance of this, and sufficient resources committed.

3. Staffing of the countertrade function is critical. Countertrade requires imagination, invention and patience. The official(s) chosen should be up to the challenge. If it is to be one man, who covers in his absence?
4. Enthusiasm for the concept of exciting countertrade deals should be tempered with realism. Communication is critical. The ultimate purpose must be remembered – sale/profitability. Communication with the external support services is vital. It is a type of activity which needs a wide range of possible participants – speak to everyone involved in countertrade.
5. The information gathered must be stored in an accessible form. A computer database is one answer (this idea is developed below).
6. Ensure the countertrade proposal is complete and fully understood. It may be necessary to 'sell' the idea to a foreign government.
7. Target a few new markets, rather than try to cover the globe.
8. Undertake a full risk analysis of the proposal, to determine where risks do or could occur, and examine how these risks can be overcome or hedged.

Storing countertrade data

It has been said that the key to countertrade is knowing who can do what to help. A common misconception is that help can only be secured from individuals or organisations with a prior knowledge of countertrade. But this is not so. As described elsewhere in this book, the purchase of countertrade goods is based on a commercial contract which will not differ to any great extent from contracts which are *not* based on a reciprocal arrangement. Potential countertrade partners are, therefore, as numerous as there are buyers of the types of goods found in countertrade transactions. Finding such buyers, or finding sources of information which will lead to the identification of such buyers, is a key element in building up a countertrade capability. As the volume of such information grows, so will the need to store the data in a flexible and retrievable form. Some people will use a cross-referenced card index system, but this could become very hard to manage and update.

A computer database is, naturally, the preferred vehicle, given the capacity and flexibility inherent in most database packages available today. As a guide, a database containing the basic data shown in Fig. 16.1 would be a solid foundation. Within this basic format, it is possible to retrieve information based on product and/or country.

Sources for the information to be stored could be as follows:

Name of company		
Postal address	Physical address	
Telephone	Telex	Fax

Contact(s)

Name	Position

Goods bought/traded

Type	STC code	Usual sources

East European expertise

Country	Product	Foreign trading organisation

Fig. 16.1 Countertrade database

1. Trade directories.
2. Chambers of commerce.
3. Trade associations.
4. Libraries.
5. Yellow Pages.
6. Purchasing department of company.
7. Examination of similar products for manufacturer's/distributor's names.
8. External databases (e.g. Kompass, Dun and Bradstreet).

Not all of the data will be of a 'positive' nature. The database will record if a company does *not* wish to be approached in countertrade deals. It is also useful to maintain a record of which cases have been referred to whom, so that successes can be repeated, and failures avoided.

CHAPTER 17

Summary

Countertrade can be costly, cumbersome and time-consuming. Regrettably, in some areas it is unavoidable. The exporter's reaction will ultimately be determined by two simple questions:

1. Do I *need* this business?
2. Can I accept countertrade and stay profitable?

There are a host of other questions but most will lead back to these.

This book has addressed the various aspects of countertrade that will affect the second question, but the first depends on the circumstances of the individual exporter. Important considerations in determining the answer to the second question are *risk* and *cost*. Whilst a fair guide can be obtained as regards cost, evaluation of risk is a far more complex matter. Not all risks can be avoided, and the risk analysis should seek to establish the following:

1. How risks can be *minimised.*
2. What risks to *assume.*
3. What risks can be *hedged, off-loaded* or *insured.*

The following notes summarise the issues:

1. Minimise risk by:
   - (a) getting advice;
   - (b) careful contract drafting;
   - (c) sound funds/goods flow management;
   - (d) careful selection of partners.
2. Assume risk by:
   - (a) careful calculation of amount at risk;
   - (b) calculating effect on profit;
   - (c) calculating effect on cash flow;
   - (d) calculating effect on other business.
3. Transfer risk by:

(a) finding a partner (e.g. bank or trader) willing to take risk on a non-recourse basis for a fee;
(b) covering specific risks through insurance, commodity/currency hedging.

The quotation from Rod Rees in the Introduction (see page 2) should be remembered. Normal commercial considerations should *not* be abandoned just because countertrade is involved. Equally, countertrade should not be seen as a panacea, or a magic wand to wave over impossible situations.

It is hoped that the ideas contained in this book will provide the exporter with a good understanding of the practical aspects of countertrade.

The future

It is unlikely that countertrade will disappear from the world trading scene for many years. The reasons which have prompted its use will still apply for the foreseeable future. We will see changes in techniques, and perhaps more involvement by Western governments or national export credit agencies like ECGD. The IMF could act as a restraining influence if it continues to fight against bilateralism in trade.

Overall, however, exporters will need to face up to countertrade, and examine how they are organised to cope with it, and where it can be used.

APPENDIX 1

Countertrade practice world-wide (with a guide to products)

For the sake of completeness, this appendix describes countertrade practice in various countries of the world. It must be noted, however, that rules, regulations, laws and practices change, often without warning or advice. (The assistance of the Department of Trade and Industry in preparing this guide is gratefully acknowledged.)

Albania

Albania is a socialist state, opposed to acceptance of medium- and long-term credits. Its lack of foreign exchange has led to demands for countertrade. Imports and exports are state controlled.

Possible countertrade goods: low-grade minerals, manufactured goods.

Algeria

It is a declared policy to balance trade bilaterally. Demands for countertrade have been seen in tender documents. Algeria has a number of bilateral clearing arrangements.

Possible countertrade goods: oil, gas, oil products, phosphate, mercury, olive oil, wine, dates, cotton, iron ore.

Angola

A number of bilateral trading arrangements exist, e.g. with Brazil and Cuba. There is no formal policy.

Possible countertrade goods: oil, cotton seed by-products, groundnuts, palm and sunflower oils, minerals, coffee, fishmeal.

Argentina

There are specific regulations aimed at keeping countertrade under tight control. One condition of countertrading here is that deals, other than straight one-for-one 'barter' deals, should always be kept in balance. There should also be a strong underlying financial arrangement covering documentation, escrow accounts and bank guarantees. Any imbalances that build up should be cleared by cash payment. The new law differentiates between single deals carried out on letters of credit and those concerning regular shipments. In the latter case, a letter of credit must be opened and payment made within 60 days either side of the delivery date. There is no specific list of goods eligible for countertrade.

Possible countertrade goods: meat, hides and skins, manufactured goods.

Australia

The Federal Government has, with effect from 1 March 1986, introduced a revised off-sets policy for overseas suppliers of civil and defence goods and services. The revised programme is intended to place greater emphasis on bringing advanced technology, skills and capabilities to Australian industry. The contract threshold against which off-sets may be sought is increased from A$1 million to A$2.5 million. This threshold applies to single orders and to orders accumulated in any one financial year. Off-sets will not be required where purchases have an import content of less than 30 per cent. The policy is applied to major overseas defence purchases as well as to purchases such as communications and electronic equipment, civil aircraft, motor vehicles and computers. From 1 July 1986, state preference policies were abolished in favour of an Australia-wide scheme under which public sector purchases at federal or state level will have preference applied to Australian content regardless of the state of origin of such content.

Austria

Countertrade is confined almost exclusively to military purchasing, and such negotiations are co-ordinated by the Ministry of Defence. The creation of employment opportunities and the encouragement of high technology production may be taken into consideration.

Bangladesh

There is an underlying desire to engage in countertrade if the circumstances and the goods are appropriate, in order to save foreign exchange and to achieve business which might not necessarily be concluded in the normal way. Enquiries are dealt with by the official Trade Corporation of Bangladesh:

TCB Bhaban, Kawran Bazaar, GPO Box 418, Dhaka 8.

An import entitlement regime for at least some sectors is operated, where imports of materials and supplies are licensed for manufacturers who export. Buy-back is sometimes proposed to assist the finance of capital investment projects.

Possible countertrade goods: jute, leather, tea, paper.

Barbados

A small amount of countertrade is carried out, mainly with other Caricom countries to alleviate debts between each other.

Belgium

To date, countertrade for the Belgian government's civil purchases in the form of off-set has only been required for selected public sector contracts for the Telephone Authority, the Civil Aviation Authority, and Sabena, the Belgian national airline.

However, countertrade – again in the form of off-set – is required for all substantial defence contracts. The Ministry of Economic Affairs – the ministry responsible for handling the off-set dossiers – says that only defence contracts having a value of over BFrs.10 million will be subject to off-set conditions, but some of those involved in preparing tender bids claim that off-set is sometimes required for contracts of a lower value than this.

Where foreign tenders for Belgian public sector contracts have been invited, whether in the civil or defence fields, the Belgian government's usual approach is to accept, as qualified, all bids which meet the technical specifications (and, where appropriate, pass test procedures) and are within the budget allocation, and then to decide between them on the basis of the relative value of their off-set proposals. The criteria they adopt for making this evaluation are varied, complex and often subjective, with usually a high political content.

Amongst the political factors to be taken into account, and one to which considerable importance is usually attached in Belgium, is the way in which the effect of the off-set proposals is split between the main regions of the country: off-set proposals for a substantial contract which are linked exclusively to firms in either Flanders or Wallonia are unlikely to win sufficiently wide support from the group of ministers who may ultimately decide on the award of the contract.

Although the dividing lines between them are not altogether clear, the Belgian authorities attempt to distinguish between three elements in the off-set concept: *direct*, *semi-direct* and *indirect* (a bidder may combine elements of all three in drawing up his proposal).

Direct

This involves the purchase in Belgium of equipment, parts or accessories to be employed in meeting the particular contract requirement, and/or assembly or manufacture of parts or accessories in Belgium under licence.

Semi-direct

The foreign bidder undertakes, on his own behalf and on behalf of his non-Belgian subcontractors, to place orders for some of these same items of equipment, parts or accessories *over and above* the contract requirement; these additional orders must be exported from Belgium.

Indirect

This can take several forms, and is not linked to the contract itself, either by the nature of the purchases, or in time. Such off-set includes purchases from Belgium by a foreign customer which can be included in the bidder's proposal without there necessarily being any link between the bidder and the purchaser. However, the purchases from the Belgian suppliers must be of a technological level equal to or higher than the contract requirement.

Whether direct, semi-direct or indirect, the off-set proposed must be new business and not part of an ongoing contract. Recent experience has shown that the Belgian government expects off-set proposals to be worth at least 100 per cent of the estimated contract value, and in some cases it seeks and receives proposals for off-set greatly in excess of that figure.

Bolivia

Legislation was passed in July 1984 (Decree 20/318) setting out the procedure for countertrade transactions. A summary of the principal clauses follows on pages 164 and 165.

Requests by private companies to purchase goods from abroad will be submitted through the appropriate ministry. Only imports for essentials will be considered, even on a countertrade basis. The ministry concerned will apply to the Banco Central de Bolivia for an allocation of foreign exchange. If the allocation is *not* made, but the goods are sanctioned for import, the importer has two alternatives:

1. If the importer's own goods qualify for use in countertrade, a quantity thereof will be made available to a state trading company which will countertrade the goods for the desired import.
2. If the importer's own goods cannot be used in countertrade, the firm will have to pay in local currency for other Bolivian goods which the state trading company can then use to acquire the approved import.

The decree covers all state-controlled enterprises' purchases of machinery, primary and raw materials, industrial inputs and essential consumer goods. In such cases, the countertrade goods will come from the same state enterprise but it is not clear whether the goods will come from the same enterprise directly or from the same industrial sector.

The approval for the countertrade will be made by the following:

(a) Ministry of Finance;
(b) Ministry of Industry;
(c) Ministry of Commerce and Tourism;
(d) Ministry of Integration;
(e) Ministry of Planning and Co-ordination;

together with the relevant industries' ministry.

Strict conditions may be imposed on the marketing of countertrade goods. In particular, the net price realised by their sale may not be less than the c.i.f. price ex Bolivia. This precludes the use of discounts to make the Bolivian goods more marketable.

Information on the availability of goods for use in countertrade is collated by the Chamber of Commerce and Chamber of Industry.

The following is a summary of the Supreme Decree 20/318 dated 3 July 1984.

1. Barter is legalised and defined as simultaneous exchange of goods.
2. Approval is required from five ministries and from the technical bodies in the relevant industrial ministry.
3. Only essential imports will be brought in under these arrangements, against the export of any product.

4. The terms of the arrangement must state the prices of the goods involved and their places of origin. Existing import/export rules will apply.
5. Provisions regarding imports under c.i.f. conditions.
6. Imports will not be permitted on f.o.b. basis.
7. The value of exports (countertrade goods) made on other than c.i.f. basis, must be equal to or greater than the value c.i.f. (Bolivian border) of the import, except where the export is by air when the c.i.f. (airport) value must exceed the import value.
8. The net value of exports (countertrade goods) under c.i.f. contracts (city or ports of destination) must be equal to or greater than the value c.i.f. (frontier) of the imports.
9. In the event of non-completion of a countertrade transaction, the Direccion de Operacion y Supervision Cambiaria will *not* provide foreign exchange to cover any resulting debts.
10. The payment of foreign exchange by the Banco Central de Bolivia will be made on presentation of the import and export licences, and the prior approval of the ministries mentioned in (2) above.
11. In 'barter' deals, the normal rules regarding payment of the foreign-exchange proceeds from the export do not apply, except if the value of exports exceeds the value of imports.
12. Compensation transactions will be accepted only when the value of the exports exceeds the value of the imports.
13. Both import and export legs of a 'barter' transaction are subject to existing customs legislation. Prices of imports will be rigorously controlled.

Possible countertrade goods: minerals, wool, hardwood, hides, clothing, agricultural goods.

Brazil

Background

The Brazilian government has not established any guidelines to regulate countertrade but countertrade activity has occurred in the past and is steadily increasing. Cacex, the trade-regulating arm of the Central Bank, does not regard countertrade as a legitimate trade instrument, yet it will consider import licence applications for countertrade deals on a case-by-case basis.

Reasons

1. To increase the export of goods and manufactured goods which do not have large foreign markets.
2. To save valuable foreign exchange.
3. To keep a favourable trade account balance.

Extent

Countertrade deals in Brazil fall into three major categories:

1. Clearing accounts with most East European nations, notably Romania, Hungary, Bulgaria and East Germany.
2. Reciprocal credit conventions arranged through Association Latinoamericana de Integracion (ALADI), the Latin American inter-governmental trade association.
3. Bilateral agreements with Brazil's oil suppliers, both OPEC and non-OPEC members.

While some private sector countertrade deals have occurred, they are, nevertheless, rare.

Procedure and implications

Approval As mentioned before, Cacex will consider private sector countertrade commitments on a case-by-case basis. Yet it must be emphasised that it is current Brazilian policy to earn hard currency through *traditional* trade with developed countries. Thus approval of countertrade contracts with developed countries has been given in only a few cases.

Because Brazil has issued no specific regulations in the area of countertrade, the standard import regulations apply. The procedure for permission involves proposals submitted in writing to Cacex and the Central Bank. Cacex examines each proposal from the commercial standpoint. The criteria used include the following:

1. Consideration of whether the proposed import was listed in the applicant's annual import programme as certified with Cacex.
2. Whether the exported Brazilian product already has a current export market.
3. Whether the proposed import is already available in Brazil.
4. The need for the proposed import.

5. The cost in foreign exchange.
6. The availability of foreign exchange at the time of application.

Cacex is likely to approve contracts which involve the import of high-priority products, otherwise unobtainable in Brazil; for example, petroleum and related products, health care goods, and technical and scientific equipment and instrumentation.

Cacex also tends to prefer the following:

1. Contracts involving 'additional' or new exports of manufactured goods.
2. Deals with a high ratio of exports to imports.
3. Deals which involve the export of Brazilian goods before the import takes place.
4. Contracts where the importing firm has a record of high export growth in relation to import levels.

The Central Bank examines the financing methods. This is done to determine whether other types of payment would serve to decrease the trade balance. The proposals should be made in letter form addressed to the relevant individuals. At Cacex, the proposals should be submitted to the appropriate division:

Primary materials:	Dr Pedro Sebastiao de Se Ferreira
Food products:	Dr Mauricio Souza Assis
Mechanical equipment:	Dr Namir Salek

At the Central Bank, proposals should be submitted to the international department. Approval may take as long as four months, depending on type of product, payment procedure and documentation.

Recent private sector countertrade The Cacex criteria mentioned above are applied stringently. As a result, private sector countertrade deals are not common, but some private sector countertrade arrangements do occur, usually involving Brazil's state-owned trading companies. In particular, Interbras, the giant trading company subsidiary of Petrobras, the government-owned oil corporation, is a main focus of countertrade activity in Brazil. Other trading companies active in countertrade include Cotia Trading and Cicatrade. Some examples of recent countertrade deals with multinational companies of developed countries include the following:

1. A US$130 million telecommunications satellite contract with Spar Aerospace of Canada and Hughes Aircraft. In return for the

contract, Spar has agreed to find markets for US$60 million worth of Brazilian products over a four-year period.

2. Negotiations between the government-owned aircraft manufacturer Embraer and small US airlines to sell six to twelve Bandeirante commuter planes. In return, Embraer has asked its US suppliers to import parts and components from the company.
3. Ferrostahl of West Germany was contracted to build the first of two submarines for Brazil in return for $200 million worth of iron ore. Construction has taken place in Brazil and thus has included technology transfer.

East European clearing accounts One way in which Western companies have become involved in Brazilian countertrade deals has been through Brazil's clearing accounts in Eastern Europe. Brazil holds such accounts with Poland, Hungary, Bulgaria, Romania and East Germany. These clearing accounts are part of bilateral trade and payment agreements which call for long-term forms of 'barter' between the two countries. Since each country buys and sells at different rates, imbalances tend to develop (usually in favour of Brazil, which often sells more to than it buys from Eastern Europe). As a result of such imbalances a Western company may enter a countertrade deal through so-called 'switch' transactions. Through a switch deal Brazil may agree to allow imports of goods from Western countries, which would not normally be permitted, since they are paid directly or indirectly through one of the East European clearing accounts instead of in valuable foreign currency.

Companies can get clearing dollars in Brazil at an 8 per cent to 10 per cent discount and obtain import licences on a one-to-one ratio to the value of those clearing dollars in Brazilian exports to the East European country. However, these clearing dollars are not marketable unless a parallel countertrade contract can be arranged with the East European country in advance.

Brazilian officials usually have no objection to such switch agreements, but encouragement is not open, since such agreements are informal and sensitive. Some sources state that as much as 30 per cent of Brazil's trade is channelled via these clearing agreements.

Additionality The Brazilian authorities usually agree to grant additional import licences either when there is a conversion of clearing balances into hard cash for the Central Bank or when an 'additional' export of Brazilian goods can be shown. (By 'additional' it is meant that the goods would not otherwise be exported.) The major obstacle in setting up countertrade agreements in Brazil for the private sector is the difficulty in convincing Cacex that the Brazilian export is in fact additional.

Other concerns While settlements with East European nations are made in clearing dollars, settlements with other nations are made in freely convertible currencies on the basis of reciprocal credit lines. Since these agreements provide the option to pay with cash, they comply with the IMF's so-called negative pledge requirement, which bars compulsory countertrade.

Many companies contemplating countertrade in Brazil are interested in its potential use as a vehicle for repatriating blocked funds, whether profits, dividends or capital.

In order to overcome the problem of remitting funds, Western companies either find local companies that can use cruzados for their expenses or buy local products in cruzados for export as countertrade goods, keeping the hard currency proceeds abroad.

The Befiex programme Another effective countertrade instrument is the Brazilian Befiex programme, under which a Brazilian company can get tax and investment benefits and permission to import components and equipment in exchange for making a ten-year commitment to export. Companies can benefit greatly by understanding the relationship of countertrade to Befiex and various other export incentive programmes. Over the next six years, for example, it will help export $250 million worth of steel slabs from Brazil. Aside from the reduced import duty and the tax benefits available through Befiex, interest rate subsidies can be obtained from Finex (Finex is a scheme administered by Cacex by which the interest rates on buyer and supplier credits are subsidised).

Through countertrade Brazil has acquired oil, corn, a communications satellite, steel products, mining equipment, aircraft and industrial equipment.

Possible countertrade goods: foodstuffs, petrochemicals, oil-drilling equipment, armoured cars, sugar, leaf tobacco, chicken meat, unrefined soya bean oil, cocoa butter, gray iron alloys, iron ore, semiprocessed hides and leather, wood pulp and paper, orange juice, footwear, machinery, electrical apparatus, coffee, cotton, nickel, tin.

Bulgaria

Countertrade is not a dominant feature of Bulgaria's external commerce but when used it takes one of three forms:

1. Multimillion-pound deals where Bulgaria requests that a proportion of the foreign exchange commitment is settled in countertrade as part of the tactics of the commercial negotiations.
2. Self-financing deals where countertrade is a precondition of the contract, financed entirely by countertrade.
3. Foreign trade organisation initiatives to offer some kind of barter deal to foreign suppliers. This is usually because the foreign trade organisation is trying to unload a commodity it is handling on the export side of its business.

Burma

The Burmese approach countertrade cautiously, on a case-by-case basis. They are most prepared to consider countertrade in rice, since world prices for their export surplus are depressed.

Possible countertrade goods: timber, rice, agricultural goods.

Cameroon

There is no official policy with regard to countertrade.

Canada

Generally, official trade policy is not in favour of countertrade but does recognise that it produces a small amount of useful exports. There is no direct governmental involvement and it is left to the exporter to decide whether to become involved in countertrade. Most official procurement over £100 million involves off-set – this is especially the case in the high-technology sector.

Chile

No regulations exist and experience is minimal. Consideration *could* be given on a case-by-case basis, and applications would need to go to the Director General of International Economic Relations at the Ministry of Foreign Relations, and the Minister of Finance and Economy.

China

In examining countertrade in China, it should be noted that the Chinese use a different terminology to that which is more widely accepted in the Western world:

Barter = one-time exchange of goods under one contract
Compensation = buy-back
Counterpurchase = compensation
Evidence accounts = agreement to balance trade

To the extent that statistics can be believed, buy-back deals reported in 1985 were US$213 million, some 35 per cent up on 1984. Barter/ counterpurchase deals were estimated to be between US$700 and US$800 million.

The emphasis in China now is on equity joint ventures/technology transfer. The Chinese see this as a way of generating foreign exchange and at the same time upgrading technology. Indeed, reference to the list of products for which import licences are required shows emphasis on 'production of . . . . . .'.

Bilateral deals with the Third World are flourishing; what is not clear is what proportion of the barter deals reported above relate to these clearing arrangements.

Control

The China International Trust and Investment Corporation claims to have a co-ordinating role, but it is likely that this is restricted to the negotiation of buy-back and bilateral deals. The Ministry of Foreign Economic Relations and Trade seems to have been given the role of co-ordinating countertrade policy and administration. Indeed it also controls the issue of export licences which is central to the whole question of countertrade.

A new Countertrade Unit was established under Yang Fan in May 1985 with the mandate to 'co-ordinate and facilitate countertrade'. Its role is that of matchmaker but questions have been posed as to whether it has the authority and power to enforce co-operation between the Chinese parties to a transaction. It is significant that it will only step in if the transaction is at an advanced stage, so it is important to work up the transaction to a point where agreement in principle has been reached with various parties. The question of co-ordination between the Chinese parties is a critical one.

It is hard enough to structure a transaction involving industries in the same economic or regional group, but it is particularly difficult if the two entities are in different provinces or ministries.

Finally it should be remembered that the Ministry of Foreign Economic Relations and Trade will not sign deals; it only co-ordinates.

Products

It has been clearly stated that only non-traditional goods would be used in countertrade. An extensive list of goods to be controlled by export licences has been issued. Another source has indicated that possible countertrade goods would be raw cotton, jute bags, black tea, minerals, machinery, PVC goods and steel products.

Summary

Without wishing to overstate the problems, countertrade in China is never going to be easy. The main difficulties lie in the areas of linkage between the Chinese entities involved, lack of knowledge of countertrade and confusion over terminology. The exporter will need to become involved in all aspects of the countertrade, although this will fall short of taking delivery of countertrade goods.

Colombia

A governmental decree was issued on 16 December 1985 reducing the scope for countertrade operations to certain compensation deals in a specific instance, such as in support of a local product having temporary difficulties in finding an overseas market. On 6 May 1986, decree 1459 of the Ministry of Economic Development was issued. As a result of this, countertrade is now reserved exclusively for commercial exchanges with the Eastern bloc.

Costa Rica

A Barter Law was passed in 1965, with administrative rules formulated in 1983. The system is regulated by the Central Bank and the Ministry of Economy and Commerce. Initial applications must go to the Ministry's Directorate of External Finance. The application is reviewed by a technical commission with members drawn from the Ministry, and the International Transactions and Finance Divisions of the Central Bank.

Attention is paid to the following:

1. Whether the countertrade would increase overall exports.
2. Whether the country's balance of trade would be improved.
3. Whether the price offered for the countertrade goods reflects world market prices.
4. The priority of the import.
5. Availability of local substitutes.
6. Whether the countertrade goods could be sold for hard currency at the same price as under a countertrade arrangement.

If the application receives a favourable recommendation by the commission, a 90-day 'Barter Licence' is issued by the Ministry. This licence carries the following information:

1. Names of exporter and importer.
1. Name of foreign consignee.
3. Description of merchandise and tariff code.
4. Country of destination.
5. F.o.b. or c.i.f. value in dollars.
6. Name of the foreign bank involved in the countertrade operation.
7. Port of exit/entry of the merchandise.
8. Expiry date of the countertrade licence.

Costa Rica has bilateral payment agreements with Colombia, Mexico and Poland.

Possible countertrade goods: coffee.

Cuba

Cuba is a full member of Comecon and conducts approximately 85 per cent of its business with Socialist countries on a countertrade basis. It is official policy to encourage countertrade with Western suppliers where possible. Recent steps to co-ordinate counterpurchase within the Ministry of Foreign Trade have not, however, resulted in the hoped-for increase. One major factor is that the Cuban authorities have very little surplus industrial or agricultural produce to offer.

A great majority of trade with the United Kingdom and other Western countries remains, and is likely to remain for some time, on a normal commercial basis.

Possible countertrade goods: nickel, fish, tobacco, sugar, molasses, fruit juices, lobsters, rum, tourism.

Cyprus

The government ministries are discussing amendments to the conditions for international tenders to allow either part or the whole of the value of a tender to be payable by the export of problematic Cypriot produce, such as wine.

Czechoslovakia

The Czechoslovaks maintain that they prefer to trade on the basis of normal international practice. However, exporters should not be surprised if the question of countertrade is raised in contract negotiations. To a great extent, whether countertrade becomes part of the deal depends on the relative bargaining strengths of the two sides. The import of goods which are viewed as less essential or unlikely to increase hard currency revenue are likely to have heavier countertrade obligations attached – up to 100 per cent. In the past there has been some lack of flexibility at the Czech end as regards availability of a wide range of goods for countertrade. Firms in the United Kingdom should press for such availability at the outset of negotiations.

Denmark

Officially, countertrade is an unwelcome practice, though Danish companies dealing with the Eastern bloc have been using countertrade on an ever-increasing scale. The Danes operate what they call compensatory trade: defence purchases from abroad have a certain degree of Danish involvement in the form of equipment. It is also practice to insist that sales of defence equipment to the Danish armed forces are off-set by purchases of Danish goods to the same value. Similar compensatory deals have been negotiated on the civilian side, including one involving the purchase of locomotives from Switzerland.

Dominican Republic

In Presidential Decree No. 20005, regulations were set out governing the operation of countertrade transactions. Applications by local or foreign entities are submitted to Cedopex (Dominican Centre for the Promotion of Exports). In making its decision, Cedopex will liaise with the Dominican Central Bank and other government agencies whose participation is essential to the transaction. The Cedopex directors determine the criteria for approving individual transactions and the kind of products which may be imported/ exported. It will also monitor fulfilment of both sides of the transaction in conjunction with the Ministry of Finance and the Central Bank. To ensure compliance of the parties involved, a bond is to be posted with the Central Bank by importers or exporters depending on which goods are shipped first.

Ecuador

Ecuador has long had an interest in countertrade. The latest regulations governing such trade were issued on 4 September 1984, and were modified on 11 December 1985.

Petroleum and its derivatives, bananas, shrimps, coffee and cocoa beans are not available for countertrade purposes, although bananas can be used when they are destined for new markets or countries with which Ecuador has bilateral non-currency trading agreements (mainly East European countries).

Transactions must start with the export of Ecuadorean products and the corresponding import licence(s) will be granted within a maximum of 180 days from the date of the export licence (though when infrastructural projects with external finance are involved, they are exempt from this 180-day term).

The Ministry of Industries, Commerce and Integration (Imports Department) is responsible for authorising all such business.

Possible countertrade goods: oil, prawns, fish, balsa, instant coffee, bean meal, fish products, tomato paste.

Egypt

Egypt is, in general, in favour of countertrade deals and much of its trade with Eastern Europe is carried out on this basis. Due to the present financial exigencies, it is likely that new provisions will be written into forthcoming tenders for government projects which will require the successful bidder to take part of his payment in Egyptian produce. However, no details have yet been announced.

Possible countertrade goods: cotton, fruit, vegetables, phosphates, perfume, cotton fabrics.

Ethiopia

Countertrade is not really favoured by the central government, but there are indications that the managers of individual state enterprises may be looking more favourably than before at barter. However, it is not clear that this will receive official approval.

Possible countertrade goods: basic agricultural goods, hides and skins.

Finland

Off-set is required in respect of sales of defence equipment. A new five-year bilateral trade agreement has been signed with the Soviet Union covering the period 1986–91. This may result in increased investment in joint ventures.

German Democratic Republic

Demands for countertrade are dependent upon the degree of priority which the German Democratic Republic attaches to the import in question.

The percentage of the cost of goods required to be covered by countertrade ranges from about 10 per cent to well over 100 per cent and is again dependent on the priority of the import. Some British companies experience difficulties in finding suitable goods which they can use in-house as the range offered is narrow and usually limited to goods produced by the foreign trade organisation to which the sale is being made. The services of countertrade agents may be useful for finding a market for such goods outside the United Kingdom.

Greece

Two policies exist in Greece, one to promote exports and one relating to off-sets under the government's procurement policy.

Counterpurchase

In pursuance of the first policy, the International Trade Company (ITCO) was established in May 1984. It is state-owned, through the Hellenic Industrial Development Bank SA, the National Investment Bank for Industrial Development, the Agricultural Bank of Greece, and the Investment Bank SA.

By August 1985 around $250 million in countertrade deals had been done, with many West European, Middle Eastern, North African and East European countries.

Whilst there is generally no compulsion for a tenderer for a government contract to offer countertrade, any proposal made will be taken into consideration at the time of evaluation.

ITCO is looking for long-term trading relationships but will assist in the construction of off-set proposals, in particular the counterpurchase of Greek goods as part of a larger package. ITCO's standard counterpurchase agreement includes the following conditions and requirements:

1. (a) The overseas supplier (supplier) may discharge the counterpurchase obligation, or may employ a third party to do so. Services purchased will also qualify.
   (b) The proposed purchases must be 'in addition to those already effected during the last 3 years by all the (third parties and/or the Supplier) as a unit, in total and by country of destination'.
2. Final destinations for the counterpurchased goods/services must be stated.
3. A time limit will be imposed, with an agreed spread of purchases over the time limit.
4. (a) A list of the goods to be counterpurchased will be agreed.
   (b) Subsequent variations to this list will only be agreed to by ITCO on a case-by-case basis.
5. Acceptable third parties for the discharge of the counterpurchase obligation would be:
   (a) the supplier and its subsidiaries or affiliates;
   (b) any other party agreed to in writing by ITCO.
6. The supplier will submit to ITCO a notarised list of purchases from Greece by product and country of destination effected during the last three years by the supplier or its subsidiaries/affiliates. If a third party is employed, the same rule applies.
7. For individual purchases to be credited to the supplier's counterpurchase obligation, the following terms and conditions must be fulfilled:
   (a) the contract must be between an eligible buyer as listed above, and a Greek company;
   (b) the products/services must be on the approved list;

(c) the purchase must exceed the levels of previous purchases as declared (see 1 (b)).

8. To have a purchase credited, the supplier will need to submit to ITCO the following:
   (a) copies of export invoices;
   (b) copies of shipping documents;
   (c) customs clearance certificates.
9. The supplier will be called on to provide a bank performance guarantee for a percentage of the counterpurchase obligation, in favour of ITCO.

   If any or all of the counterpurchase offer remains unfulfilled at the end of the agreed period, ITCO will claim from the supplier a penalty pro rata with the amount outstanding. In the event of non-payment, ITCO will claim under the bank guarantee.
10. In the event of *force majeure*, the performance period and the performance bond will be extended accordingly. If conditions of *force majeure* continue for more than 12 months, the parties may denounce further execution.
11. If the supplier causes the suspension (partly or wholly) of the principal contract, the counterpurchase obligation will continue, but the remaining fulfilment period will be halved.
    (a) If the principal contract is suspended temporarily by the buyer, the period of fulfilment, etc., will be extended.
    (b) If the contract is suspended permanently, the supplier's obligations cease and any counterpurchase which has been made in excess of the then required amount will be carried forward, subject to certain restrictions.
12. Assignment or transfer of this obligation may only take place with the prior written consent of ITCO.
13. The agreement with ITCO can only be modified if both sides agree.
14. English is the operative language.
15. ITCO will assist the supplier with introductions to competent Greek companies, and will assist in resolving any disputes.
16. (a) Six-monthly reports on the progress made in discharging the obligation will be called for, and meetings with ITCO may take place when necessary.
    (b) The conversion rates for contracts discharged in currencies other than the one determined in the original offer, will be based directly on the rates of the related currencies without the intervention of European Currency Units.

(c) Arbitration will be held in the country agreed between ITCO and the supplier.
(d) The supplier will be credited with the value of the purchases of goods and services at the date of the customs clearance certificate or payment for the services. The performance guarantee will be reduced accordingly and proportionately.

Off-set (Industrial Off-set Benefit = IOB)

These notes summarise the main points from the Greek IOB policy. The IOB is a programme designed to:

(a) create employment;
(b) acquire technology;
(c) conserve/replace foreign exchange;
(d) reduce reliance on foreign suppliers for strategic needs;
(e) create new markets for Greek goods.

1. *Method of discharging IOB* Industrial Off-set Benefit (IOB) is considered as the fulfilment of one or more of the following transactions between a local Greek firm and any eligible party:

(a) Purchase through subcontracting of subsystems, accessories or parts of the specific system under procurement, or a similar one, in quantities larger than the ones required for the specific procurement (buy-back).
(b) Purchase of software or services (e.g. repairs, design studies and training) with *Greek Added Value* (GAV) larger than or equal to 50 per cent. Transportation and insurance services are not considered as IOB except in the case where Greek-owned transportation means are used for the fulfilment of an approved IOB.
(c) Purchase of defence material manufactured in Greece with GAV greater than or equal to 40 per cent.
(d) Purchase of local industrial products, from an approved product list, with GAV greater than or equal to 40 per cent.
(e) Technology transfer under favourable conditions (joint venture, licence agreement, partial absorption of products or services, exclusive rights in a particular geographical area, etc.).

2. *Use of third parties* The supplier of equipment, etc. to Greece will retain full responsibility for the discharge of the IOB obligation,

notwithstanding the fact that the obligation may be discharged by a third party. Acceptable parties are as follows:

(a) The system manufacturer including all its divisions and subsidiaries.
(b) The manufacturers of subsystems or accessories of the system under procurement, including all its divisions and subsidiaries.
(c) The subcontracting companies, their divisions and subsidiary firms.
(d) Any other entity after written authorisation by the competent authority, which is granted after an investigation of the particular transaction and with the provision that from all other aspects it complies with the requirements of this Article.

Use of a third party must be approved by the Greek authorities prior to its appointment.

3. *Eligibility of IOB activity* Before an 'activity' is credited to the supplier's obligation, the following requirements must be met:

(a) It must emanate exclusively from the supplier's or other eligible party's exclusive efforts resulting from his responsibility in fulfilling the IOB commitment for the specific procurement and not from previously existing relations or obligations towards the Greek economy.
(b) It must have suitable pre-authorisation from the competent Greek authority, responsible for the verification and supervision of the IOB programme.
(c) It must comply with the Greek laws and the development targets of the Greek economy.
(d) A final and irrevocable agreement must have been signed between the interested parties in which prices, quantities, qualities, time and place of delivery, procedures and terms and conditions for the fulfilment of the agreement must be specified.

4. *Valuation of IOB credit* The method of calculating the value of each IOB activity is complex. Credit will be given as follows (each paragraph refers to the points made in paragraph (1) above):

(a) The net foreign exchange rate benefit from subsequent exports. Not included, therefore, would be the extra foreign exchange costs of the Greek producer nor the value of any materials supplied from abroad.
(b) and (c) The FOB value of the transaction will be credited.

(d) If the buyer is a new buyer, 100 per cent of the FOB value is credited. If the buyer is an existing buyer, the value which corresponds to the increase in value over the level of the previous three years will be credited.

(e) In the case of technology transfer, a formula will be applied for each of the five years following the start of production:

$$C = K\ (ES + 1/2\ DS)$$

where ES is the value of sales abroad, DS is the value of domestic sales and K is a factor that represents the share of the value of said technology in the overall investment. The value of K is calculated by dividing the commercial value of the technology by the total capital (including the value of the technology) employed in the production.

The credit to the supplier in the case of (a)–(d) will be granted at the time of submission to the competent authority of the final contract between the supplier or his appointed agent, and the declaration from the Greek company.

5. *IOB offers*

(a) The IOB offer will be expressed as a percentage of the principal supply contract, and in the same currency.

(b) The IOB offer will be increased when the contract is awarded by an amount relating to the level of inflation in the supplier's country.

(c) The IOB policy is designed to counterbalance the cost of the procurement by 100 per cent of its value *but* with a minimum of 10 per cent. In evaluating the offer, account will be taken of the amount, quality and probability of fulfilment.

(d) In the case of defence procurements, the supplier must attempt to maximise the portion of IOB applied to the Greek defence industry, with a minimum portion of 30 per cent of the IOB.

6. *Implementation of IOB offers*

(a) The supplier must include in his IOB offer full details of the specific programmes and particulars of Greek subcontractors in the case of 1(a).

(b) Reference must be made to the category of off-set, types, quantities and estimated values.

(c) Signing of final contracts, or at least advance agreements in general terms, represents a prerequisite to the signing of the principal contract.

(d) Such contracts/agreements should specify the types, quantities, prices, delivery schedules, general terms of co-operation and the estimated maximum limit of any additional foreign currency cost.

7. *Additional costs of IOB* Details of any additional costs caused by the IOB offers must be provided.

8. *Co-operation with Greek IOB partners* All assistance must be provided by the supplier to the Greek participating companies to enable them to carry out the work. Any approvals from the supplier's government must be obtained by the supplier.

9. *Time-scales*

(a) The overall duration of the IOB offer must be specified, and must not exceed five years.
(b) The IOB period must be split into at least two sub-periods.
(c) It is desirable that at least 50 per cent of the total IOB commitment be discharged in the first half of the total IOB period with the balance as evenly spread as possible.

10. *Penalty guarantees/payments*

(a) A bank guarantee of a value of 10 per cent of the IOB offer will be required from the supplier.
(b) The penalty will be paid pro rata with any unfulfilled portion of the obligation.
(c) Such penalties paid are deposited in a special account at the Bank of Greece and are refunded when the obligation is fulfilled.
(d) Special rules apply for IOB commitments unfulfilled after the first half of the implementation period, or if the IOB is discharged with benefits of a lesser category.

11. *Evaluation criteria* The criteria taken into account for the evaluation of an IOB offer are as follows:

(a) Level and category of offered IOB.
(b) Technology transfer.
(c) Support of the Greek industry by the supplier.
(d) Guarantee and fulfilment probability.

(e) Effects on employment.
(f) Portion of the total contractual value payable in drachmas.
(g) Capital return of the required investment and additional cost of the Greek industry.
(h) Implementation time schedule.
(i) Specific programmes proposed.

12. *Competent authority*

(a) The competent authority for the administration, control and supervision of the IOB programme is the Defense Industry Directorate (DID) in co-operation with the corresponding governmental and collective authorities of the productive classes involved. The supplier must address himself to DID for any subject relating directly or indirectly to his obligations in IOB.
(b) DID in co-operation with the interested collective authorities will help the supplier to locate eligible Greek manufacturers and he, in turn, will inform DID about his final choice of manufacturers, the progress of the negotiations and the type, the quantity, the delivery schedule and the value of the products that he (the supplier) intends to have manufactured by each of them.
(c) Any dispute that might arise between the two parties during the fulfilment of the IOB will be resolved between them within the framework of the contract and with a spirit of mutual understanding and collaboration.
(d) If, despite the goodwill of both parties, no compromise solution can be found, such a dispute will be resolved according to the provisions of the relevant article of the main supply contract.

Guatemala

Countertrade applications are considered on a case-by-case basis, and must be referred to the Department of Foreign Exchange at the Banco de Guatemala.

Traditional exports such as coffee, sugar, meat, cotton and cardamom are generally not permitted for use in countertrade.

Guyana

The Guyanese Department of Economic Co-operation has become very concerned with the countertrade deals that have been undertaken with other countries in the last two years. Straight 100 per cent barter deals are no longer envisaged and the emphasis appears to be changing towards semi-joint-venture types of deals where foreign equipment is provided with a guaranteed overseas market for some of the goods produced. All foreign firms wishing to enter into countertrade deals will have to do so through suppliers or firms established in Guyana.

Possible countertrade goods: rice, bauxite.

Honduras

Relatively speaking, Honduras is believed to be an 'active' countertrading country, with over 25 years' experience. Countertrade deals could involve both primary and non-traditional exports.

Applications must be submitted through the Ministry of Economy which will act in conjunction with the Ministry of Finance, Central Bank and Consuplane (an *ad hoc* government committee that reviews application documentation).

Hungary

The Hungarians officially disapprove of countertrade but in practice some foreign trade organisations are insistent in their demands for some forms of counterpurchase. These demands increased in 1983 when Hungary had an urgent need to improve its hard currency position. Companies are often faced with a very limited choice of goods to take from the Hungarians; it seems to be very difficult to sell to one foreign trade organisation and buy from another. Evidence accounts are maintained by some firms. However, many Hungarian companies, encouraged by the government, are now looking for alternatives to countertrade, e.g. direct investment in Hungary by Western companies in the form of joint venture activities and local manufacture under licence.

India

With the current drive to increase export earnings, the Indian government is increasingly making requests for countertrade in the context of major import deals with foreign countries.

Barter arrangements have long been a feature of trade with Comecon countries, but they have recently become increasingly frequent in dealings with South East Asian countries, and during 1986 there have been signs of increased Indian interest in countertrade with West European countries, although so far the actual volume of such trade remains relatively small. Technology transfer packages and buy-back deals also frequently feature in major project deals. The organisations principally involved are the State Trading Corporation, the Minerals and Metals Trading Corporation, and the Project Equipment Corporation.

India is purchasing sugar, vegetable oils, fertilisers, chemicals and newsprint against counterpurchase commitments. The seller is required to furnish a performance bond of 5 per cent of his counterpurchase commitment to fulfil the same within a period of six months. The seller is given a wide choice of items, out of which the counterpurchase commitments are to be fulfilled.

Indonesia

Background

Indonesia has issued clear regulations for countertrade, entitled 'Guidelines for the implementation of linking government procurements of imports with Indonesian export products excluding petroleum and natural gas' based on a decision of the Special Cabinet Session on Economics, Finance and Industry on 2 December 1981. A revised directive was issued on 8 April 1983.

Reasons

The government of Indonesia wishes to exploit its strengths as a buyer in a buyer's market by insisting that suppliers assist Indonesia in the sale of Indonesian products and to overcome what it calls the 'growing protectionism in industrialised countries'.

Extent

Countertrade offers will be required for all government (departments, non-departmental government institutions and state-owned enterprises) procurements financed by the state budget and by export credits on the basis of 100 per cent countertrade for all non-local costs.

The following are excluded:

1. Military procurements.

2. Imports based on loans and credits from the World Bank, Asian Development Bank and Islamic Bank.
3. Technology purchases.
4. Licences and patents.
5. Consultants' services.
6. All procurements below 500 million rupiah.
7. Joint ventures.

Penalty

Non-fulfilment of the countertrade obligation will incur a penalty of 50 per cent of the unfulfilled portion.

Time-scales

Fulfilment of the obligation must commence at most six months after contract signature and must be completed by the latest three months before expiry date of the original export contract.

Restrictions

Sales of countertrade goods are subject to certain restrictions as to product, market and buyer. In view of the system for discharging obligations, these restrictions need not concern the exporter.

System

1. When tendering for a project, companies are obliged to sign a letter of undertaking, in which they confirm their willingness to buy Indonesian products should they be awarded the contract.
2. The Department of Trade accepts the undertaking with a letter of approval – called 'Annexe A' – which sets out the ground-rules for completion of the countertrade obligation.
3. When countertrade goods have been purchased, copies of the export form (PEBs) and related bills of lading are submitted to the Department of Trade.

Procedure for exporter

1. The counterpurchase obligation may be transferred to a third party (on a subsequent payment to that party of a fee) with whom an agreement will be signed.
2. On signing the letter of undertaking (see specimen below), the exporter nominates the third party.

3. On issue of 'Annexe A' the Indonesians acknowledge acceptance of the third party's involvement.
4. A copy of 'Annexe A' must be given to the third party as evidence of the extent of its obligation.
5. The third party will submit forms PEB, etc. to the Department of Trade.
6. Evidence of completion of the obligation will be submitted by the third party and the exporter will then pay the third party the agreed fee.

Implications for exporter

The facility for passing over the countertrade obligation and the attendant penalty means that the discharge of countertrade in Indonesia is, for the exporter, a relatively simple task. The fee payable to the third party can be pre-determined and either built into the export price or absorbed. As the fee is only payable on successful conclusion of the obligation, the exporter is protected against non-fulfilment.

Specimen documents

(LETTERHEAD OF TENDERER)*

-----------,198–

Department of Trade
Republic of Indonesia
Directorate General for Foreign Trade
Jalan Abdul Muis 87
Jakarta
INDONESIA

c/o (Insert name of Department, Agency or
Corporation issuing Tender)

Dear Sirs:

We refer to (describe subject matter of tender and tender number) issued on ––––––, 198– by (insert name of Indonesian department,

* This letter should be signed and submitted by the Tenderer. If the Tenderer is a foreign contractor/supplier, this letter should be signed by the foreign contractor/supplier and not by its Indonesian agent, partner or representative, if any.

Agency or Corporation issuing tender) and to our tender document no. ------ submitted on -------, 198– in response thereto.

We hereby irrevocably undertake during the period from the date of award of the contract relating to such tender until final acceptance (or equivalent) of our work and services thereunder or until completion of deliveries thereunder, as the case may be:

1. to purchase, or to cause to be purchased by one or more of our affiliated companies in the country or countries** to be confirmed by the Department of Trade in a letter in the form of Annex A hereto or by third parties located in any other country or countries acceptable to you, agricultural and/or industrial products contained in Books A.1 and A.2, each entitled "List of Indonesian Export Commodities Available for Additional Exports in 1982", published in January 1982 and March 1982, respectively, by the Department of Trade, and/or such other Indonesian products as you may approve in writing (hereinafter, collectively, the "Products"), from one or more of the commodity associations or exporters named in Books B.1 and B.2, each entitled "List of Indonesian Commodity Associations and Exporters", published in January 1982 and March 1982, respectively, by the Department of Trade, and/or from other duly licensed Indonesian exporters (hereinafter, collectively, the "Exporters"), in an amount at least equal to the foreign currency value of all equipment, materials and products to be supplied by you from non-Indonesian sources pursuant to the terms of the above-described contract, such value to be agreed with the Department of Trade and confirmed in a letter in the form of Annex A hereto;

2. to use the products, or to resell the products for use, or to cause the products to be used or resold, in the country or countries to be confirmed as aforesaid, unless with your specific authorization we are permitted to use the products, or to resell the products for use, or to cause the products to be used or resold, in any other country or countries;

3. to purchase the products, or to cause the products to be purchased, before the end of the term of the contract relating to the above-described tender and, in any event, to start the purchase or to cause to be purchased, within six (6) months after the date of award of such contract; and

4. to submit, or to cause to be submitted from time to time to the

** The Department of Trade will normally only confirm the country of nationality of the contractor/supplier. However, depending upon the circumstances of any given contract, other countries may be confirmed by the Department.

Department of Trade, by letter in the form of Annex B the relevant PEB forms and such other evidence of the shipment of products purchased pursuant to this undertaking as will permit the Department of Trade to monitor compliance herewith.

In connection with our irrevocable undertaking contained herein, this will confirm our understanding that:

a. the commercial terms, including those relating to price and delivery, in respect of each purchase of products from an Exporter shall be negotiated by us or by other purchasers thereof at the time of actual purchase;

b. the amount of each such purchase to be applied towards our obligation hereunder shall be equal to the invoiced purchase price of the products purchased, excluding, however, any shipping costs included in such invoice and any taxes or customs duties charged in connection therewith;

c. the amount of each such purchase (if measured in a currency other than the currency in which our obligation hereunder is measured) shall be applied against our obligation hereunder at exchange rates (as quoted by Bank Indonesia) prevailing at the date of the Exporter's invoice issued in respect of such purchase;

d. if we or our affiliated companies in the country or countries to be confirmed as aforesaid have traditionally purchased Products from Indonesian exporters, our undertaking contained herein shall be viewed as representing a commitment over and above such traditional level of purchases, it being the spirit and intention of such undertaking that purchases of Products hereunder shall be in addition to such traditional level of purchases;

e. if the contract relating to the above-described tender should be prematurely terminated, our undertaking contained herein shall also terminate without further obligation on our part; and

f. (i) if, during the course of performance of our obligations contained herein, we should be of the view that sufficient products either are not available in Indonesia or are not of suitable export quality or internationally competitive in price, you shall, at our request, review with us the actual circumstances at the time and,

(ii) if, after both parties have reviewed the matter in good faith and in the spirit of cooperation with a view to reaching a mutually acceptable solution you and we agree that we are not able to comply with the requirement of our undertaking contained herein because sufficient products either are not available in Indonesia or are not of suitable export quality or internationally competitive in price, you shall modify such requirements to take account of actual circumstances at the time which modifications may include, an extension of the time during which our obligations contained herein must be satisfied.

If we fail to comply with our undertaking contained herein, we hereby agree to pay to you as liquidated damages an amount equal to 50% of the difference between the total value of Products actually purchased pursuant to this undertaking and the foreign currency amount to be confirmed as aforesaid.

In connection with our undertaking contained herein, we hereby represent and warrant to you that (i) we have full power and authority and legal right to enter into this undertaking and to perform and observe the terms and provisions hereof, (ii) we have taken all necessary legal action to authorize, execute and deliver this undertaking, (iii) this undertaking constitutes our legal, valid and binding obligation, and (iv) no law, rule or regulation or contractual or other obligation binding on us is or will be contravened by reason of our execution and delivery of this undertaking or by our performance and observance of the terms and provisions hereof.

This undertaking shall be binding upon our successors.

Very truly yours,
(NAME OF TENDERER)
Affix
25 Rp.
Stamp

By ------
Name:
Title:

ANNEX A

(LETTERHEAD OF DEPARTMENT OF TRADE)

– – – – – – –, 198–

(Address of Tenderer)
(Please refer to code no. C/P)

Dear Sirs:

We refer to – – – – – – tender No. – – – – – – issued on – – – – – –, 198–, by (insert name of Indonesian Department, Agency or Corporation issuing tender) (the "Tender") and to your tender document submitted in response thereto and the Letter of Approval No. – – – – – – issued on – – – – – – –, 198– by the Minister/State Secretary acting as the Chairman of the Government Supervising Team for the Government Procurement.

We acknowledge receipt of your Letter of undertaking of – – – – – –, 198– a copy of which is attached hereto and initialled for identification by the Department of Trade.

In accordance with the provisions of paragraph number 1 of such Letter of Undertaking, we confirm the following:

1. The foreign currency value of all equipment, materials and products to be supplied by you from non-Indonesian sources pursuant to the terms of the contract relating to the tender shall be – – – – – –.

2. The countries referred to in such paragraph shall be – – – – – – and other countries provided that your counterpurchase shall not cause any friction in the respective destination, nor to cause any friction with existing trade activities by Indonesian traders.

3. Affiliated companies which may purchase Indonesian agricultural and industrial products in satisfaction of your obligation under such Letter of Undertaking shall be – – – – – –.

4. The Counterpurchase obligations contained in such Letter of Undertaking must be satisfied by you on or before – – – – – – (insert date of final satisfaction) unless, pursuant to paragraph 4.f thereof, such date is extended.

Your signature in the space marked "Agreed" below shall be conclusive evidence of your agreement to be bound by the terms of your Letter of Undertaking of – – – – – –, 198–, as supplemented by the provisions hereof.

Very truly yours,
DEPARTMENT OF TRADE

AGREED: (TENDERER)

By – – – – – –

By – – – – – –

ASSIGNMENT AGREEMENT

THIS AGREEMENT, dated ______________ between (insert name of Assignor) of (insert address of Assignor) and (insert name of Assignee) of (insert address of Assignee).

WHEREAS, the Assignor has undertaken certain obligation with respect to the purchase of commodities/goods from Indonesia as evidenced by a counterpurchase Letter of Undertaking dated ______________ and an Annex A Letter, ref. No. ______________ dated ______________ code No. C/P ______________ (such Letter of Undertaking and Annex A letter hereinafter collectively referred to as the "Letter of Undertaking").

WHEREAS, the Assignor desires to assign to the Assignee, without recourse to the Assignor, all of his rights and obligations under and with respect to the Letter of Undertaking;

WHEREAS, the Assignee desires to accept such assignment; and

WHEREAS, the Department of Trade of the Republic of Indonesia is willing to consent to such assignment;

NOW, THEREFORE, the Assignor and the Assignee hereby agree as follows:

1. The Assignor hereby assigns to the Assignee, without recourse to the Assignor, all of his rights and obligations under and with respect to the Letter of Undertaking.
2. The Assignee hereby accepts such assignment and specifically agrees, for the benefit of the Department of Trade of the Republic of Indonesia, to assume and be bound by all of the terms and conditions of the Letter of Undertaking, and in particular those relating to the payment of liquidated damages in the event the Assignee fails to comply with the terms of the Letter of Undertaking, as if Letter of Undertaking had originally been signed by the Assignee.
3. This Assignment Agreement shall become effective on and as of the date on which the Department of Trade of the Republic of Indonesia shall consent thereto.

IN WITNESS WHEREOF, the Assignor and the Assignee have executed this Assignment on the date and year first above written.

By: By:

CONSENT

The Department of Trade of the Republic of Indonesia hereby consent to the foregoing assignment, thereby releasing (insert name of

Assignor) from his obligations under and with respect to the Letter of Undertaking, in consideration of such obligations, together with all rights relating thereto, having been assigned to and assumed by (insert name of Assignee).

DEPARTMENT OF TRADE

By:

Iran

The fall in the price of oil and the consequent shortage of foreign exchange in Iran has increased the attractiveness of countertrade. However, oil 'barter' deals are at present particularly difficult to arrange because of fluctuating prices. Attempts are being made to identify markets for Iran's non-oil and manufactured goods which might be countertraded. All oil 'barter' deals are overseen by the Bilateral Transactions Committee of the Ministry of Commerce, and the relevant division of the National Iranian Oil Company. Countertrade involving other commodities or finished products is overseen by the Ministry of Commerce and any other ministry concerned. Western exporters contemplating countertrade with Iran will need to approach the appropriate ministry to offer their wares and at the same time propose a market for the Iranian export commodity concerned.

Possible countertrade goods: crude oil, carpets, dried fruits, minerals.

Iraq

Iraqi authorities express a dislike of countertrade, but 'barter' is now more attractive owing to the drain on its finances resulting from the war with Iran. Foreign contractors bidding for major oil-related projects usually have to offer two forms of payment: credit or oil 'barter'.

Possible countertrade goods: dates, minerals, oil and oil derivatives.

Israel

Under Israeli law a counterpurchase clause must be included in contracts for purchases valued at over US$50,000 made by government agencies, state corporations or state-assisted institutions.

The law does not apply to contracts with the Israeli Ports Authority. The clause obliges the supplier to buy Israeli goods or services to the value of 35 per cent of the contract. There is growing interest in countertrade in the Israeli private sector. CLAL, one of the largest Israeli industrial groups, and Bank Leumi and Hapoalim have set up organisations to deal with countertrade. Other major industrial organisations, such as Koor Industries and the Eisenberg Group, although not having specific firms or branches for the purpose, do enter into countertrade arrangements when the need arises. Suppliers to the Israel Government who are involved in countertrade arrangements should note that the competent body to administer, control and supervise such arrangements is the Israel Cooperation Authority:

35 Shaul Hamelech Boulevard, PO Box 33231, Tel Aviv 61231; Telex 032139; Telephone 03–262172/4.

Jamaica

Jamaica tends not to use bauxite and aluminium for private sector deals, because of the effect on world prices. She has concluded deals with the United States where the bauxite was for the US stockpile. However, Jamaica may offer local products as part of a countertrade proposal.

Jordan

The gentle but steady decline of the economy combined with a depression in the world phosphate market has obliged Jordan to look for opportunities to trade off its phosphate production in payment to successful foreign contractors and suppliers.

There is now no doubt that Jordan will favour those foreign companies bidding for major contracts who are willing to take fertilisers, potash or phosphate rock in part-payment for contracts or to arrange triangular deals. Exporters bidding for major contracts should be aware of the possibility of facing requests for countertrade.

Kenya

The Kenyan Government is studying countertrade proposals and has yet to formulate an official policy. The parastatal organisation primarily responsible for countertrade is the Kenya National Trading Corporation. However, the Central Bank and the Ministry of Commerce and Industry also have to approve any company-to-company countertrade agreements. The commodities involved are not likely to be those with a ready world market such as coffee, tea and horticultural products.

Possible countertrade goods: fluorspar, pyrethrum, sisal, leather goods.

Korea (South)

Objectives

1. To assist in developing and expanding Korean manufacturing and industrial capability.
2. To gain new technology, and provide design and development work.
3. To assist under-utilised sectors of industry.
4. To stimulate activity in selected sectors of the economy – particularly national defence.
5. To create new employment opportunities.

Basic guidelines

1. The policy may be applied to any/all major purchases of equipment, materials or services made by the Korean government, for more than US$1 million.
2. The aim is for each contract to attract 50 per cent value in off-sets, 10 per cent of which will be in the direct off-set category. (See 'Definitions' (1) below.)
3. The quality and quantity of the off-set offer will be an important element in contract tender evaluations.
4. The Defence Industry Bureau (DIB), Ministry of National Defense (MND) will review the off-set proposals.
5. Tenderers will sign a Memorandum of Agreement in respect of the off-set programme, when the contract is awarded. The Memorandum will be attached to the principal supply contract.
6. The MND hopes to achieve off-set in category C or better (see page 200).
7. The MND will seek fulfilment of off-set within the period of the principal contract.

Definitions

There are two off-set categories:

1. *Direct* – activities which relate to the principal contract:

(a) Technology transfer relating to parts and components.
(b) Provision of opportunities to manufacture and export parts and components.
(c) Transfer of technology to obtain a maintenance capability.
(d) Assistance in establishing industrial facilities and/or provision of equipment or tooling.
(e) Assistance in obtaining maintenance opportunities in overseas markets for which the Republic of Korea has the technological capability.

2. *Indirect* – activities *not* related to the principal contract:
   (a) Korean Industrial Participation (KIP):
      (i) As for (1) above which are not directly related to the principal contract.
      (ii) Opportunities to participate in major research and development projects.
      (iii) Assistance in creating new employment opportunities.
      (iv) Any approved activity that will further enhance Korean national, economic or industrial interests.
   (b) Counterpurchase:
   Subject to the prior approval of the MND, the following may be included:
      (i) Direct purchase of, and/or assistance in selling, self-defence articles from original Korean sources.
      (ii) Direct purchase of, and/or assistance in selling, general commodities from original Korean sources.

Evaluation

1. The technological sophistication, the total dollar value and the length of time to complete the off-set programme will be major factors in the evaluation process.
2. It is expected that Korean equipment, material and services will be used to the maximum extent possible. Priority will be given to those off-set proposals containing a greater amount of Korean material and services.
3. The MND will not approve those activities that do not meet selection criteria.
4. In calculating off-set credits for projects where Korean companies are utilised, only the value of the equipment, material or services provided by the Republic of Korea will be considered for off-set credit.

5. Values, weighted in most cases, will be applied to the various types/categories of off-set proposals (see Summary below).
6. The evaluation formula is as follows:

$$\frac{\left(\text{Off-set percentage} \times \text{Weighted value}\right) \div \text{Weighted off-set execution period*}}{\text{MND's objective off-set percentage} \times 3} \times 100$$

Terms and conditions

1. All calculations are made in US dollars.
2. Programmes will be phased, wherever possible, in annual increments in parallel with the payment schedule of the principal contract, and should be completed within the period of the principal contract.
3. Expenses incurred in the execution of the off-set programme will not be allowed as an off-set credit.
4. The terms of the principal contract will apply, where appropriate, to the off-set commitment.
5. The scope of the off-set commitment will be varied in line with any changes in the principal contract.
6. Applications for off-set credits should be accompanied by copies of irrevocable letters of credit or shipping documents or export permits with purchase order.
7. Credits accumulated in excess of the commitment may be carried forward and used in follow-on contracts.
8. If the contractor requests an extension of the off-set period beyond the expiry date of the principal contract, MND approval must be sought and a 10 per cent performance bond will be called for.
9. A 10 per cent penalty will be paid on the unfulfilled portion of the commitment, at expiry.
10. Contractors will be required to report quarterly to the Offset Program Office on the progress of implementation of off-set commitments. Reports will include details of opportunities offered to Korean industries and contracts concluded. Upon conclusion of off-set commitments, both parties will sign a statement certifying the conclusion of the off-set programme.

* The weighted off-set execution period is calculated as follows:

$$\frac{1 + \text{Time exceeded basic contract period}}{\text{Basic contract period}}$$

Form of proposal

The following points must be covered in the submission of off-set proposals:

1. Estimated principal contract value.
2. Off-set value and percentage; KIP value and percentage; counter-purchase value and percentage.
3. Fulfilment time-period (months/years).
4. Commitment to, or assurance of, fulfilment.

Procedure for submission of proposals

1. Off-set proposals should be submitted to the Offset Program Office (DIB, MND) in writing together with a draft Memorandum of Agreement within the period specified in the Request for Proposal, indicating in detail a contractor's commitment to the off-set programme and outlining the off-set programme execution plan.
2. Within four weeks after the receipt of the off-set proposal and draft Memorandum of Agreement by the Offset Program Office, each foreign contractor will meet with the assigned off-set project manager and discuss the details of the proposal. If the submitted proposal is not feasible or does not satisfy the MND's basic off-set objectives, continued revisions and supplemental actions will be taken. If a satisfactory proposal is not submitted within the closing period, it will be disadvantageous to the contractor.
3. All discussions beweeen the contractor and the off-set project manager will be completed before signing the Memorandum of Agreement, which will be signed by a designated representative of the MND and a representative of the contractor.

Summary of Korean off-set proposals and procedures

Off-set proposal	*Value* (x=multiple)
Provision of infrastructure, equipment and tooling (considered on a case-by-case basis)	Cost × 3 – × 10
Where contractor acts as intermediary in (a) provision of opportunities for KIP	

Off-set proposal	*Value* (x=multiple)
(b) assistance in selling self-defence articles	Cost × .5 – × 1
(c) assistance in selling specific products which have never been previously exported to a third party	
(d) assistance in selling general commodities which have never been previously exported to a specific country	

Technology transfer	
1. Direct off-set technology (defence)	11–15 per cent of work value provided by contractor
2. Indirect off-set technology (defence)	8–12 per cent of work value provided by contractor
3. Indirect off-set technology (commercial)	4–7 per cent of work value provided by contractor
Technology assistance	
Transportation, lodging, food and associated costs	Cost
Training	
Training classes, etc.	$5,000 per class
Financial assistance and other intangible assistance	Case-by-case basis

Weighting

Weighting will be applied according to the category of importance of the proposals (this weighting at the discretion of the MND)

Category	*Activity*	*Weighting*
A	High national priority activities which greatly affect economic and industrial development objectives related to direct off-set. (a) Creation, or improvement of,	5

Category	Activity	Weighting
	self-reliance by providing for: – ability to independently produce equipment (components) – ability to jointly produce equipment (components) – ability to produce spare parts independently – ability to maintain equipment independently. (b) Provision of opportunities to manufacture and export parts and components. (c) Assistance in obtaining maintenance opportunities in overseas markets for which the Republic of Korea has the technological capability. (d) Assistance in establishing industrial facilities and/or provision of equipment or tooling. (e) Other activities which greatly contribute to national interests.	
B	Priority activities which contribute to economic and industrial development and diversification. (a) Direct off-set which does not extensively contribute to national interests. (b) Indirect off-set (KIP) which extensively contributes to national interests.	4
C	Desirable activities which support economic/industrial growth and favourably affect the international balance of payments. (a) Indirect off-set (KIP) which extensively contributes to national interests. (b) Direct purchase of, and/or	3

Category	*Activity*	*Weighting*
	assistance in selling, self-defence articles from original Korean sources.	
D	(a) Acceptable activities which contribute to economic growth in areas that do not require extensive assistance. (b) Direct purchase of, and/or assistance in selling general commodities approved by the MND from original Korean sources.	2
E	Incidental activities which satisfy unique requirements of the MND. These activities will be considered on a case-by-case basis (e.g. studies, management development assistance and other assistance).	1
F	Unacceptable activities which do not satisfy MND requirements and/or activities which do not require external assistance such as exhausted export quotas or production capacity which has been exceeded.	0
Costs for technology related to execution of the Offset Program	Cost	
Royalties and licence fees for products currently being purchased in Korea	Cost	

Notes: 1. The imported element of goods manufactured and retained in Korea will not be allowed as off-set credit. If goods are subsequently exported, credit will be allowed.
2. Shipping costs relating to the off-set programme will not be allowed as a credit, but Korean shipping used to transport other goods *will* be allowed.

Procedures for off-set programmes	
Foreign contractor	Requests survey of Korean industrial capabilities and marketing related to off-set programmes.
	If required, requests recommendations for Korean industrial sources.
Defence Industry Bureau (Offset Program Office)	Arranges for foreign contractor's requests after consulting proper Republic of Korea government agencies.
	Informs foreign contractors of arrangements.
Foreign contractor	Surveys Korean industries recommended by DIB.
	Submits acceptable off-set proposals and a draft Memorandum of Agreement to DIB within a specified period of time.
Defence Industry Bureau (Offset Program Office)	Defines foreign cantractor's proposal and prepares alternatives for negotiations.
	Concludes negotiation upon completion of discussions and signs an appropriate agreement (Memorandum of Agreement).
	Evaluates off-set proposals and submits results to Review Council.

Libya

Libya offers surplus oil for countertrading purposes, and state enterprises producing oil and oil products prefer counterpurchase arrangements. Libya has a number of bilateral agreements involving oil.

Malta

The Malta government frequently seeks to include a compensation trading clause in contracts governing the purchase of major capital goods by the government itself or by parastatal companies. Specific contract conditions are subject to negotiations but performance guarantees are normally included.

Car importers are also required to generate exports of Maltese goods or services to become eligible for import licences.

Malaysia

Background

In early 1983, the Malaysian Cabinet directed that a special unit be created within the Ministry of Trade and Industry, to oversee countertrade activities. This unit is called 'Unit Khas Countertrade'. Two booklets are available, but the contents are summarised here. The Unit acts as a clearing house for information, and as a monitoring body to review the progress of countertrade deals. Its activities are not confined to government deals.

Reasons

1. To increase export of primary products and manufactured goods.
2. To improve the unfavourable balance of trade with certain countries.
3. To save foreign exchange.

Extent

All government departments and statutory bodies submit procurement proposals subject to international tender, to Unit Khas, where a directive will be made whether countertrade proposals will be called for.

For 'works' contracts, the value which will be considered for 'countertrade' (i.e. against which the countertrade proposals will be measured) is the portion involving payments in foreign currency.

Tenderers are encouraged to make countertrade offers *even* where no reference is made to countertrade in the tender documents.

Countertrade offers are *not mandatory* but will be one of the factors considered in tender evaluation. Countertrade offers are not needed for tenders funded by international lending agencies.

Penalty

A guarantee to ensure fulfilment of counterpurchase obligations may be called for, to an extent determined when negotiating the countertrade agreement.

Time-scales

These are fixed when the countertrade agreement is signed.

Restrictions

There are marketing restrictions on Malaysian countertrade goods, but the system for discharging countertrade obligations means that the exporter is not concerned with these restrictions.

System

1. Countertrade offers, in the form of the letter of undertaking (see below), should initially give a general indication of the value, time period and products involved. This letter should be signed and submitted by the tenderer.

   If the tenderer is a foreign contractor/supplier, this letter should be signed by the foreign contractor/supplier and not by its agent, partner or representative, if any. Copies of the 'List of Malaysian Products for Export' referred to in the Letter of Undertaking are available from the Ministry of Trade and Industry upon request.
2. Once tenders have closed and the offers are being evaluated, the department or agency will require full particulars of offers.
3. When tendering, it must be stated whether the countertrade system proposed is compensation (i.e. payment in goods) or counterpurchase (i.e. payment in foreign exchange with a parallel obligation to buy Malaysian goods).
4. Unit Khas will negotiate the countertrade contract once the tender has been awarded. Copies of sample counterpurchase and compensation agreements are available.

Procedure for exporter

1. The exporter must decide on whether to choose compensation or counterpurchase, or a combination.
2. The exporter will decide the extent of his countertrade offer.

3. The offer will be made when tenders are submitted.
4. The counterpurchase obligation may be transferred with the approval of Unit Khas, to a third party. The exporter will need to identify an appropriate third party and negotiate a suitable fee.
5. When the contract is awarded, the third party and the tenderer negotiate the countertrade agreement with Unit Khas.
6. If countertrade is implemented in the form of compensation, payments will be made direct to the local exporting companies, under the guidance of Unit Khas, and in terms of the countertrade agreement.
7. If counterpurchase is used, normal commercial conditions will apply, and Unit Khas will include counterpurchase conditions – including penalties – in the countertrade agreement.
8. The countertrade agreement is separate to the main procurement contract, and is normally signed before the main contract.
9. Fulfilment is monitored by submitting to the Unit Khas various export documents, who will then issue a Letter of Confirmation.

Specimen document

(LETTERHEAD OF TENDERER)

______________ 198 ______

The Secretary General,
Ministry of Trade and Industries,
International Trade Division,
(Countertrade Special Unit),
9th Floor, Block 10,
Government Office Complex,
Jalan Duta,
KUALA LUMPUR.

c/o

Secretary General,
Ministry of Finance,
Contract & Supplies Division,
5th Floor, Block 9,
Government Office Complex,
Jalan Duta,
KUALA LUMPUR.

Dear Sirs,
We refer to the Tender for the Supply of Tender No. ______ issued on ____________ 1985 by Ministry of Finance, Malaysia and to our tender document No. ______ submitted on ______________, 1985 in response thereto.

We hereby irrevocably undertake during the period from the date of award of the contract relating to such tender until final acceptance (or equivalent) of our work and services thereunder or until completion of deliveries thereunder, as the case may be:

1. to purchase, or to cause to be purchased by one or more of our affiliated companies in the country or countries to be confirmed by the Ministry of Trade and Industry located in any other country or countries acceptable to you, the agricultural and/or industrial products contained in the 'List of Malaysian Products for Export' issued by the Ministry of Trade and Industry and/or such other products as you may approve in writing, from one or more of the suppliers in Malaysia, in an amount equal to the total FOB value of the goods to be supplied by us from non-Malaysian sources pursuant to the terms of the above described contract. The value of the contract is to be agreed with the Ministry of Trade and Industry and confirmed by letter from the Ministry.
2. to use the products, or to resell the products for use, or to cause the products to be used or resold, in the country or countries to be confirmed as aforesaid, unless with your specific authorization we are permitted to use the products, or to resell the products for use, or to cause the products to be used or resold, in any other country or countries;
3. to purchase the products, or to cause the products to be purchased, before the end of the term of the contract relating to the above described tender according to a fixed schedule to be negotiated and agreed upon with the Ministry of Trade and Industry.
4. to submit, or cause to be submitted, to the Ministry of Trade and Industry the relevant document and such other evidence of the shipment of products purchased in pursuance to this undertaking as will permit the Ministry of Trade and Industry to monitor compliance herewith.

In connection with our irrevocable undertaking contained herein, this will confirm our understanding that:

(a) the commercial terms, including those relating to price and delivery, in respect of each purchase of products from a Supplier shall be negotiated by us or by other purchasers thereof at the time of actual purchase;

(b) the amount of each such purchase to be applied towards our obligation hereunder shall be equal to the invoiced purchase price of the products purchased, or Custom Export Declaration value, whichever is lower, excluding, however, any shipping costs included in such invoice and any taxes or customs duties charged in connection therewith;

(c) the amount of each such purchase (if measured in a currency other than the currency in which our obligation hereunder is measured) shall be applied against our obligation hereunder at exchange rates (as quoted by Bank Negara Malaysia) prevailing at the date of the supplying invoice issued in respect of such purchase; and

(d) if we/our affiliated companies in the country or countries to be confirmed as aforesaid have traditionally purchased products from Malaysia, our undertaking contained herein shall be viewed as representing a commitment over and above such traditional level of purchases, it being the spirit and intention of such undertaking that purchases of products hereunder shall be in addition to such traditional level of purchases;

If we fail to comply with our undertaking contained herein we hereby agree to pay to you as liquidated damages an amount equal to a minimum of fifteen per cent (15%) of the value of Malaysian goods and commodities not purchased.

In connection with our undertaking contained herein, we hereby represent and warrant to you that (i) we have full power and authority and legal right to enter into this undertaking and to perform and observe the terms and provisions hereof, (ii) we have all necessary legal action to authorise, execute and deliver this undertaking, (iii) this undertaking constitutes our legal, valid and binding obligation, and (iv) no law, rule or regulation or contractual or other obligation binding on us is or will contravene by reason of our execution and delivery of this undertaking or by our performance and observance of the terms and provisions hereof.

This undertaking shall be binding upon our successors.

Very truly yours,

(Signature)

Name : ____________________
Title : ____________________
Official Seal : ____________________

Witness:

Signature : ____________________
Name : ____________________
Title : ____________________
Official Seal : ____________________

Mexico

Currently, the official policy is to permit countertrade only as a means of increasing non-oil exports. However, the Banco de Mexico and the Ministry of Trade and Industrial Development which authorise countertrade deals may refuse authorisation if exports could be sold for foreign exchange. Each countertrade proposal is assessed case by case on its potential to create a flow of foreign exchange into the country (the authorities have created a list of export products they are keen to promote).

Extent

Mexico has clearing arrangements within ALADI, as well as with several countries in Central America, Cuba, the Dominican Republic, Iran, East Germany and Bulgaria. Mexico has countertraded non-ferrous metals and agricultural produce for chemicals and machine tools over a five-year period from 1981, cocoa beans for rubber with Malaysia in 1983 and steel for steel technology with the USSR in 1984. Other deals in recent years were completed with Canada, Guatemala and the United States.

Procedure

The importing party must obtain authorisation from the Banco de Mexico and the approval of the Ministry of Trade and Industrial Development. In March 1983 Mexico established the 'Supplementary

Exchange Control Rules Applicable to the Use and Transfer of Foreign Exchanges Generated by Exports'. They were amended and expanded in February 1984. The rules stipulate the following:

1. Local exporters are officially authorised to receive imports as a means of payment for the goods exported.
2. A Mexican firm interested in countertrade must receive authorisation from the Banco de Mexico and approval of the Ministry of Trade and Industrial Development.
3. If a countertrade proposal is approved the Mexican exporter will receive a permit.
4. If the Mexican exporter receives cash in partial payment the cash can be used legally for four purposes:
   (a) import goods and services needed for their production process;
   (b) cover other expenses authorised by the government needed for exports;
   (c) carry out barter trade with authorised merchandise for importation to Mexico;
   (d) open a 'special account' in a Mexican bank that can only be increased through deposits of additional foreign exchange earned abroad converted to pesos at the controlled rate.

   Any foreign currency not used for one of the allowable purposes must be sold for pesos at the controlled rate.
5. Exporters required to sell their foreign exchange earnings to the government receive foreign exchange receipts called *comprobantes*.

Countertrade goods should be non-traditional exports. If they are traditional exports (e.g. oil) then they should be sold in an area or market in which Mexico has not sold yet. Apart from firms which create such 'additional' exports, the government also gives special consideration to those firms which import the technical know-how and marketing skills that would make domestic Mexican goods marketable in the world economy.

The most significant countertrade deals have involved Mexico's large state-owned companies. Senior officials in Mexico's Ministry of Energy, Mining and Parastatal Industries foresee a major role for countertrade in the food and food-processing sector, primarily through Conasupo, the state-owned food retailing network. Countertrade is expected to figure substantially in the communications and transportation sectors, particularly in the Combinado Industrial Sanagun consisting of Diesel Nacional (trucks and buses), Constructora Nacional de

Carros de Ferrocarril (railroad cars) and Siderugica Nacional (steel machinery and engine blocks for Renault and Datsun).

Possible countertrade goods: coffee, cocoa, avocado pears, honey, textiles, footwear, clothing, minerals, vehicle parts.

Morocco

The government is not favourably inclined towards countertrade. Countertrade deals have been carried out using phosphates and wine, but this is uncommon. Since mid-1985 an attempt has been going on to enforce a law of 1982 requiring local vehicle assemblers to achieve 40 per cent (50 per cent for trucks) of either local content and/or counter-purchase of parts by the overseas suppliers of the CKD kits.

The required figures are not thought to have been achieved, or perhaps achievable, and in one case the government has accepted countertrade in a mineral (barytes) which is being sold below market price to achieve disposal.

The Netherlands

The Netherlands countertrade policy is similar to that employed by many European countries. Key points are as follows:

1. The industrial participation/off-set requirement is imposed in every case, except where the value is too small to make it worth while.
2. Although the off-set offers of tenderers are not considered in the initial evaluation of tenders, the off-set aspect could be used as a tie-breaker.
3. A standard agreement is available, and a short form could be obtained on the telex provided the client asked for it.
4. The goods to be purchased should be of the same technological level as those being supplied.
5. The Dutch government expects 100 per cent of the non-Dutch contract value to be off-set.
6. The key element in the counterpurchase of Dutch goods is that it should represent new business.
7. This would not rule out the involvement of a trader but the Dutch will test whether the individual purchases represent additional trade.

8. In need, the Ministry of Economic Affairs will give advance clearance for the purchase of certain goods if it is approached.
9. There are no penalty guarantees or clauses in the countertrade agreement, but a dispute clause is included.
10. If there is any difficulty in locating suitable countertrade products the Ministry of Defence will help.

New Zealand

New Zealand would like to receive both off-set and counterpurchase offers on public sector procurement. Tenderers for government purchases or other publicly funded purchases likely to exceed NZ$2 million in value, are invited to submit proposals for both. Off-set can be in the form of local manufacture, technology transfer, joint research and market assistance for locally produced technological products. Countertrade proposals can be a deciding factor in the award of contracts when all else is more or less equal. It is for the tenderer to identify the products to be exported, where they will go, what value will be taken and the time period over which the exports will be spread. Firms which can show a history of trade beneficial to New Zealand can quote this as an alternative to making a counterpurchase proposal.

Nicaragua

There is recourse to countertrade owing to the lack of foreign currency. All countertrade dealings have to be channelled through the Ministry of Foreign Trade, more specifically the Ministry's 'Direccion General de Integraction Economica'.

Nigeria

Nigeria concluded a number of bilateral oil barter arrangements. Such deals included oil for car kits with Brazil. These deals were not popular amongst all the Nigerian ministries and, following the counter-coup that brought Major General Babangida to power, a Committee of Investigation was set up. Its brief was to examine countertrade deals signed by the previous military government of General Buhari. The Committee's report spoke of serious procedural irregularities but found it 'difficult to fault the use of countertrade as a short-term measure for national economic revival and sustained development'.

Consequently, the government has given the go-ahead to a cautious resumption of oil 'swap' negotiations. As far as possible, agreements would be on a government-to-government basis, which would cut out the trading company intermediaries blamed for charging excessive margins on the deals. Priority areas have been defined as follows:

1. Completion of ongoing core projects including petrochemicals, iron and steel and liquid natural gas.
2. Liquidating or servicing selected and verified debts.
3. Importing essential raw materials, machinery and agricultural equipment.
4. Creating employment and building up the industrial sector.

Pakistan

Pakistan is entrusting a large volume of its barter business to three international trading groups in a bid to develop its exports of industrial goods. The government is dividing its aim for $1 billion of its exports handled this way between Mitsubishi of Japan ($200 million), Marcotrade of Switzerland ($400 million) and Sukab of Sweden ($400 million). These were chosen from over 50 applicants but the Prime Minister has intervened to ensure that further companies may become involved. The government aims for $1 billion of its exports to be handled this way, though there is concern that this may result in higher import prices. Pakistan wishes to import oil, tea, edible oil and fertiliser.

Possible countertrade goods: cotton, garments, leather, hide, skins, fruit and vegetables, engineering goods, foods, rugs and carpets, surplus steel mill products.

Peru

The government is keen to develop countertrade and the existing regulations will be revised. Incentives are likely to be introduced to encourage firms to deal in countertrade, and to deal in non-traditional products. Under Budget Law 24030 of 14 December 1984, a Countertrade Committee was created to approve export operations of different kinds, payable in goods and services. The Committee is headed by the Vice-Minister of Commerce; the members are from the Central Bank, the Government Exporters' Organisation and one representative from the private sector.

Transactions considered by the Committee will be judged by the following criteria:

1. A strengthening of exports, especially of the non-traditional kind and contributions to the stability of Peruvian overeas markets and their expansion.
2. An effective export substitution in those markets where traditional mechanisms are not at present working.
3. The harmony of export and import prices by comparison with world market conditions.
4. Contributions to the balance of payments.
5. The professional competence and economic solvency of bodies involved in intermediate services and the level of guarantees offered.

The Philippines

Countertrade is not new to the Philippines. It has been used on a limited scale and in various forms for many years. The Philippine International Trading Corporation (PITC) was set up several years ago to facilitate trade between the Philippines and Eastern Europe and China. Countertrade with non-communist countries is dealt with on a case-by-case basis but will always be subject to Central Bank approval. Although the PITC will in all cases be willing to assist in the formulation of countertrade deals, it is not essential that it is involved. Deals can be arranged directly between negotiating companies. The commodities involved are not likely to be those with a ready world market (such as coconut oil, fruits, tobacco and wood products). Countertrade is viewed in the Philippines more as a means of finding new markets for Philippine exports than as an alternative method of paying for imports.

Poland

As a result of her severe economic and financial problems, Poland is importing only what is absolutely necessary from the West. Counterpurchase and/or buy-back are usually demanded, especially where relatively large projects are concerned. Contracts requiring a 50 per cent plus counterpurchase commitment are quite common. Legislation to permit the establishment of joint ventures is expected to be introduced.

Portugal

Portugal is increasingly demanding off-sets on civil and defence public sector contracts. The usual requirement is related to the provision of local employment, foreign currency, goods and services off-set, although other forms of countertrade are becoming common.

Qatar

Qatar has been known to barter crude oil in part or full payment for construction contracts and to settle large longstanding claims.

Romania

Due to the ongoing severe economic difficulties, countertrade is a predominant and long-term feature of commercial dealings with Romania. The Romanian system of offering goods only from the foreign trade organisation to which the exporting company is selling makes for a lack of flexibility. The quality may be lower and the price may be higher than that expected for cash transactions.

The position has been exacerbated by a Foreign Trade Law introduced at the beginning of 1981 which requires enterprises engaged in foreign trade to balance their hard currency accounts at the end of every quarter.

Saudi Arabia

There is no publicly declared Saudi policy on countertrade and the government normally prefers to deal on a cash basis for public sector contracts and supplies. In very rare special cases, however, there have been oil 'barter' deals. In certain projects (e.g. petrochemicals) the foreign joint-venture partner has been obliged to take responsibility for the sale of a percentage (normally 50 per cent) of the product. Off-set conditions have been applied to one giant defence contract, requiring the contractor to reinvest 35 per cent of the contract price in high technology local industry over ten years. There is otherwise a general regulation that non-100 per cent Saudi contractors must subcontract 30 per cent of a contract in the public sector to a 100 per cent Saudi company.

Sierra Leone

There is no officially stated government policy on countertrade. However, due to a serious lack of foreign exchange the government has entered into several agreements with various countries by which vital imports such as oil and certain consumer items have been exchanged for diamonds, gold and agricultural produce. At present the government is prepared to negotiate countertrade arrangements on an *ad hoc* basis, considering each case on its merit.

Singapore

Until as recently as the end of 1984 Singapore discouraged countertrade, although a little was carried on with Indonesia involving timber, poultry and eggs. A Countertrade Service Unit was established in May 1985 to serve as a catalyst in developing Singapore as a countertrade services centre. Singapore hopes to act as a middleman using specialist countertrade companies, which will be encouraged to open local offices there using such incentives as tax exemption for five years and a subsequent concessional tax level of 10 per cent. It is hoped that these companies will conduct countertrade with China, India, Africa and Latin America. This is seen as a response to growing local interest in countertrade rather than any move away from Singapore's commitment to an open, cash-based multilateral trading system.

South Africa

A Secretariat for non-conventional trade was established in March 1986 in the Department of Trade and Industry, following the government's announcement that countertrading would be actively promoted as part of South Africa's trading policy.

Soviet Union

The USSR has for several years favoured the use of countertrade as an alternative to conventional methods of trading. Changes in the system for marketing Soviet goods will greatly affect countertrade deals. Buy-back has been used extensively to help finance large capital projects, particularly in the chemical and gas sectors. According to Soviet claims, some 45 large industrial projects had been commissioned on this basis by 1983.

However, countertrade is not obligatory in Soviet foreign trade contracts and, where proposed, usually represents a relatively low proportion of contract value, for example less than 10 per cent, although higher rates may apply in some cases (e.g. consumer goods).

Syria

Due to an acute shortage of foreign currency, countertrade is favoured. Oil is used, but this is on the whole pledged (largely to Romania).

Possible countertrade goods: cotton garments, skins and hides, phosphate, garlic, kitchen and sanitary utensils, salt.

Tanzania

Countertrade accounts for 10 per cent of the export trade. There is no official government policy towards countertrade but the basic rule is that traditional exports must be sold for hard currency and not countertraded. Such exports include coffee (beans), cotton, sisal fibre, tea (unblended), cashew nuts, tobacco, and cloves (Zanzibar only). Countertrade deals are restricted to those bringing in vitally needed spare parts and necessities not available in Tanzania. No import licences have been granted for luxury goods obtained by barter.

Possible countertrade goods: blended tea, instant coffee, beeswax, softwoods, spices, hides and skins, textiles.

Thailand

The Thai government is increasingly interested in developing countertrade as a means of procuring certain imports which it might otherwise be reluctant to finance. It sees countertrade, too, as a way of improving its export performance, particularly in those commodities which it has difficulty in selling in sufficient quantities on the international market. Hitherto, Thailand's shopping list has tended to concentrate on chemicals, fertilisers, agricultural equipment, oil and steel. It is likely that Thailand's state enterprises may be increasingly tempted to consider countertrade as a means of financing imports, although the government remains cautious of the risk of undermining the country's normal trading patten. There is no defined Thai policy on countertrade, though a high-level committee has been appointed by the government to examine the use of countertrade. Despite this lack of policy, countertrade is beginning to figure more prominently than hitherto in the bidding for major local projects.

Possible countertrade goods: tobacco, rice, maize, tapioca, sugar, paper.

Tunisia

Countertrade is playing an increasing part in commercial negotiations. It is thought that the Tunisians intend to set up a new countertrade organisation, but for the time being negotiations are handled by the Centre de Promotion des Exportations.

Possible countertrade goods: phosphates, olive oil.

Turkey

Under bilateral agreements with her major oil suppliers (Iraq, Libya and Iran), Turkey's oil purchases are made under arrangements involving barter and counterpurchase. For certain major projects and sales, particularly in the defence field, successful bids also sometimes involve an element of counterpurchase though this is usually not insisted upon by the authorities.

However, a willingness to include countertrade in the financial package can enhance an offer which would not otherwise enjoy full credit backing. Off-set arrangements are rather more common, though here the purpose is not so much to reduce the foreign exchange costs of a contract as to encourage the development of local manufacturing industry and the transfer of technology through direct foreign capital investment. Recently the Turkish government has been trying to persuade foreign companies and consortia bidding for major projects such as power plant to accept an arrangement whereby they undertake to install and run the plant, paying themselves from the profits thus generated. After a certain number of years, when the costs have been fully repaid, the plant would be transferred to Turkish ownership.

Uganda

Ugandan authorities do not favour countertrade (which would consist almost entirely of coffee). Uganda prefers to sell surplus coffee where it can for foreign exchange.

United States of America

It has been said that America's 'Buy America' policy is a form of countertrade, in that foreign suppliers are sometimes required to sell their products through US corporations. Large defence contracts awarded to foreign suppliers may call for that supplier to enter into a joint production agreement with a US company. As a general policy, however, the US government is against countertrade, viewing it as a restrictive practice and a non-tariff barrier to trade.

Uruguay

Present legislation requires all Uruguayan public organisations to give preference to foreign suppliers who include a countertrade element in their offers.

Possible countertrade goods: rice, fish, footwear, textiles, leather.

Venezuela

State entities are looking for the first time at countertrade to finance major expansion programmes. Iron ore and aluminium are the principal commodities involved. With falling dollar revenues resulting from the slump in oil prices, countertrade could become a feature particularly in terms of project finance.

Yugoslavia

Yugoslavia has severe economic problems and has adopted a policy of restricting imports whilst maximising exports in order to keep the balance of payments under control. It is thought that about 20 per cent of all foreign trade exchanges in 1985 were linked to countertrade and the level was certainly at least 15 per cent. Yugoslav enterprises who wish to engage in countertrade must seek authorisation from the Federal Secretariat for Foreign Trade. Approval will only be given if the value of the export exceeds the value of the import. The Yugoslav authorities aim to regulate countertrade to secure the sale abroad of goods which are usually difficult to export, or to markets which have proved difficult to penetrate. Therefore, goods which could normally expect to find ready markets overseas are unlikely to be offered. Approval may be given if the deal involves an export which will facilitate the import of commodities in short supply on the domestic market. Countertrade deals have been attractive to Yugoslav enterprises in so far as such transactions were exempt from regulations which required part of the hard currency proceeds from export sales to be converted into dinars. These regulations have been replaced and the new legislation in force from 1 January 1986 requires all foreign currency earnings deposited with a designated bank to be converted into dinars within 48 hours.

The new law on trading with foreign countries has added no particular encouragement to Yugoslav firms to develop this mode of commerce. Under the old law, for example, it was possible for Yugoslav firms to circumvent the imports regime by using countertrade, but under the new one they have to comply with the various import categories whether countertrade or normal methods are used. There may be, therefore, a more cautious reaction by Yugoslav firms to countertrade but equally there will be those who see other commercial benefits from engaging in it. It is understood from the Federal Secretariat for Foreign Trade that countertrade arrangements will be more flexibly applied, but all such deals will have to be kept within the overall annual ceiling for the importation of equipment.

Zambia

Zambia has recently reviewed its policy on countertrade and is encouraging barter deals in all areas except mineral ores (copper, cobalt, lead, zinc, etc.), although 'special transactions' have been arranged which could be construed as countertrade.

Zimbabwe

Zimbabwe would prefer not to indulge in countertrade, but regards it as necessary for trade with certain countries such as those in Eastern Europe. Countertrade also provides an outlet for Zimbabwe's own surplus products such as maize and tobacco.

Countertrade proposals are examined and decided by a Special Trading Committee, chaired by the Deputy Minister of Trade and Commerce. Past deals have involved the export of Zimbabwean tobacco, maize, asbestos and ferrochrome in exchange for machinery, spare parts for machinery, consumer items and raw materials. In approving deals the Committee will seek to ensure that the goods for export are not re-sold to a country which would normally purchase the goods for cash.

APPENDIX 2

Bank export trading companies operating in the United States in mid 1985

Bank holding company	*Export trading company*
Frontier Bancorp Vista, CA	Interbank Trading Co. San Diego, CA
Florida Park Banks Inc. St Petersburg, FL	Park Services International St Petersburg, FL
Capital Bancorp Miami, FL	Capital Trade Services Inc. Miami, FL
CoreStates Financial Corp. Lancaster, PA	CoreStates Export Trading Co. Philadelphia, PA
North Valley Bancorp Redding, CA	Casia-Pacific Redding, CA
Maryland National Corp. Baltimore, MD	MN Trade Corp. Baltimore, MD
Marine Corporation Milwaukee, WI	Marine Financial Services Inc. Milwaukee, WI
*Ramapo Financial Corp. Wayne, NJ Ultra Bancorporation Bridgewater, NJ and Trenton, NJ	Florida Interbank Trading Co. Inc. Jacksonville, FL
*First Wisconsin Corp. Milwaukee, WI	InterContinental Trading Co. Inc. Rolling Meadows, IL
Commerce Union Corp. Nashville, TN	Commerce Trading Corp. Nashville, TN
Valley National Corp. Phoenix, AZ	Valley International Trading Co. Phoenix, AZ
Manufacturers Hanover Corp. New York, NY	Manufacturers Hanover World Trade Corp. New York, NY

Bank holding company	*Export trading company*
Marine Midland Banks Inc. Buffalo, NY	Marine Midland Trade Inc. New York, NY
United Bancorp of Arizona Phoenix, AZ	United Bank Export Trading Co. Phoenix, AZ
Security Pacific Corp. San Francisco, CA	Security Pacific Export Trading Co. Los Angeles, CA
Citicorp New York, NY	Citicorp International Trading Co. New York, NY
First Interstate Bancorp Los Angeles, CA	First Interstate Trading Co. Los Angeles, CA
First Kentucky National Corp. Louisville, KY	First Kentucky National Corp. Louisville, KY
Union Bancorp Inc. Los Angeles, CA	StanChart Export Services Co. Inc. Los Angeles, CA
Crocker National Corp. San Francisco, CA	Crocker Pacific Trade Corp. San Francisco, CA
*Ramapo Financial Corp. Wayne, NJ Ultra Bancorp Bridgewater, NJ New Jersey National Corp. Trenton, NJ	Bancorp's International Trading Co. Somerset, NJ
State Street Boston Corp. Boston, MA	State Street Trade Development Corp. Inc. Boston, MA
International Bancshares Corp. Laredo, TX	IBC Trading Co. Laredo, TX
US Bancorp Portland, OR	US World Trade Corp. Portland, OR
*First Chicago Corp. Chicago, IL	First Chicago Trading Co. Chicago, IL
Rainier Bancorp Seattle, WA	Rainier International Trading Co. Seattle, WA
Shawmut Corp. Boston, MA	Shawmut Export Corp. Boston, MA

Bank holding company	*Export trading company*
Hongkong and Shanghai Banking Corp. Hong Kong	Equator Trading Co. Hartford, CT
Banking America Corp. San Francisco, CA	BankAmerica World Trade Corp. San Francisco, CA
Bankers Trust New York Corp. New York, NY	Bankers Trust International Trading Corp. New York, NY
First National State Bancorp Newark, NJ	First International Trading Co. Newark, NJ
Chase Manhattan Corp. New York, NJ	Chase Trade Inc. New York, NY
*Society Corp. Cleveland, OH	Export Partnership for International Trade Inc. Cleveland, OH
Fleet Financial Group Inc. Providence, RI	Fleet Trading Co. Providence, RI
First National Bancshares Inc. Houma, LA	First Export Corp. Houma, LA
Manufacturers Hanover Corp. New York, NY	CIT International Sales Corp. New York, NY
First Union Corp. Charlotte, NC	First Union Export Trading Co. Charlotte, NC
Alaska Mutual Bancorp Anchorage, AK	Mutual International Corp. Anchorage, AK

* Joint-venture investment
Source: US Commerce Department

APPENDIX 3

Penalty guarantees

East European Bank Guarantee

Appendix No. ________________ to Contract No.

In accordance with the instructions of A, we give the following guarantee in favour of B.

We, ________________ Bank, are informed that Contract No. for the supply of a complete installation for the production and packing of has been signed by Company A, as Vendor, and B, as Buyer.

Under Contract No. Company A undertakes to send B, one month after the contract comes into force, a bank guarantee for the amount of £500,000, guaranteeing B in the event of A, or another Company authorised by A, not buying, or paying for, the goods purchased from ________________ export Companies, the value per annum of these goods being fixed by Contract No. as follows:

Year	Value
1983	1,000,000
1984	1,000,000
1985	1,000,000
1986	1,000,000
1987	1,000,000

In fulfilment of the a/m obligations of A, we, ________________ Bank, undertake to pay, irrevocably, unconditionally and without reserve, and irrespective of any objections or protests on the part of A or any third parties, at your first request, by transferring the amounts claimed by yourselves to your account with ________________ Bank, up to a maximum amount of £500,000 distributed over a number of years, as follows:

Year	Value
1983	100,000
1984	100,000
1985	100,000
1986	100,000
1987	100,000

For payment of sums in accordance with this bank guarantee, you should send us a registered letter specifying the extent of the obligation not fulfilled by A and the method of calculating the penalties due by A.

The bank guarantee comes into effect on the date of issue thereof and is reduced in proportion to the fulfilment of the obligations referred to above, or on payment of the penalties in your favour, and becomes null and void after fulfilment of the obligations on the part of A, on which date it must be returned to us if you have not submitted a claim for payment of penalties by that date.

Romanian Bank Guarantee (1)

To: Romanian State Trading Company.

We are informed that ______________ Limited (hereinafter called the sellers) have entered into a contract with ______________ dated ______________ for the supply of a drilling machine and that in this connection the sellers have undertaken to arrange for the purchase of goods of Romanian origin by a third party to a value of not less than 15% of the amount of the above-mentioned contract and that in this connection a bank guarantee is required.

On behalf of the sellers we hereby give you our guarantee and undertake to pay you any amount or amounts not exceeding in total a maximum of US$ ______________ on receipt of your first demand in writing accompanied by your signed statement that the sellers have failed to fulfil their obligations for the purchase of goods of Romanian origin by a third party.

This guarantee will only become operative when the full contract price of US$ ______________ has been received for the credit of the special blocked account in the name of sellers at Barclays Bank PLC and we have advised you to this effect by way of an amendment to this guarantee.

This guarantee is valid for written demand received by us on or before ______________ after which date our liability to you under this guarantee will cease and this guarantee will be of no further effect.

Draft of letter of guarantee for countertrade obligations

Under terms of Contract No. ______________ with ______________ Bucharest, Romania, UK Party has undertaken to purchase Romanian goods under internationally competitive conditions of price, quality and delivery time.

1. We ______________ Bank PLC hereby guarantee irrevocably to the amount of £______________ (say Pounds Sterling ______________ Pence) representing 10% agreed penalties under the counterpurchase clause of contract ______________ with Romania Bucharest in which UK Limited undertakes to

purchase direct or cause to be purchased by third parties, Romanian commodities as per item 3 of frame contract number ______________ amounting to the value of £______________ (say Pounds Sterling ______________).

2. If by 12 months from receipt of Letter of Credit from Romania ______________ Limited has not fulfilled or caused to be fulfilled all counter-purchase obligations as expressed in frame contract no. ______________ (Romanians) may claim all or the part of the penalty agreed for the amount of the goods to be purchased.
3. Consequently, we the undersigned Barclays Bank PLC, Bank of Seller, of ______________ shall pay the amount of £______________ within a period of 10 days from the date of receiving the simple demand of (Romanians), deliberately renouncing the benefit of division, discussion, opposition, jurisdiction, protest, *force majeure*, currency restrictions or any other exception or objection, which UK Party could avail itself of, save that counterpurchase obligations have been actually fulfilled.
4. This guarantee is valid from the date of issue and automatically expires 14 months after receipt by ______________ Limited, of Uzinexport Letter of Credit for £ ______________

This original Letter of Credit shall be cancelled 14 months after receipt by ______________ Limited, of Uzinexport Letter of Credit for £ ______________ or upon the prior entire fulfilment of counter-purchase obligations.

Romanian Bank Guarantee (2)

Under terms of Contract No. ________________ with Uzinexportimport Bucharest, Romania, ________________ Limited has undertaken to purchase Romanian goods under internationally competitive conditions of price, quality and delivery time.

1. We ________________ Bank PLC hereby guarantee irrevocably to the amount of ________________ representing 10% agreed penalties under the counterpurchase clause of contract ________________ with Uzinexportimport Bucharest in which ________________ Limited undertakes to purchase direct or cause to be purchased by third parties, Romanian commodities as per item 3 of frame contract number ________________ amounting to the value of
2. If by 12 months from receipt of Letter of Credit from Uzinexportimport, ________________ Limited has not fulfilled or caused to be fulfilled all counterpurchase obligations as expressed in frame contract no. ________________ Uzinexportimport may claim all or the part of the penalty agreed for the amount of the goods to be purchased.
3. Consequently, we the undersigned ________________ Bank PLC, Bank of Seller ________________ Limited, shall pay the amount of £ ________________ within a period of 10 days from the date of receiving the simple demand of Uzinexportimport, deliberately renouncing the benefit of division, discussion, opposition, jurisdiction, protest, *force majeure*, currency restrictions or any other exception or objection, which ________________ Limited, could avail itself of, save that counterpurchase obligations have been actually fulfilled.

Malaysian Bank Guarantee

THIS AGREEMENT is made the ______________ day of ______________ 198 ______________ BETWEEN ______________

(insert name of Bank)

of ______________

(insert principal address of business of Bank)

(hereinafter called the 'Guarantor') of the one part and the (Government/Government Agency) (hereinafter called the ______________) of the other part.

WHEREAS:

(1) This Agreement is supplemental to the Counterpurchase Agreement (hereinafter called the 'Agreement') dated the ______________ day of ______________ 198 ______________ made between the (Government/Government Agency) of the one part and the (Contractor) (hereinafter called ______________) of the other part whereby the (Contractor) agreed and undertook to Counterpurchase such amount of Malaysian Goods and Commodities directly from Malaysian Companies in Malaysia to the total value of Ringgit ______________ (M$ ______________) based on the F.O.B. prices of the Malaysian Goods and Commodities to be purchased.

(2) The Guarantor has agreed to guarantee the due performance of the Agreement in the manner hereinafter appearing;

NOW THE GUARANTOR HEREBY AGREES WITH THE (GOVERNMENT/GOVERNMENT AGENCY) AS FOLLOWS:

(1) If the (Contractor) shall in any respect fail to execute the Agreement or commit any breach of his obligations thereunder then the Guarantor shall pay to the (Government/Government Agency) up to and not exceeding the sum of Malaysian Ringgit ______________ ______________ (M$ ______________) representing ______________ % of the value of the Agreement on the (Government's/Government Agency's) demand notwithstanding any contestation of protest by the (Contractor) or by the Guarantor or by any other third party. Provided always that the total of all partial demands so made shall not exceed the sum of M$ ______________ and that the

Guarantor's liability to pay the (Government/Government Agency) as aforesaid shall correspondingly be reduced proportionate to any partial demand having been made as aforesaid.

(2) The Guarantor shall not be discharged or released from this Guarantee by any arrangement between the (Contractor) and the (Government/Government Agency) with or without the consent of the Guarantor or by any alteration in the obligations undertaken by the (Contractor) or by any forbearance whether as to payment, time, performance or otherwise, but the Guarantor shall be entitled to be informed of such arrangement or alteration.

(3) This Guarantee is a continuing guarantee and shall be irrevocable and shall remain in force and effect until the ______________ day of ______________ 198 ______________

Given under our hands the date first above mentioned

Signed for and on behalf of) ______________________
the said
Guarantor in the presence of) Name: ______________

Designation: ______________
Banker's Seal: ______________

____
(Witness)
Name: ______________
Designation: ______________
Company's Seal/
Banker's Seal: ______________

Signed for and on behalf of) ______________________

Name: ______________
Designation: ______________
Department's Seal: ______________

____
(Witness)
Name: ______________
Designation: ______________

Cyprus Bank Guarantee

Penalty guarantee (Cyprus)

To: The ______________ of Cyprus.
We are informed that ______________ (hereinafter called 'the Contractors') have entered into Contract Number ______________ dated ______________ with ______________ of Cyprus (hereinafter called 'the Employers') for the supply and installation of ______________ equipment etc., as appropriate) ______________ and in this connection the Contractors have undertaken to arrange in accordance with the terms and conditions of Countertrade Agreement Number ______________ dated ______________ by way of Countertrade for ______________ (general description of the Countertrade deal) ______________ the value of such Countertrade to be not less than Cypriot Pounds ______________ (amount) ______________ as determined in their sole discretion by ______________ of Cyprus, and in support of the aforementioned Countertrade Agreement a bank guarantee is required.

On behalf of the Contractors, we hereby give you our guarantee and undertake to pay you any amount or amounts not exceeding in total a maximum of Cypriot Pounds ______________ (amount in figures and in words) ______________ upon receipt of your first demand in writing accompanied by your signed statement certifying that the Countertrade Contract has expired unfulfilled within the time limit specified in the relevant Countertrade Agreement and as a consequence the Contractors have failed to fulfil their obligations under such Countertrade Agreement, such statement to be countersigned by ______________.

It is understood and accepted as a term of this guarantee that any failure or default on the part of a third party engaged or induced by the Contractors to execute the Countertrade Contract shall be deemed to constitute a failure on the part of the Contractors to honour their obligations under the relevant Countertrade Agreement will not affect the rights of action under the Countertrade Contract.

This Guarantee is valid for written demands received by us on or before ______________ (completion date mentioned in Countertrade Agreement plus three months) ______________ after which date our liability to you under this guarantee will cease and this guarantee will be of no further effect.

This Guarantee shall be governed by and construed in accordance with the laws of Cyprus.

APPENDIX 4

Agreement with third party

Agreement between:

Exporter Limited

and

Trading House Limited

with regard to the agreement concluded between Exporter Limited and Foreign Countertrade Goods Supplier Limited, for purchase of ________________ products or services, which agreement has been assigned and transferred by Exporter Limited to Trading House Limited and a copy of which is attached hereto together with original Assignment and Transfer Agreement, both agreements to be considered integral parts of this present agreement,

1. Exporter Limited shall pay to Trading House Limited for having accepted all of Exporter Limited rights and for having assumed all of Exporter Limited obligations under the agreement concluded between Exporter Limited and Foreign Countertrade Goods and Supplier Limited as above stated, a subsidy at the rate of (percent) of the CIF purchase value, payable when the following documents have been submitted to Foreign Countertrade Goods Supplier Limited under the Exporter Limited/Foreign Countertrade Goods Supplier Limited Agreement:
   - 1.1 copies of duly authorised export invoices,
   - 1.2 Copies of shipping documents,
   - 1.3 Customs clearance certificate;
   - 1.4 Evidence that the purchase has been credited to the obligation of Exporter Limited
2. A commission of percent is payable by Exporter Limited to Trading House Limited on the full contract value within one month

of the ratification of the underlying contract between Exporter Limited and the Bank of Buyers Country.

3. If part of the purchase obligation in the Exporters Limited/Foreign Countertrade Goods and Supplier Limited agreement as assigned and transferred to Trading House Limited remains unfulfilled at the end of the fulfilment period and payment of a penalty to Foreign Countertrade Goods and Supplier Limited becomes due as foreseen in the Exporter Limited/Foreign Countertrade Goods and Supplier Limited agreement, Trading House Limited will pay that penalty to FCGS Limited and Exporter Limited will pay to Trading House Limited a subsidy at the aforementioned rate of percent of that unfulfilled remaining amount.
4. The total maximum liability of Exporter Limited towards Trading House Limited under this agreement is restricted to the payment of % of subsidy, plus, % commission, totalling % of contract value.
5. Any disputes arising between Exporter Limited and Trading House Limited shall be resolved through amicable negotiations in a spirit of mutual understanding and collaboration.

If no solution is obtained, the difference shall be finally settled under the Rules of Conciliation and Arbitration of the International Chamber of Commerce by three arbitrators appointed in accordance with the Rules. Arbitration will be held in London and the English substantive law shall be applicable.

Signed:

ASSIGNMENT AND TRANSFER

________________ having its principal offices at ________________ (hereinafter called '________________') assigns all of its rights under the Agreement concluded between Foreign Countertrade Goods and Supplier Limited per attached photostat copy of such Agreement to Trading House Limited having its principal offices at ________________ and Trading House Limited accepts such assignment, and Exporter Limited transfers to Trading House Limited who assumes all of Exporter Limited's obligations under the same Agreement, and Exporter Limited after such assignment and transfer shall have no longer any rights or obligations under the herein referenced Agreement. Exporter Limited understands that Trading House Limited will enter the assigned and transferred Agreement within the framework of the Trading House

Limited – Foreign Countertrade Goods and Supplier Limited Agreement No. ________________

Enclosure: Photostat copy of Agreement between Exporter Limited and Foreign Countertrade Goods and Supplier Limited.

London ________________
FOR Trading House Limited

Foreign Country ________________
FOR Foreign Countertrade Goods and Supplier Limited

APPENDIX 5

Insurance

Pre-quotation questionnaire

THE ASSURED:	(a)	Name and address
	(b)	Period established
	(c)	Annual turnover
	(d)	Assured's experience of the 'product being sold'
	(e)	Period over which Assured has traded with Buyer/other buyers in the Buyer's country
	(f)	Has Assured traded with this Buyer on similar payment terms? If Yes was payment received when it was due?
THE BUYER:	(a)	Name of the Buyer
	(b)	Private or government owned
	(c)	Buyer's size/turnover (if private)
	(d)	Buyer's need for 'product'
THE GOODS:	(a)	What is 'product' being sold?
	(b)	Standard or prototype?
	(c)	What will the product be used for?
	(d)	Will it earn foreign exchange for the Buyer?
	(e)	Does the Buyer's country really need it?
THE CONTRACT:	(a)	Delivery period of 'product'
	(b)	Terms and method of payment
	(c)	Guarantees of payment if any
COVER REQUIRED	(a)	Pre-delivery Sum insured Period
	(b)	Post-delivery credit Sum insured Period
ADDITIONAL INFORMATION:	(a)	If things go wrong is there any action the Assured can take to exert pressure on the Buyer?
	(b)	Please provide any other available information which you feel may be relevant

PRIVATE AND CONFIDENTIAL

Proposal form for insurance against political risks on contracts

1. Name and address of Assured
   It would be helpful to have:
   (a) copies of your last two years' financial accounts
   (b) the name and nationality of your ultimate parent
   (c) literature describing the activities and products of your company

---

2. Buyer
   Name and address:
   (a) Is the Buyer a part of the Government?
   (b) If not, it would help to have information that demonstrates their financial standing and respectability

---

3. Contract
   With regard to the Contract, please supply:
   (a) Date
   (b) Value
   (c) Nature of goods/services to be supplied
   (d) Please supply a breakdown of the contracted time scale under the Contract including as applicable:

(i)	manufacturing	from	to
(ii)	delivery	from	to
(iii)	provision of services	from	to
(iv)	erection	from	to
(v)	civil works	from	to
(vi)	commissioning	from	to
(vii)	warranty	from	to

   (e) (i) What is the extent of the contractual obligations? (i.e. delivery: ex-works/f.o.b./c.i.f./supervision/completion of erection/commissioning turnkey, provision of services, etc.)
   (ii) Where does delivery and acceptance take place?
   (iii) When and where does title pass to Buyer?
   (f) (i) What per cent of the Contract is subcontracted out?
   (ii) Names and nationality of the principal subcontractors

and details of any previous dealings with them
(iii) Is the Buyer aware of the identity of the principal subcontractors?
(g) (i) To which country's law is the Contract subject?
(ii) Is there an arbitration provision? If so, where will it take place and under whose rules?
(iii) Is there an adequate *force majeure* clause?
(h) (i) What are the precise terms of payment?
(ii) What is the currency of payment?
(iii) When is the Buyer required to open letter(s) of credit?
(iv) What is the precise method and currency of payment (if letters of credit are to be used when is the Buyer required to open these)?

---

4. Previous experience
Please give details of other current or previous contracts undertaken in the Buyer's country
Date Buyer Contract value Due date Due payment received

Please give FULL details of any problems encountered on such contracts:

---

5. (a) Who is the engineer/consultant on this contract?
(b) What is his nationality?
(c) Have you worked together before?
(d) If so, was his work satisfactory?
(e) Do you have a local partner/agent/representative?
(f) If so who is he and for who else does he act?
(j) Does the Buyer have to supply or do anything to enable you to complete this Contract? If yes, what does he have to do or supply? and by what date?
(k) Does the Buyer hold the necessary licences/permits to import the goods and pay for them as contracted?
(l) Are the licences/permits valid for the duration of the Contract?

(m) Is the Buyer financing the Contract from external sources?
(n) If so from whom?
(o) Has this been arranged?
(p) How important do you consider this Contract is to the Buyer, and why?
(q) How easily could the Buyer find an alternative supplier?
(r) Was this an invited Contract or open to competitive tender?

---

6. Cover required
What limit of cover do you require:

	Limit	Period of cover
(a) Work in progress, i.e. losses suffered up to the date of completion of the contracted works	________	________
Post-completion cover, i.e. losses suffered after the date of completion of the contracted works	________	________
(b) Unfair calling of on-demand guarantee:		
Advance payment	________	________
Performance	________	________
Others	________	________
(c) Do you wish to insure against specific perils only, i.e. embargo, war, repudiation, non-payment or exchange transfer?		

7. Do you want to investigate the availability of commitment cover? (See note IV)

---

8. It would be helpful to have a copy of the General Conditions of the Contract.

---

9. If cover required for unfair calling of bank guarantee, please supply the following information:
   - (a) Type of guarantee
   - (b) Value
   - (c) Does the guarantee reduce pro rata with deliveries/work done
   - (d) Expiry date
   - (e) Name of local bank
   - (f) Name of your bank
   - (g) Please provide a copy of the wording of the bond given to the Buyer

---

10. Additional information
    ANY OTHER INFORMATION THAT UNDERWRITERS SHOULD BE AWARE OF.

The information disclosed herein will be treated as strictly confidential.

We hereby declare that the statements made by us in this questionnaire are complete and true to best of our knowledge and belief and that we have not withheld any other material information.

We undertake not to disclose to the buyer the existence of any policy that may be issued.

We agree that the questionnaire shall form the basis of and be part of any policy issued.

Date ________________ Signed________________________________
Name and Title________________________

Please note:

I. Premium is charged on the Underwriter's limit of liability and the period of risk. It is therefore in the Assured's interest to restrict the amounts and the period to that which is needed.

II. It is suggested that the limits sought for the net loss after the deduction of all likely savings and recoveries and that the period of cover is kept to the minimum necessary.

III. Your attention is drawn to the fact that all indications given by Underwriters are on *today*'s rate basis and therefore Underwriters are free to withdraw their indication or to revise the terms of it at any time whatsoever. Cover can only be bound when an order to bind cover is accepted by Underwriters.

IV. It may be possible to guarantee the availability of cover at today's rate subject to payment of a suitable premium.

V. Non-disclosure of any material underwriting information may void any policy issued.

COUNTERTRADE INSURANCE
QUESTIONNAIRE TO OBTAIN INDICATIVE QUOTATION

Details of proposed insured

1. Name and address of applicant
2. Name and address of exporter/importer if different

Details of contract

3. Host country
4. Name and address of importer/exporter
5. Legal status
6. Products/services being sold/delivered
7. Priority of products/services
8. Total contract value
9. Currency of contract (if any)
10. Is this a bid or firm contract? If firm, when signed or signature expected
11. Shipment dates
12. Method of payment
13. Guarantees/support available from the importer/exporter's government or central bank
14. External financing of exporter
15. Detailed previous experience of applicant (or exporter/importer) with:
    (A) Country involved
    (B) Exporter/importer involved

Risk to be insured

16. Risk to be insured:
    - (A) Contract repudiation
    - (B) Importer's default
    - (C) Exporter's default
    - (D) Import/export embargo
    - (E) Exchange transfer/currency inconvertibility
    - (F) Arbitration award refusal
    - (G) *Force majeure* termination
    - (H) Other perils (please specify)

Barter transaction questionnaire

AMERICAN INTERNATIONAL UNDERWRITERS (UK) LIMITED TRADE AND POLITICAL RISK DIVISION

ANTICIPATORY CREDIT/BARTER TRANSACTIONS APPLICATION FORM

This application form is designed to accommodate a wide range of transactions and contractual structures.

All questions must be answered. Where a question is deemed not applicable please answer 'N/A' and explain why this is so.

Section A – THE APPLICANT
Section B – FINANCIAL STRUCTURE
Section C – THE SALES CONTRACT
Section D – THE PURCHASE CONTRACT
Section E – GENERAL AND SIGNATURES

Should answers to any of the following questions require more space than is provided, attachments providing particulars are welcomed.

Copies of the following documents are required by the Underwriters:

(a) the Call for Tenders and Tender Documents;
(b) the Contracts or Sales Agreements;
(c) copy debt instruments, e.g, copy letters of credit, promissory notes and bills of exchange;
(d) drawdown or delivery schedules;
(e) schedule of exposures;
(f) latest audited financial statements of the Applicant, the Seller on the Sales Contract and the Buyer on the Purchase Contract.

Section A

1. Name of Applicant and Parent ______________________

   ____

   Nationality of Applicant and nationality of Parent

   ____

   Address ______________________

   ____

   ____

2. Brief information about applicant
Founded ______
Capital and reserves last 3 years ______
______
Turnover last 3 years ______

Profit/loss last 3 years ______
______
Working capital net worth (equity) ______
Number of employees ______
Major shareholders ______
Auditors ______
Have audited accounts been qualified in the last 5 years? ______
______
If so, for what reason? ______
______
______
Applicant to supply their most recent audited statement.

3. Has the applicant previous experience in transactions with:
   (a) the Seller under the Sales Contract? ______
   (b) The host country buyer under the Sales Contract?
   ______
   (c) The host country seller under the Purchase Contract?
   ______
   (d) The Buyer under the Purchase Contract? ______
   FULL DETAILS BY ATTACHMENT PLEASE.

Section B

FINANCIAL STRUCTURE

It is particularly important that the applicant be descriptive and co-operative in his replies to the following section.

Often a diagram proves to be the most effective method of showing how the transactions work.

4. Please provide a detailed description of the transaction.
   Barter [ ] Buy-back [ ] Counterpurchase [ ]
   Anticipatory credit [ ] Other ______
   Description ______

5. Identify the nature of the LEGALLY ENFORCEABLE INDEBTEDNESS

6. Terms of payment on the contracts

7. Identify 'instruments of payment'

   ILCs

   Guarantees

   Escrow accounts

   Other collateral

8. Were Ministry of Finance or Central Bank guarantees available?

   Were they sought?

   Were they obtained?

   Please describe/identify these in detail

9. Please supply drawdown or delivery schedules by attachment

10. Please supply schedule of exposures (by attachment if necessary)

11. Limit(s) of liability required

12. Policy period required ______________________________

Section C

DETAILS OF SALES CONTRACT

13. Name of Seller ______________________________
(if different to Applicant)
Address ______________________________
Nationality ______________________________
14. Name of Buyer ______________________________
Address ______________________________
Nationality ______________________________
15. Buyer's legal status (i.e. private company, majority government owned or nationalised company, government ministry, official import organisation, etc.)
____
16. If buyer is majority government owned does it carry full faith and credit of the government?
____
17. Describe the products and/or services which are the subject of the Sales Contract, noting any unique or unusual features.
____
____
____
____
18. (a) Is the subject matter of the Sales Contract standard or custom made?
____
(b) How important is this Sales Contract to the Buyer's country (details by attachment if necessary)? Give reasons.
____
____
____
(c) How easily could an alternative Buyer be found?
____
____
(d) Would subject matter need modification if sold to another Buyer and how extensive would such modification be?
____

19. (a) Where does delivery and acceptance of the products by the Buyer take place?

(b) Where and when does title pass to the Buyer?

Was Sales Contract open to competitive bids or was the Seller invited to tender?

20. Identify sales agent in Buyer's country if applicable

21. (a) Who is responsible for obtaining all licence(s) or consent(s) necessary for fulfilment of the contract from
   (i) the Buyer's country ______
   (ii) the Seller's country ______
(b) Are these now in force? ______
(c) If not, when expected? ______
(d) For what period are licences valid? From ______
   To ______
(e) If not for full Contract period, why not?

22. (a) Does Seller have previous experience with
   (i) this Buyer, or [ ]
   (ii) this Country? [ ]
(b) Details of recent previous experience:

Month and year	Buyer	Amount	Terms of payment	Payment delay
				days
				days
				days
				days
				days

(c) Does the Applicant and/or the Seller have other exposures with the Buyer or with other Buyers in the host country? If so, for what amounts?

23. Are any further Sales Contracts being considered with
(a) this Buyer, or [ ]
(b) this Country? [ ]
Details

24. Does the Sales Contract contain the following clauses?
(a) Termination clause
(b) Arbitration clause If yes, where is it to take place and under which laws?
(c) *Force majeure* clause
(d) Conditions precedent to effectiveness of Sales Contract
What are these?

25. Has any external financing been obtained in connection with this Sales Contract?
YES/NO
If so, from whom? (e.g. World Bank, AID, ECGD, general government revenues, etc.)

26. BRIEF INFORMATION ABOUT THE SELLER (if different to the Applicant)
Founded
Capital and reserves last 3 years
Turnover last 3 years
Working capital net worth (equity)
Number of employees
Major shareholders
Auditors
Have audited accounts been qualified in the last 5 years?
If so, for what reason?

Applicant to supply the Seller's most recent audited statement.

Section D

DETAILS OF PURCHASE CONTRACT

27. Name of Buyer ______
(if different to Applicant) ______
Address ______
Nationality ______
28. Name of Seller ______
Address ______
Nationality ______
29. Seller's legal status (i.e. private company, majority government owned or nationalised company, government ministry, official import organisation, etc.)
______
30. If Seller is majority government owned does it carry full faith and credit of the government?
______
31. Describe the products which are the subject of the Purchase Contract noting any unique or unusual features, production or harvest times
______
______
______
32. (a) Is the subject matter of the Purchase Contract standard or custom made?
______
(b) What proportion of the Seller's total output of this product does this Purchase Contract represent?
______
(c) How easily could an alternative supply of the product be found?
______
(d) How easily could an alternative Buyer be found by the Seller?
33. (a) Where does delivery and acceptance of the products by the Buyer take place?
______
(b) Where and when does title pass to the Buyer?
______

34. (a) Who is responsible for obaining all licence(s) or consent(s) necessary for fulfilment of the contract from
    (i) the Buyer's country? ______________________
    (ii) the Seller's country? ______________________
(b) Are these now in force? ______________________
(c) If not, when expected? ______________________
(d) For what period are licences valid? From ______________
    To ______________
(e) If not for full Contract period, why not?

____

____

35. (a) Does Buyer have previous experience with
    (i) this Seller, or [ ]
    (ii) this Country? [ ]
(b) Details of recent previous experience

Month and year	Buyer	Amount	Terms of payment	Payment delay
				days
				days
				days
				days
				days

(c) Does the Applicant and/or the Buyer have other exposures with the Seller or with other Sellers in the host country? If so, for what amounts?

____

____

(d) Are these other exposures insured or otherwise secured? If so, by whom or how secured?

____

____

(e) Does the Applicant and/or the Buyer have any overdues on any exposures in the host country as of the date of this Application? If so, please give details of status

____

____

____

____

____

(f) Please supply detailed information of the Buyer's previous experience in on-selling or marketing the subject matter of the Purchase Contract.

____

____

____

36. Are any further Purchase Contracts being considered with
 (a) this Seller, or [ ]
 (b) this Country? [ ]
 Details:

____

____

____

37. Does the Purchase Contract contain the following clauses?
 (a) Termination clause ______________________
 (b) Arbitration clause ______________ If yes, where is it to take place and under which laws?

____

____

 (c) *Force majeure* clause ______________________
 (d) Conditions precedent to effectiveness of Purchase Contract ______________________
 What are these? ______________________

____

38. Has any external financing been obtained in connection with this Purchase Contract?

YES/NO

If so, from whom? (e.g. World Bank, AID, ECGD, general government revenues, etc.) ______________________

____

39. BRIEF INFORMATION ABOUT BUYER
 Founded ______________________
 Capital and reserves last 3 years ______________________
 Turnover last 3 years ______________________
 Working capital net worth (equity) ______________________
 Number of employees ______________________
 Major shareholders ______________________
 Auditors ______________________
 Have audited accounts been qualified in the last 5 years? ______

____

 If so, for what reason? ______________________

Applicant to supply the Buyer's most recent audited statement.

Section E

GENERAL

THIS SECTION TO BE COMPLETED BY ALL APPLICANTS

40. (a) Has the Applicant been declined coverage on any part of this transaction by any other Insurer?

YES/NO

(b) If so, by whom and state reasons ______________________

____

____

____

41. Does the Applicant have any knowledge of any facts not readily available from the financial press which might give rise to a claim under the policy?

____

It is agreed that if such knowledge or information exists, any claim arising therefrom that has not been notified to the Company may be excluded from the proposed policy.

THE COMPANY AGREES TO TREAT AS CONFIDENTIAL ALL MATTERS PERTAINING TO THIS APPLICATION

THE APPLICANT AGREES NOT TO DISCLOSE THE EXISTENCE OF ANY POLICY WHICH MAY BE ISSUED TO ANY OUTSIDE PARTY WITHOUT THE PRIOR CONSENT OF THE COMPANY.

Signed ______________________
Title ______________________
Corporation ______________________

____

Date ______________________
Broker ______________________
Address ______________________

____

____

The above authorised officer of the Applicant declared that, to the best of his knowledge, the statements set forth in this Application are true and no material information has been withheld.

SIGNING OF THIS APPLICATION DOES NOT BIND THE ABOVE TO COM-

PLETE THE INSURANCE BUT IT IS AGREED THAT THIS APPLICATION SHALL BE THE BASIS OF THE INSURANCE SHOULD A POLICY BE ISSUED AND WILL BE ATTACHED TO AND FORM PART OF THE POLICY.

Please note that all indications given by underwriters are on a 'Today's Rate' basis. Underwriters reserve the right to withdraw their indication or to revise the terms at any time whatsoever. Cover can only be bound when an order to bind cover is accepted by underwriters, after submission of all required information and documentation.

APPENDIX 6

Forfaiting

Countertrade is a feature of trade with Eastern Europe; Chapter 14 explains why. Another technique often found there is forfaiting, and the two can often go together – forfaiting as a financing mechanism, with countertrade a parallel issue. To complete the picture, therefore, this appendix describes forfaiting.

'Forfaiting' or 'a forfait' is derived from the French meaning 'to surender something' (in this case giving up rights to a payment under a bill). Basically, it describes a form of export finance, which was developed in Vienna and Zurich, mainly to finance trade with East European countries. It has been used extensively in certain parts of Europe for the last 30 years. However, its wider use is relatively new. In recent years international debt problems have caused official export credit agencies to restrict their range of cover and increase their premia. This has made bankers and exporters look at alternatives and has focused attention on forfaiting with its many positive features. The result is that today there is much greater interest among exporters and banks in a more competitive forfait market, largely centred in London. Forfaiting should not be seen as being in competition with other export finance schemes. It is an extra option for exporters.

So what exactly is forfaiting?

Forfaiting is a form of credit where the forfaiting bank purchases an exporter's receivables, discounting them, usually at a fixed rate. This is done without recourse to the exporter (provided he has fulfilled his obligations); the bank looks only to the overseas buyer and the guarantor for payment. Put another way, credit can be offered in the sale contract to the buyer, and then the amounts due under the credit can be sold at a discount to the bank. The discounted amount in cash is received, i.e. the receivable has been converted into cash. The buyer receives the agreed period of credit with the pre-arranged repayment programme and interest rate. The bank purchases the receivables (usually evidenced by bills of exchange or promissory notes) which it either retains for presentation at the maturity dates or sells to another bank in the forfait market.

Although forfaiting is a highly flexible form of export finance, it does not compete with the more complex forms of export finance, e.g. buyer credits, that are used to finance the much longer-term multimillion turnkey projects, such as chemical plants and power stations. These projects will often have long drawdown periods, complex contractual relationships, commissioning periods and retention monies.

How does it work?

The start point will be the negotiations with the buyer, when the following questions will arise: Does the buyer want credit? If so, for how long and at what interest rate? There may be constraints here: it may be that the buyer is required by local law to pay no more than a certain interest rate or to obtain credit for not less than a certain period. As early as possible enquiries should be made as to whether the bank is prepared to quote on the deal and, if so, on what terms. The bank, if it is ready to do business, will quote a discount rate, taking into account the risk represented by the buyer, the buyer's guarantor and their country. A guarantee is normally required; the bank can advise on acceptable banks to guarantee the transaction or on alternatives such as guarantees from a ministry or even the buyer's parent company. Occasionally, when the buyer is undoubted, a guarantee will not be necessary.

The bills or notes need to be 'avalised' by the importer's bank (or whoever is standing surety). That means that the bills or notes will be endorsed by the guarantor, usually with the addition of the words 'pour aval'. This is simply an accepted method of guaranteeing payment. However, if the guaranteeing bank is unable for legal reasons to do this, it will probably issue a formal letter of guarantee instead (or, in the United States, a standby letter of credit).

The discount rate quoted by the bank will only be an indication at this stage, but it will enable the finance costs to be calculated approximately and the price structured accordingly. Neither the bank nor the exporter is yet committed and quotations can be revised as the negotiations progress. For instance, buyer and seller may later agree on a different currency or a different down-payment. Delivery dates and the scope of delivery may be changed. And of course, market interest rates will change from time to time. The bank can make and revise these calculations as often as necessary.

At about the time of contract, the exporter will wish to be certain that the bank will 'purchase' the transaction and to establish exactly what the net proceeds of the discount will be. The bank will then provide a firm offer which commits it to a specified discount rate, provided all the agreed conditions are met within a certain time period.

The exporter will then have to decide within a few days whether to accept the bank's offer. Once the offer letter has been countersigned to show acceptance, the exporter too is committed and will need to pay the bank the necessary fee for its commitment. (As a guide, this will be about 0.1 per cent per month from the date of commitment until the date the bills are presented.) At that stage, the exporter can be sure of precisely how much will be received when the bills or notes are presented for discounting. Provided the bank is satisfied with the documents when they are presented, and all other conditions have been fulfilled, the bank will buy the bills or notes without recourse.

Normally these bills or notes are obtained under a letter of credit, but they can also be obtained by sending them out with the shipping documents on a collection basis or even by getting the buyer to sign them in advance (the bank would be prepared to hold these in trust if required).

Why is it used?

Forfaiting complements existing methods of export finance and provides the following benefits:

1. It is without recourse, i.e. the receivable does not feature on balance sheets; the exporter is running a risk on the buyer or the buyer's country.
2. There are no exchange risks or interest rate risks, because payment is received in cash against presentation of documents to the bank soon after shipment. Those risks are eliminated from the day of discounting. To cover those risks from the date of signature of the commercial contract, it is possible to cover the interest rate risk by obtaining the bank's prior commitment on the discount rate and the exchange risk (where invoicing is not in the exporter's own currency) by taking out forward cover.
3. Finance at 100 per cent can be offered to the buyer with the first repayment, say, six months after shipment.

4. Once the bills or notes have been discounted, cashflow is improved.
5. Banking facilities are not affected by forfaiting.
6. The exporter is relieved of receivables' administration and payment collection problems.
7. It is possible to select which sales will be financed in this way.
8. Finance for certain goods may be available for longer terms than the official export credit agency will offer. Also, a transaction not eligible for the agency's support (e.g. goods of foreign origin) may well be financed through the forfait market.
9. The forfait transaction is not publicised so the importer need not know about the discounting of the bills or notes and competitors will not know that forfaiting is being used as the method of export finance.

Note: The exporter is of course responsible for the satisfactory performance of the commercial contract, and must also undertake to the bank that the liability of the buyer to pay is legal and binding and the bills or notes evidencing that liability are authentic.

What are the benefits to the importer?

The credit that can be offered to the importer under a forfait transaction brings with it a number of key benefits for the importer too:

1. The importer is able to obtain up to 100 per cent fixed rate finance.
2. The repayment programme can be tailored to the importer's needs.
3. The importer can obtain credit in any one of a number of freely transferable currencies.
4. The commission paid by the importer for the bank guarantee or *aval* may be less than the commission on a letter of credit.
5. The goods covered by the commercial contract can be sourced from any country or number of countries.
6. The financing can be arranged quickly.
7. The finance costs, which are based on commercial interest rates, may be lower than if the deal was arranged under OECD consensus arrangements.
8. Finance may be considered for markets for which official export credit insurers are unwilling to provide cover.
9. Details of the deal will not be publicised.

What does forfaiting cost?

Any commercially based credit transaction carries two costs: that of raising the funds, and the bank margin to cover the risks involved and other costs.

Obviously, the cost of raising the funds depends on the currency involved, the amount, the credit period and the number of repayment instalments. The risks relate to the creditworthiness of the buyer, the buyer's guarantor and country.

In forfait transactions, these two elements are combined and expressed either as an interest rate (usually compounding every six months) or more often as a 'straight discount rate' (i.e. simple discount, not compounding). Some banks periodically issue rate sheets giving straight discount rates in various currencies for the countries in which they are prepared to do business. But since interest rates change frequently and the political and economic situations in different countries also change, most banks prefer to give forfait quotes in response to specific enquiries.

What information does the bank need?

To determine what discount rate will be applied the bank needs to know the following:

1. The currency, the amount and the period to be financed.
2. The nature of the goods.
3. The name and address of the buyer's guarantor (usually a bank).
4. The repayment programme.
5. The rate of interest the buyer has agreed to pay (and how the interest is to be calculated).
6. The date the goods will be shipped.
7. The date the bills or notes and other documents will be presented to the Bank for discounting.
8. Where the bills or notes will be payable.

Later on, but before the bank is ready to give a firm undertaking to buy the bills or notes, it will need additional information:

1. What form the receivables will take (bills of exchange, promissory notes, drafts under letters of credit, invoices, etc.).
2. What form the guarantee will take (*aval* or separate guarantee, preferably the former).

3. Confirmation that the necessary import licences, exchange control authorisations and so on have been obtained (export licences may also be necessary).

If the bank is to give a firm commitment in advance of shipment and is assisting with interest calculations and contract terms of payment, it will need a copy of the commercial contract.

How does forfaiting compare with official export credit arrangements?

Forfaiting is not intended to replace such arrangements but to complement them. There are often cases where forfaiting may be more appropriate. Here are some examples:

1. Where goods are being supplied from a country or countries, other than the supplier's own, the contract may not meet the requirements on domestic and foreign content under the official credit arrangements of the supplier's country.
2. The buyer insists on 100 per cent finance, but official arrangements only permit a maximum of 85 per cent finance.
3. The buyer wants a different repayment programme from that officially laid down; e.g. the buyer may want annual repayments or one lump sum repayment.
4. The equipment being exported does not qualify under the export credit arrangements for the period of credit the buyer wants or does not qualify at all.
5. The finance has to be arranged very quickly, and the various steps under the official arrangements cannot be compressed into that time-frame.
6. The exporter may not want any right of recourse to be retained against him.
7. The overall cost of the credit provided may be lower via forfaiting.
8. The official agency is not prepared to provide cover for the particular country risk.

What do the technical terms mean?

(To) Accept	A buyer accepts a bill of exchange by signing on the front, thus undertaking to make the payment required. The buyer is then the acceptor.

Aval — A short form of guarantee where the 'avalor' signs on the bill of exchange or promissory note, adding the words 'Pour aval' or similar, e.g. 'Payment guaranteed at maturity'. The 'avalor' thereby stands surety for the obligation of the drawee of the bill or the maker of the promissory note.

Bill of exchange — An instruction signed by one party (the drawer, in this case the supplier) requiring a second party (the drawee, in this case the buyer) to pay a specific sum of money on demand or on a future date (the latter in a forfait transaction). The second party accepts the bill of exchange, signifying his undertaking to make the payment.

Buyer credit — A loan by a bank to an overseas buyer, usually guaranteed by the exporting country's official export credit agency. The loan is normally paid out direct to the exporter.

Consensus — An agreement between OECD governments on minimum interest rates, maximum credit periods and minimum downpayments to be applied to certain fixed-rate medium-term export finance transactions, which those governments' export credit agencies are prepared to support.

Discount —
(a) The amount of money deducted from a debt due at a future date in return for immediate payment.
(b) The purchase (by a bank) of a debt due at a future date.

Draft — A bill of exchange; in the context of forfaiting it is a bill to draw funds under a documentary letter of credit.

Drawdown — The action of drawing funds from a bank under an agreed loan or credit facility, usually against presentation of stipulated documents.

Endorsement	A signature on the back of a bill or note, with or without further words, which transfers rights or obligations under the bill or note to another party. Usually the endorser becomes liable on the bill or note, but in forfaiting the exporter adds the words 'without recourse' and thus is not normally liable.
Forward cover	A contract between a bank and a customer whereby the two undertake to buy or sell a specified amount of foreign currency at a fixed exchange rate at a future date.
Guarantee	An undertaking by one party (the guarantor) given to another party (the beneficiary, in this case the forfaiting bank or the supplier directly) to pay the debt of a third party (the debtor, in this case the buyer), on written demand by the beneficiary.
Margin	The difference between a bank's cost of funds and the rate at which it lends that money. The latter varies according to the period involved and the creditworthiness of the borrower and the borrower's country.
Official export credit agency	An organisation owned or supported by a country's government with a duty to promote exports from that country, by providing insurance against non-payment by overseas buyers and financing those exports (or enabling other institutions to provide such finance). Such organisations include ECGD (UK), Eximbank (USA), EDC (Canada), ERG (Switzerland), COFACE (France), Hermes (West Germany), SACE (Italy), CESCE (Spain), OKB (Austria), NCM – Nederlandsche Creditverzekering Maatschappij n.v. (Netherlands).
Promissory note	A written promise signed by one party (the maker, in this case the buyer), promising to pay a second party (the payee, usually the

supplier) a specific sum of money on demand or at a future date.

Receivables — Debts receivable; amounts owed by one party to another in payment for goods and services.

Recourse — The right to seek payment from other parties to a bill or note, should the drawee or the maker not pay.

(To) Source — To buy goods from a particular country for inclusion in a supply contract. Multisourcing is buying goods from a number of countries for this purpose.

Supplier credit — An arrangement whereby an exporter provides credit to the buyer as part of the contractual arrangements and receives refinance from a bank by selling to it bills of exchange or promissory notes signed by the overseas buyer covering the goods exported. The bank buying the bills or notes often receives the guarantee of the exporting country's official export credit agency.

Surety or guarantor — A person who undertakes to be liable for a debt contracted by another person.

APPENDIX 7

Further reading

Countertrade – Some Guidance for Exporters
Department of Trade and Industry
Projects and Export Policy 3A
1 Victoria Street
London SW1

East-West
10 Bd. St-Lazare
1030 Brussels
Belgium

Countertrade and Barter Quarterly
16 Lower Marsh
London SE1 7RJ

Euromoney Trade Finance Report
Euromoney Publications Limited
Nestor House
Playhouse Yard
London EC4V 5EX

Countertrade Outlook
3141 Park Fairfax Station
Alexandria
Virginia 22302
USA

Business Eastern Europe
Business International (plus a series of specific countertrade guides)
12.14 Chemin RieU
CH 1211
Geneva 17
Switzerland

Aceco
28 Avenue Hoche
75008
Paris
France

International Countertrade 'A Guide for Managers and Executives'
Pompiliu Verzario
US Department of Commerce
International Trade Administration
Washington DC
USA

APPENDIX 8

Acronyms and abbreviations

ACECO	Association pour la Compensation des Exchanges Commerciaux
AIG	American Insurance Group
ALADI	Associacion Latinoamericana de Integracion
CESCE	Compania Espanola de Seguros Credito a la Exportacion (Italy)
c. & f.	cost and freight
c.i.f.	cost, insurance, freight
COFACE	Compagnie Française d'Assurance pour le Commerce Exterieur (France)
Comecon	Council for Mutual Economic Assistance (Eastern Europe)
DID	Defense Industry Directorate (Greece)
DOTI	Department of Trade and Industry (UK)
DREE	Direction des Relations Economiques Exterieures
ECGD	Export Credit Guarantee Department
EDC	Export Development Corporation (Canada)
EEC	European Economic Community
ERG	Office of Export Risk Guarantees (Switzerland)
Eximbank	Export Import Bank of United States
f.o.b.	free on board
GATT	General Agreement on Tariffs and Trade
GAV	Greek added value
GE	General Electric
GETC	General Electric Trading Company
GTS	General Trade Suppliers International n.v.
IMF	International Monetary Fund

ITCO	International Trade Company
NCM	Nederlandsche Creditverzekering Maatschappij n.v.
OECD	Organization for Economic Co-operation and Development
OKB	Oesterreichische Kontrollbank Ag (Austria)
OPEC	Organization of Petroleum Exporting Countries
PITC	Philippine International Trading Corporation
SACE	Sezione Speciale per l'Assicurazione del Credito All'Esportazione (Italy)
TDB	Trade Development Board (Singapore)
UIC	Universal Investment Consultants
VAIT	Voest-Alpine Intertrading

Index